HEROIN ADDICTION
Theory, Research, and Treatment

VOLUME 2
The Addict, the Treatment Process,
and Social Control

HEROIN ADDICTION
Theory, Research, and Treatment

VOLUME 2
The Addict, the Treatment Process,
and Social Control

JEROME J. PLATT

Medical College of Pennsylvania
and
Hahnemann University
School of Medicine

Philadelphia, Pennsylvania

KRIEGER PUBLISHING COMPANY
MALABAR, FLORIDA
1995

Original Edition 1995

Printed and Published by
KRIEGER PUBLISHING COMPANY
KRIEGER DRIVE
MALABAR, FLORIDA 32950

Copyright © 1995 by Krieger Publishing Company

FROM A DECLARATION OF PRINCIPLES JOINTLY ADOPTED BY A COMMITTEE
OF THE AMERICAN BAR ASSOCIATION AND COMMITTEE OF PUBLISHERS:

This Publication is designed to provide accurate and authoritative information in regard to the
subject matter covered. It is sold with the understanding that the publisher is not engaged in
rendering legal, accounting, or other professional service. If legal advice or other expert assistance is required, the services of a competent professional person should be sought.

Library of Congress Cataloging-in-Publication Data
(Revised for vol. 2)
Platt, Jerome J.
  Heroin addiction.
  Includes bibliographical references and indexes.
  Contents: v. 1. [without special title]—v. 2. The
addict, the treatment process, and social control.
   1. Heroin habit. 2. Heroin habit—Treatment.
3. Narcotic laws—United States. I. Title.

RC568.H4P55   1986   362.2'93   83-19584
ISBN 0-89874-694-9 (v. 1)
ISBN 0-89464-267-7 (v. 2)
ISBN 0-89464-881-0 (v. 3)

10 9 8 7 6 5 4 3 2

Table Of Contents

PART II
ADVANCES IN CONCEPTUALIZING AND UNDERSTANDING
THE TREATMENT PROCESS

PART III
ADVANCES IN UNDERSTANDING THE HEROIN ADDICT

PART IV
CONTROL APPROACHES TO HEROIN ADDICTION

Foreword

Most of society's problems including crime, disease, and substance abuse are unlikely to ever disappear. Our optimism, nevertheless, is guarded but hopeful, and we pursue solutions to them. Generally, researchers in the field of substance abuse treatment research (I am pleased to be in that fraternity along with Jerome J. Platt) seek to bring the best of our skills to bear in aid of that cause. We do this by suggesting possible solutions and evaluating the outcome—evaluation products which speak to the critical issues of effectiveness and cost. Still, the value of the best of such products are not ultimately judged by academic standards, but rather by society's utilization of them. Jerome J. Platt's research efforts, particularly Volume 2 of his three volume work on heroin addiction, typifies that approach. In other words, his research publications are in aid of the making of public policy.

Moreover, it is not enough that our professional skills are judged as optimal from the standpoint of our peers—other evaluation researchers. Those engaged in the process of implementing solutions—the policy makers—have to feel the same way, or at least sufficiently confident that the evaluation outcome is clear, accurate, and reliable. The best quality evaluation study, the report of which never leaves the shelf (i.e., is never utilized), may as well never have been undertaken. Jerome J. Platt's work leaves the shelf frequently to serve policy making as well as to serve other researchers, teachers, and students.

It is axiomatic in today's scientific arena, particularly in that aspect of science dealing with human problems such as substance abuse, that professional researchers be concerned in an unbiased (nonpartisan) way with the values or interests of the whole society. The social science credo as expounded in graduate schools is that we should analyze problems with an eye on the public interest rather than on the special interests of some group within the society. We hold, as it were, that the evaluator's responsibility is to avoid bias and to accord equal legitimacy to every value or interest. Status in the field of evaluation research and policy analysis in part rests upon how freely one pursues public interest research questions in a nonpartisan manner. The more one is seen as allied to a particular special interest, the greater the loss of status in the eyes of other scientists and analysts, and the greater the loss of credibility in the eyes of competing agencies, policy makers, and legislators. Dr. Platt's writings reflect both his passion that the results of his efforts serve the public's interest, as well as his compassion for the victims of substance abuse and the difficulties faced by clinicians engaged in the often tedious and frustrating process of bringing people to recovery.

Evaluation research queries to efficacy of a solution or method, tests outcomes using conventional statistical techniques, and presents conclusions regarding the solution's utility and the probable stability of that finding. Much of today's guidance for policy scientists criticizes the fact-finding role as insufficient, and suggests that the process should yield advice to the decision maker on what to do and which vetted alternatives are worth his or her final consideration. Dr. Platt's work, in contrast to much of the more academic evaluation literature, is replete with both implicit and explicit recommendations flowing logically from the results of research.

Unfortunately, there has often been poor communication between evaluators and the consumers of evaluation. Such communications has even been referred to (with some truth) as "a dialogue among the hearing and speaking impaired." Jerome J. Platt is conscientious in his work to speak clearly, seldom employing the jargon and the esoterica of research. Thus, his work is quite understandable by lay readers as well as by his colleagues.

This new volume is current and of immediate importance. One of the most urgent concerns regarding drug use trends across the nation and in the Philadelphia-New York City area, where Dr. Platt and I work, is the resurgence of heroin use. For several years now, drug experts and law enforcement officials have alluded to the resurgence of heroin use, as a result of bumper crops of opium in Myanmar and new growth in Latin America. In many locations around the country, drug researchers and treatment programs are reporting signs of the growing availability, heightened use, and increased medical problems associated with heroin. Cocaine, however, which has been growing to its dominant status as the major drug of choice since the early eighties, is not disappearing. In fact, the combined use of both heroin and cocaine is also being seen with greater frequency among drug users, along with increased numbers of cases of dual addiction.

More than likely, the resurgence of heroin and its increased use is due in part to the current high level of its purity when sold on the street. The Drug Enforcement Administration has shown the average purity (in selected cities in the U.S.) to be about 35 percent—up by *1000*% from a decade and half ago! In New York City, the purity of street heroin is about 65%. These levels of street bag purity, unheard of in my career of 30 years, permit drug users a "good" high through snorting, allowing drug users to avoid the high-risk-for-HIV injection route. Nonetheless, there are consequent increases in emergency room admissions and overdose deaths particularly among injectors unused to the higher purity levels. A truly unfortunate circumstance is the return to active drug use of "success-fully" recovered heroin addicts. Such addicts are often lured into resumption of drug use by street reports of outstanding drug purity. It is within this context that Dr. Platt's book is incredibly timely. It can and should help reeducate and update his experienced colleagues, as well as newly inform and enlighten professional initiates into the treatment and epidemiologic world of heroin addiction.

DOUGLAS S. LIPTON, PH.D.

Preface

It has been 18 years since the first edition of *Heroin Addiction: Theory, Research, and Treatment* was published in 1976. What originally began as a review article on the etiology and treatment of heroin addiction has now expanded, with the simultaneous publication of this volume and Volume 3, into a three volume work of some 900 pages. So much for brevity! In many ways, this expansion in size is reflective of the state of the field, which incorporates a wide range of contributions from disciplines as disparate as neurochemistry and cultural anthropology.

Twenty years ago, methadone maintenance treatment had been in existence for less than a decade, psychoanalytic thinking was still influential (if not predominant) in treatment programs, the search for the addictive personality was moving ahead at full speed, little was known about relapse prevention, and even less was known about the internal processes related to change. Our knowledge of opiate receptors was still rudimentary, methadone was the only pharmacological agent approved for the treatment of opiate addicts, and HIV had yet to arrive on the drug abuse scene.

Today, we know a great deal more about heroin addiction, its etiology, pharmacology, and treatment than we did 20 years ago. At the same time, the number of problems related to heroin addiction which are foci of attention has expanded dramatically, in part because of the introduction of the Human Immunodeficiency Virus into the injection drug-using population, but also because of research advances in understanding and treating addiction in general. In this writer's opinion, we now have a true science of treatment for heroin addiction, in that we have an armamentarium of treatments, both pharmacological and behavioral, as well as sufficient knowledge of the interaction of patient characteristics and treatment outcome, to allow us to make treatment assignments, as well as to implement interventions, with some reasonable assurance of being able to predict outcomes. Yet, as will be seen, treatment settings have not been universally successful in applying this new knowledge.

Finally, it should be noted that heroin addiction is not only a chronic, relapsing disease at the individual level, but also at the societal level. The 1980s have seen heroin use eclipsed to some extent by cocaine use. Yet, heroin use has not disappeared. The number of heroin users remains significant and, at the time this is being written, heroin use appears to be increasing. The work being carried out by addiction researchers in laboratories and clinics will likely contribute to a increasingly effective response to this problem.

To make maximal use of this series of volumes, the reader should be aware of the plan according to which they were written. The second edition of Volume 1 of *Heroin Addiction: Theory, Research, and Treatment* was published in 1986, and like the first edition published in 1976, attempted an overview of the then current status of all aspects of heroin addiction, from the legal and historical points of view, to the underlying pharmacology and physiology of heroin addiction, through pharmacological and psychosocial interventions. The purpose of the second edition was to update the volume with respect to advances having taken place during the 10 years between 1975 and 1985. Since then, the momentum of progress in understanding and treating heroin addiction has increased dramatically, and it is with a continued purpose of informing the readership of rapidly unfolding developments in this field that the author and publisher have decided to produce a series of volumes at appropriate intervals. The second edition was thus designated Volume 1 at the time of a second printing in 1988. Volume 2, *Heroin Addiction: The Addict, The Treatment Process, and Social Control,* has as its aim, to provide an overview of new findings with respect to the understanding of heroin addiction and their application to the development and improvement of treatment, while Volume 3, *Heroin Addiction: Treatment Advances and AIDS*, describes recent developments in treatment, as well as an overview of AIDS as it relates to heroin addiction. In order to both minimize the time required to produce each volume, and maintain as low a cost as possible for each volume, repetition of material in prior volumes in the series has been avoided.

While Volume 1 attempted, to some extent, to be a broad review of the entire field of knowledge pertaining to heroin addiction, no such attempt has been undertaken with the preparation of Volume 2. The content of each volume is now more delineated in nature, and it is expected that future volumes addressing other topical areas will appear subsequently.

As previously noted, the material in Volumes 2 and 3 is new, and does not overlap with earlier volumes, except as is absolutely necessary for continuity. Where substantial knowledge of earlier material not repeated in this volume is deemed necessary for a full understanding of the context of current developments, the reader is referred to the specific location in the relevant earlier volume. Additionally, in order to provide the reader with more rapid access to the literature reviewed in each of the volumes, author and subject indexes from Volume 2 on have been made cumulative for all previous volumes in the series.

This volume is intended to serve as a review of, as well as a means of access to, the scientific and related literature on heroin addiction and its treatment. While every effort has been made to accurately report the ideas, concepts, research findings, and opinions therein, the author cannot assume any responsibility for the validity, accuracy, or effectiveness in practice of the ideas, concepts, opinions, and data which are presented. This volume is not intended to serve as a treatment manual in actual clinical situations nor to substitute in any way for appropriate clinical training, experience, or supervision. Readers should consult the original sources for more detailed information concerning the ideas, findings, and interventions described, and should employ them only after appropriate consideration.

A number of individuals have contributed to the completion of this volume. Thanks are extended to Arthur Meyerson, then chairman of the Department of Mental Health Sciences at Hahnemann University, for having made the time available so that this volume could be prepared, Daniel O. Taube and Mindy Widman, for their assistance in assembling and managing some of the huge amount of material which was reviewed, as well as in drafting parts of several chapters, Diane Mathis, Torbjörn Järbe, and Mindy Widman for their critical reading and comments on the manuscript, and to Kay Platt for her critical reading, proofreading, and assistance in preparing the indexes (but most of all for her generous tolerance during the preparation of the manuscript). Mindy Widman supervised, and Lee Sinclair and Stacey Chestnut assisted with the onerous task of assembling the bibliography, and this assistance is also appreciated. Finally, Robert E. Krieger of Krieger Publishing Co. graciously granted extensions for the completion of this work, ever faithful that the proposed volumes would one day appear. I am pleased that he was right!

Jerome J. Platt

Philadelphia, Pennsylvania

Acknowledgment

Parts of Chapter 7 are based upon, and reprint material from, "Major Psycho-therapeutic Modalities for Heroin Addiction: A Brief Review," by J. J. Platt, S. D. Husband, and D. O. Taube, which appeared in *The International Journal of the Addictions* (1990–91, volume 25, number 12A, pages 1453–1477). This material is used by courtesy of Marcel Dekker, Inc.

PART ONE

The Continuing Problem of Heroin Addiction

CHAPTER 1

Overview: The Continuing Problem of Heroin Addiction

THE EXTENT OF THE PROBLEM

Heroin use in the United States remains a significant national problem. Although overtaken by cocaine as the primary "hard drug" being used and now more likely to be part of an overall pattern of multiple drug use (Hubbard, Marsden, Rachal, Harwood, Cavanaugh, and Ginzburg, 1989), the level of heroin use is still considerable. According to the National Institute on Drug Abuse's 1991 National Household Survey (NHSDA; NIDA, 1992a), 1.3% of the U.S. population aged 12 and older, or some 2.5 million people, had used heroin at some point in their lives. Preliminary data from the 1992 National Household Survey (SAMHSA, 1993) indicated a drop from 1.3% to .9%, a change statistically significant at the .05 level. Yet, even at this lower level of heroin use, the percentage corresponds to a population figure of 1,840,000 people.

When annual trends in heroin use are examined as a function of age, there is clear variation. For example, the overall percentage of the population aged 12

Table 1.1
Percentages of Respondents Reporting
Use of Heroin for Lifetime, Past Year, and Past Month by Age

	Lifetime				*Past Year*				*Past Month*		
1988	*1990*	*1991*	*1992*	*1988*	*1990*	*1991*	*1992*	*1988*	*1990*	*1991*	*1992*
Ages 12–17											
1.0	0.8	1.3	0.9	0.3	0.2	0.2	0.2	0.0	0.0	0.0	0.1
Ages 18–25											
0.3	0.6	0.8	1.3	0.3	0.5	0.3	0.5	0.1	0.1	0.1	0.2
Ages 26–34											
2.1	1.4	1.8	1.6	0.5	0.2	0.3	0.2	NA	0.0	0.1	1.4
Ages 35 and over											
0.8	0.7	1.5	0.7	0.2	0.1	0.1	0.1	0.0	NA	0.0	0.0

Source: SAMHSA, Office of Applied Studies, National Household Survey on Drug Abuse. (June, 1993). *Preliminary estimates from the 1992 National Household Survey on Drug Abuse.*

and older, who had used heroin at some point in their lifetimes, showed an over-all decline between 1991 and 1992 (to the levels of 1988 through 1990). At the same time, lifetime use of heroin for the U.S. population aged 18 through 25 showed a steady increase from 1988 through 1992 (see Table 1.1). In addition to this being the case for the Lifetime category, an increasing trend for this age group was true for the Past Year and Past Month categories of use as well. These figures suggest a steady rate of increase in heroin use for the age group in which such use is most likely to begin.

According to the 1992 National Household Survey, 1.84 million Americans, or just under 1% of the population, have tried heroin (Substance Abuse and Mental Health Services Administration, 1993). However, it should be noted that the household surveys of substance abuse do not adequately measure the prevalence of heroin use and are believed to result in significant underestimates, particularly with respect to current use (Secretary, Department of Health and Human Services, 1991).

Two recent reports have raised questions concerning current methods and findings about the extent of drug use in the United States. In the first report, the General Accounting Office (GAO, June, 1993) questioned the accuracy of several measures of drug use in the United States, including the NHSDA, discussed above. The National Household Survey was found by the GAO to be seriously flawed in its estimates of heroin use, both through overestimation and underestimation. The NHSDA was found to have overestimated heroin users in households by 46% through a faulty system of imputing drug use to reconcile contradictory responses. However, the GAO noted that "heroin users frequently do not live in stable household environments of the sort sampled" (1993, p. 56) resulting in underestimation, the extent of which was not posited. While it is thus impossible to determine the net effects of these over-/underestimations, it can be assumed that the household survey data are less accurate for heroin use across the United States than would, at first glance, be thought. The second report (Eisenhandler and Drucker, 1993) provided the results of an attempt to estimate the prevalence of opiate use among subscribers to a large private insurance plan, Empire Blue Cross and Blue Shield of New York. Some 141,000 opiate users were found to have been insured by the plan between 1982 and 1992, with 85,000 still insured at the time of the study. Eisenhandler and Drucker (1993) concluded that

There is a large population of insured opiate users who may be excluded from the estimates of the overall number of opiate users as insured opiate users are less likely to be counted via contact with governmental agencies (p. 2890).

Data from the Drug Abuse Warning Network (DAWN; NIDA, 1992b), another large scale, ongoing drug abuse data collection system, provide another source of information concerning the current level of heroin use. During 1991, there were an estimated 400,079 drug abuse episodes and 685,233 drug abuse mentions at hospitals eligible for inclusion in the DAWN system. Of these cases, there were 36,576 mentions of heroin/morphine use during emergency room episodes, which accounted for 9.14% of all episodes. This figure was exceeded only by alcohol-in-combination with other drugs (123,758 mentions, accounting for 30.93% of all episodes) and cocaine (102,727 mentions, accounting for 25.68% of all episodes). In the 21 DAWN metropolitan areas, the highest numbers of drug mentions from central city hospitals were for methadone (83%), heroin/morphine (77%), cocaine (77%), haloperidol (74%), and PCP/PCP combinations (70%).

When heroin and morphine mentions were examined as a function of age, they were the third most frequently mentioned drugs for both the groups aged 26 through 34 years and 35 years and older, but were seventh in mentions among patients aged 18 to 25 years. When mentions were classified by ethnicity, heroin/morphine use retained its rank as the third most frequently mentioned drug among both African American (14.21%) and Hispanic (15.55%) patients; it ranked sixth in mentions among white patients (6.06%).

While the overall distribution of heroin and morphine mentions did not show an increase between 1990 and 1991, there were statistically significant increases in a number of metropolitan areas. These included Baltimore (134%), St Louis (69%), Buffalo (46%), Boston (26%), and Chicago (10%). At the same time, there were significant decreases in numbers of mentions in Los Angeles (30%), Dallas (25%), Denver (16%), San Francisco (16%), and New Orleans (11%).

Finally, it should be noted that preliminary data from DAWN for the third quarter of 1992 indicated a record number (13,400) of heroin-related emergency room episodes during this period. This finding was particularly evident among persons aged 35 and over, in whom heroin emergencies increased by 42%. This finding occurred while total episodes (109,200) were up only slightly from the third quarter of 1991 (105,100) and the second quarter of 1992 (106,000) (*Alcohol and Drug Abuse Weekly*, May 10, 1993). This trend was also present in the final annual figures for 1992. Heroin overdoses rose to 48,000 during 1992, a 34% increase over the previous year, while cocaine overdoses also rose 18%, to 119,800. Both of these figures reflected all-time highs (Treaster, October 5, 1993).

Medical examiner data for drug abuse-related deaths in 27 metropolitan areas (NIDA, 1992c) also exist. These data concerning heroin use are also compiled by the National Institute on Drug Abuse. Although not representative of all areas of the United States because of its focus on metropolitan areas (at least through 1991, although this limitation will change for the 1992 data year), these data provide a third national data base. Here, again, heroin/morphine retained third place with respect to the frequency of mentioned drugs, being found in 35% of drug-related deaths. Cocaine was mentioned in 46% of drug-related deaths, while alcohol-in-combination was mentioned in connection with 37% of drug-related deaths. These numbers do not represent a significant change from the previous year in terms of the proportion of cases in which deaths involving heroin/morphine was mentioned (this figure was 34% for 1990). In cases where the death was accidental or unexpected, heroin/morphine was the second most frequently mentioned drug (42% of all such cases), while cocaine and alcohol-in-combination were mentioned in 56% and 40% of deaths respectively.

Consistent with data from the DAWN system, there were significant changes in the number of mentions of heroin/morphine in medical examiner cases in a number of cities. Increases occurred in Baltimore (268% increase), Newark (252%), and St. Louis (109%), while decreases occurred in Dallas (35% decrease), Los Angeles (23%), San Francisco (13%), and San Diego (11%).

Data from the National Household Survey, DAWN system, and the annual medical examiner data all indicate a consistent use of heroin in the United States, although primarily centered in the 26 to 34 year old age group. When data from a number of cities are considered, the overall pattern is one of increasing use, although primarily centered in the Eastern United States.

The 1991 Drug Abuse Warning Network (DAWN) report also contained other, disturbing, information suggesting an overall increase in heroin use. Drug-related emergency room episodes showed a 12% increase from the fourth quarter of 1990 to the second quarter of 1991. While, during this period, there was a 31% increase in persons seeking emergency room assistance for cocaine-related incidents, there was a 26% increase in heroin-related emergency room incidents (*Alcoholism and Drug Abuse Weekly*, January 1, 1992). In order to confirm the existence of this trend, Inciardi, Tressell, Pottieger, and Rosales (1992) conducted a street survey of 224 current heroin users (average age = 38 years) in the Miami/Dade County metropolitan area addressing, among other issues, street addicts' opinions of current availability, cost, and quality of heroin (and crack). Respondents were both long-term (mean age at first use, 19.5 years), and current users (all but one respondent had used heroin by injection in the past month, and 88% had used daily in the past month). Respondents had increased their heroin, but not their crack, use during the previous year, 76% reported greater availability than a year earlier, and 62% reported greater quality, while only 47% thought it was cheaper. Interestingly, the perceived quality of the available drug appeared to have most influenced increased use.

Overall, then, heroin use appears to be an endemic problem in the United States, although it has been displaced as the drug of choice by cocaine. Data from a number of sources showed a decrease in heroin use among new entrants into drug abuse treatment. For example, the Client Oriented Data Acquisition Process (CODAP) showed a decrease from 61% to 36% between 1976 to 1981 (NIDA, 1982), a trend also reflected in data from TOPS (Hubbard et al., 1989).

When drug abuse patterns from the three major national surveys of characteristics of drug abuse treatment (see Appendix A) are examined (see Table 1.2), a steady decline in the rates of *regular* opioid use over time is found. For instance, the examination of daily opioid use rates among entering cohorts in the Drug Abuse Reporting System (DARP), Treatment Outcome Prospective Study (TOPS), and Drug Abuse Treatment Outcome Study (DATOS), reveal a regular decline in daily opioid use for methadone, long-term residential, and outpatient nonmethadone treatment modalities. At the same time, for clients in methadone maintenance treatment, nonopioid use increased dramatically, and a much greater number of clients used nonopioids in combination with daily opioid use (DARP: 49%, DATOS: 74%). A similar increase occurred among clients in long-term residential treatment (DARP: 17%, DATOS: 74%), while a somewhat smaller, but not inconsequential increase occurred among outpatient non-methadone patients (DARP: 48%, DATOS: 81%).

The figures cited above should not, however, be taken as the actual number of persons who are in need of drug abuse treatment and related services. That number is significantly larger. Gerstein and Lewin (1990) provided an estimate by noting that the data included in the Institute of Medicine report (Gerstein and Harwood, 1990) on drug-treatment programs yielded a point-prevalence estimate of 5.5 million people who were dependent on or abusing drugs, close to half of whom were in the criminal-justice system. This estimate, they concluded, was the " ... number of people for whom drug treatment is clearly or probably appropriate" (p. 844).

Most recently, however, indications of increased heroin use have appeared. Not

Table 1.2
DARP Drug Use Patterns, by Modality:
Comparison of DARP, TOPS, and Preliminary DATOS Data (in percent)

	DARP	TOPS	DATOS
	Methadone		
Drug Use Pattern	(n = 11,023)	(n = 3,223)	(n = 877)
Daily opioid use only	45	21	13
Daily opioid/some nonopioids	49	60	74
Less than daily opioid use	5	15	11
Nonopioid use only	1	4	2
Total	100	100	100
	Long-Term Residential		
	(n = 4,505)	(n = 1,192)	(n = 943)
Daily opioid use only	23	6	1
Daily opioid/some nonopioids	40	24	12
Less than daily opioid use	20	29	13
Nonopioid use only	17	41	74
Total	100	100	100
	Outpatient Non-Methadone		
	(n = 5,785)	(n = 1,949)	(n = 663)
Daily opioid use only	17	2	1
Daily opioid/some nonopioids	16	8	5
Less than daily opioid use	17	26	13
Nonopioid use only	48	64	81
Total	100	100	100

Note: These data exclude clients with no recent drug use or those who have been institutionalized longer than 10 months in the past year.

Note: Missing data are excluded separately for each characteristic.
Source: Hubbard, R. L. (1993). Drug Abuse Treatment Outcome Study (DATOS) research. Presented at the NIDA Second National Conference on Drug Abuse Research & Practice, Washington, D.C., July 14–17.

only has the sheer number of admissions to emergency rooms with heroin-related problems increased by some 30% between comparable periods of 1992 and 1993 (*Alcohol and Drug Abuse Weekly*, May 10, 1993), but the percentage of drug arrests in New York involving heroin increased from 28% in 1988 to 55% in 1992 (Treaster, August 1, 1993).

CHARACTERISTICS OF CLIENTS ENTERING TREATMENT

Table 1.3 presents demographic characteristics for persons entering the four primary modalities of drug abuse treatment in the DATOS study: methadone maintenance; long-term residential; outpatient nonmethadone; and short-term inpatient treatment. Some clear similarities and differences exist across modalities. For example, across modalities, approximately two-thirds of all new admissions tend to be male, while African Americans account for approximately one-half of admissions to all modalities, with the exception of methadone maintenance where they account for slightly under one-third of entering clients. Hispanics tend to be overrepresented in methadone maintenance treatment and underrepresented in short-term inpatient treatment. Non-Hispanic Caucasians, on the other hand, tend to be overrepresented in methadone treatment. Clients entering methadone maintenance treatment tend to be somewhat older than clients entering other modalities, and clients entering residential treatment tend to be slightly younger. Finally, clients entering both methadone maintenance and short-term inpatient treatment are more likely to be married or living as married than clients entering the other two modalities.

CONSEQUENCES OF ADDICTION PROBLEMS IN THE UNITED STATES

Mortality

Injection drug use in the era of AIDS has greatly increased the risks of drug-related death for heroin users. Joe and Simpson (1990), for example, reported the results of an analysis of mortality risk factors for a sample of 555 addicts who had survived at least 6 years in the 12-year DARP follow-up. The rate of mortality for this group, 13.8 per 1,000 person-years, was approximately seven times that for an age-comparable general population comparison group. Four variables were found to successfully predict mortality: (a) alcohol consumption (daily intake equivalent to over eight ounces of 80 proof alcohol beverage); (b) pattern of opioid drug use (including continued use of alcohol and opioids); (c) age (over 36 years of age at time of admission to DARP); and (d) marital status (where unmarried people were at greatest risk). When drug related deaths occurred, they frequently involved heroin (37%), cocaine (49%), or the use of these drugs in combination; the latter practice is often called "speedballing" (Secretary, Department of Health and Human Services, 1991).

Examining the long-term consequences of heroin use, Hser, Anglin, and Powers (1993) followed 581 addicts admitted to the California Civil Addict Program during the years 1962 through 1964. Interviews, investigating patterns of drug use over a period of approximately 15 years, were conducted during 1974–1975

Table 1.3
Client Demographics: Preliminary DATOS Data (in percent)

Characteristic	Methadone (N = 986)	Long-Term Residential (N = 1,639)	Outpatient Non-Methadone (N = 1,516)	Short-term Inpatient (N = 1,927)
Gender				
Male	60.4	66.8	66.4	67.7
Female	39.6	33.2	33.6	32.3
Total	100.0	100.0	100.0	100.0
Race/Ethnicity				
African-American	29.8	48.3	48.2	50.3
Hispanic	22.7	12.9	11.9	6.1
Non-Hispanic Caucasian	45.6	35.7	36.4	40.9
Other	1.8	3.1	3.5	2.6
Total	100.0	100.0	100.0	100.0
Age				
18–20	0.1	3.9	4.6	3.9
21–25	5.0	19.0	15.2	12.5
26–30	14.0	31.2	26.3	25.1
31–44	69.1	42.9	48.9	51.7
45 and older	11.9	3.1	5.0	6.7
Total	100.0	100.0	100.0	100.0
Marital Status				
Married	21.5	12.2	18.8	27.0
Separated	8.7	7.0	7.8	6.3
Divorced	15.4	13.5	13.0	14.8
Widowed	3.6	1.2	1.3	1.9
Living as Married	21.0	10.7	12.2	8.5
Never Married	29.7	55.5	46.8	41.5
Total	100.0	100.0	100.0	100.0

Note: Missing data are excluded separately for each characteristic.
Source: Hubbard, R. L. (1993). Drug Abuse Treatment Outcome Study (DATOS) research. Presented at the NIDA Second National Conference on Drug Abuse Research & Practice, Washington, D.C., July 14–17.

and 1985–1986. At the time of the first follow-up interview in 1974–1975, 13.8% of the sample had died, while 27.7% had died by the time of the second interview in 1985–1986. An addict who had been actively using narcotics in 1974–1975 had a slightly higher risk of death (.21 versus .16) by 1985–1986 when compared with inactive users. Average age of death was 40.2 years. When cause of death was examined, 32.3% were the direct result of drug overdose, and 39.1% were the result of alcohol use, smoking, or other factors. Homicide, suicide, or accident accounted for 28.6% of the deaths. The variable found to be most strongly related to mortality during the first 10 years of the follow-up was age, i.e., higher mortality among older addicts. This variable was not significantly associated with mortality during the second 10 years. Instead, this variable had been replaced by self-reported disability status, while three other variables were marginally related to early death: the percentage of time alcohol was used heavily; mean number of arrests; and level of cigarette smoking. Length of addiction was not found to be related to early death. Most likely this finding resulted from a lack of statistical variation among the subjects followed in this study, almost all of whom had extensive addiction histories.

Financial Expenditures and Treatment

The costs of addiction to alcohol and drugs in general, and heroin addiction specifically, represent a major problem in the United States. In its 1993 report on the costs of treating preventable behavioral problems in the United States, the American Medical Association (1993) estimated that more than $171 billion is spent annually on such preventable problems as alcohol, tobacco, and drug abuse. The cost of drug abuse problems alone was $58.3 billion in health care, law enforcement, and lost productivity in 1988. In comparison, costs associated with alcohol abuse totalled $85.8 billion, reflecting an estimated two million persons hospitalized, 125,000 visits with a drug abuse diagnosis to office-based physicians, and 6,100 deaths in 1985; three-fourths occurred among persons aged 15 to 44 years of age. Estimates of funding sources paying the bill for direct costs of treating and supporting drug abusers may be divided into private sources (36%) and public sources (64%). The latter figure can be allocated to Federal funds (39%) and state and local funds (25%; Rice, Kelman, and Miller, 1991).

According to the 1991 National Drug and Alcohol Treatment Unit Survey (Office of Applied Studies, Substance Abuse and Mental Health Services Administration, 1993), the total capacity of drug and alcohol abuse treatment programs in the United States, both public and private, exceeded one million treatment slots, with a utilization rate of 81.1%. When utilization by type of problem was considered, 45% of patients were classified as alcoholic, 29.2% as primarily having a drug problem, and 25.8% as having a combined alcohol and drug problem. Utilization by type of program indicated that 81.4% of available outpatient slots were filled, as were 79.9% of inpatient slots and 65.2% of detoxification slots. A total of $4.144 billion was spent on drug and alcohol treatment in 1991, a figure only slightly up from $4.082 billion in 1990.

It would be difficult, if not impossible, to determine the costs of treatment or prevention for heroin addiction alone. However, on a given day, 11,277 treatment and prevention programs provide services to 811,819 substance abuse patients. While not directly comparable because of yearly variations in reporting, the increase from 755,079 patients served in 1990 suggests more than a chance fluctuation. Ambulatory treatment (outpatient, intensive outpatient, or outpatient detoxification) was the most common type of program, with 87.8% of the patient total, while residential programs (hospital-based inpatient, short- or long-term residential) accounted for 10.8% of patients. Full-time detoxification programs (hospital inpatient or free-standing residential) accounted for the remaining 1.4%. Eighty percent (9,057) of these 11,277 programs provided treatment to their patients. Of this number, 79.2% were combined alcohol and drug abuse units, 9.9% served only drug abuse patients, and 10.9% serviced only alcoholic patients. Occupancy rates by source of funding were as follows: State and local government—87.7%; private nonprofit, with some public funding—82.4%; tribal government—76.7%; federal—74.7%; and private for profit—70.0%.

Criminal Activity

Criminal activity has long been seen as a common characteristic of heroin addicts (see, e.g., Ball, Rosen, Flueck, and Nurco, 1981; Inciardi, 1981; Musto, 1973; Terry and Pellens, 1970; see also Volume 1, pp. 184–185, and this Volume, Chapter 7). Ball and Ross (1991), for example, calculated that the addicts in their study committed an average of 484 crimes per year during their periods of active heroin use! In a more conservative estimate, Nurco, Ball, Shaffer, and Hanlon (1985) calculated that, on average, a narcotic addict commits 178 criminal offenses a year. Extrapolating this figure to the estimated 450,000 addicts in the United States, narcotics addicts commit some 80 million crimes a year! Of this figure, some 38% were assumed to be drug-related, 22% were the so-called "victimless" crimes of prostitution, gambling and alcohol violations, and 40% were major crimes (including robbery and assaults, vehicle·theft, shoplifting, selling stolen goods, forgery, counterfeiting, and burglary). When crime-days per year-at-risk, a concept reflecting the commission of one or more crimes during a 24-hour period was used, the annual number of crime-days per year-at-risk was found to consistently average over 230. This rate was not only persistent on a day-to-day basis, but also tended to continue over an extended number of years and periods of addiction. Heroin-using offenders also account for a significant amount of crime. Chaiken (1986) reported heroin-using offenders to have committed 15 times as many robberies, 20 times as many burglaries, and 10 times as many thefts as other offenders; Johnson, Goldstein, Preble, Schmeidler, Lipton, Spunt, and Miller (1985) reported that active drug use increases crime rates by a factor of 4 to 6.

Thus, with regard to crime, the Third Triennial Report (Secretary, Department of Health and Human Services, 1991) concluded that the results of several studies

... indicated that narcotic addicts commit a disproportionate number of crimes, almost equally divided between 1) drug dealing/possession crimes and "victimless" offenses; and 2) personal and property offenses (p. 24).

Given the more than 32,800 admissions to federal and 390,000 to state prisons in 1990 (Bureau of Justice Statistics, 1993), the sheer magnitude of the drug abuse problem among those adjudicated by the criminal justice system is staggering. Some 20% of the convicted jail population, over 20% of the total state prison population, and 54% of the federal prison population in 1990 were drug offenders. At the far end of the criminal justice pipeline, some 30% of the approximately 70,000 federal probationers at the end of June, 1989 were drug offenders, a significant increase from 23% in 1985 (Bureau of Justice Statistics, 1992). While comparable figures are not available at the state levels, there is no reason to believe the level to be different. The number of prisoners incarcerated for drug abuse-related offenses has, in fact, threatened to overwhelm the criminal justice system, and has led to an unprecedented protest by senior judges on the federal bench, including a refusal by several to continue being parties to what they perceive as an ineffective and cruel war on drugs characterized by an emphasis on punishment rather than prevention, education, and treatment (*New York Times*, April 17, 1993, p. A1).

Costs to the Individual

Injection drug use, which almost all heroin addicts engage in at some point in their addiction careers, has been found be a marker for a wide range of drug-use related problems experienced on a life-time basis. Dinwiddie, Reich, and Cloninger (1992b), for example, found the following rates of complications among a sample of male and female injecting drug users: (a) physical (males, 73.8%; females, 58.1%); (b) psychological (males, 83.6%; females, 54.8%); (c) social impairment (males, 77.1%; females, 64.5%); (d) drug-related antisocial behavior (males, 19.7%; females, 16.1%); and (e) any drug-related problem (males, 95.1%; females, 80.7%). Only with respect to psychological complications did the difference between males and females reach significance. When "heavy" versus "light" (experimental) intravenous use was examined, heavy users were found to have had significantly more physical complications and more social impairment, as well as to have had more treatment for drug abuse.

THE CHANGING NATURE OF THE PROBLEM

Heroin addiction, while a persistent problem in the United States, represents proportionally a much smaller percentage of the overall drug problem than it did 20 years ago. This change is evident in the results summarized in Table 1.4. The table compares data collected by the TOPS study, which was conducted on admissions to treatment during 1979–1981, and the DATOS study, which was conducted during 1991–1993. Not surprisingly, heroin addicts using the drug daily or weekly accounted for 66.5% of all admissions to methadone maintenance treatment in the TOPS study, and 87.6% in the DATOS study. Cocaine use among methadone maintenance clients, however, increased from 27.6% in the TOPS study to 41.9% in the DATOS study. Cocaine was in fact the most widely abused drug across the other modalities in DATOS, with 67% of those in both short-term inpatient and long-term residential programs, and 41% of outpatient non-methadone clients reporting cocaine as their primary drug of abuse.

Cocaine and Heroin Use

As seen above, the increasing prevalence of cocaine use has had an impact on heroin use in two ways: (a) an increasing substitution of cocaine for heroin as a primary drug of abuse for many populations; and (b) the use of heroin and cocaine in combination ("speedballing"). Examining how the use of crack cocaine has had an impact on the heroin subculture, McBride, Inciardi, Chitwood, McCoy, et al. (1992) studied the relationship between crack use on the one hand, and injection drug use, other drug use, and high-risk behavior on the other, in a national population of out-of-treatment street heroin users. This study was carried out with 22,072 injecting drug users selected from the National AIDS Demonstration Research population (of over 48,000, 38,000 of whom had injected heroin) who had reported any use during their lifetimes of both cocaine and heroin by injection. The results indicated a strong relationship between the use of crack and higher rates of other drug use. The use of alcohol, marijuana, and amphetamines more than once a day was more than twice as likely among injection drug users (IDUs) who had used crack in the past six months. Over 60% of those injection heroin users who used crack more than once a day also snorted cocaine, and some 40% used amphetamines daily. McBride et al. (1992) concluded that (a) heavy use of crack cocaine was part of a pattern of frequent use of stimulants; (b) frequent crack users among heroin IDUs also injected cocaine and amphetamines more than once a day; (c) crack use was not a replacement for injecting

Table 1.4
Weekly or Daily drug Use, by Modality:
comparison of TOPS and Preliminary DATOS Data (in percent)

	TOPS (1979–81)	DATOS (1991–93)
	Methadone (Outpatient)	
Drug	(n = 4,184)	(n = 986)
Heroin	66.5	87.6
Other Opioids	28.3	23.1
Cocaine	27.6	41.9
Barbiturates/Sedatives	28.0	10.9
Amphetamines	9.0	2.8
Marijuana	55.0	17.7
Alcohol	47.4	29.8
	Long-Term Residential	
	(n = 2,891)	(n = 1,639)
Heroin	30.9	15.3
Other Opioids	29.7	5.0
Cocaine	30.0	66.9
Barbiturates/Sedatives	39.5	5.3
Amphetamines	30.0	6.0
Marijuana	65.0	28.0
Alcohol	65.0	56.7
	Outpatient Non-Methadone	
	(n = 2,914)	(n = 1,516)
Heroin	10.3	5.8
Other Opioids	15.1	4.5
Cocaine	16.8	41.0
Barbiturates/Sedatives	28.0	2.7
Amphetamines	22.7	5.1
Marijuana	68.1	25.7
Alcohol	61.7	47.0

continued on next page

Table 1.4   *continued*

	Short-Term Inpatient	
		(n = 1,927)
Heroin	N/A	5.9
Other Opioids	N/A	10.6
Cocaine	N/A	66.0
Barbiturates/Sedatives	N/A	9.7
Amphetamines	N/A	4.7
Marijuana	N/A	30.4
Alcohol	N/A	64.9

Note: The numbers are the percentage who indicated weekly or daily use as a proportion of the total number of respondents.
Source: Hubbard, R. L. (1993). Drug Abuse Treatment Outcome Study (DATOS) research. Presented at the NIDA Second National Conference on Drug Abuse Research & Practice, Washigton, D.C., July 14–17.

drugs, but rather was associated with more frequent injection use of stimulants; and (d) frequent crack use was associated with an increased frequency of needle sharing and the use of shooting galleries.

Most recently, however, with the availability of higher purity heroin, there has been a return to heroin use. Possible explanations are the ability to now obtain a heroin high without injecting, and the increasing use of heroin to avoid or reduce the cyclic effects of anxiety triggered by cocaine use, as well as the depression which often follows (Treaster, August 1, 1993).

Changing Routes of Administration

In recent years there has been a shift in the routes of administration. This shift is particularly pronounced among recent initiates to heroin use. Thus, rather than injecting opiates, inhalation ("sniffing," "snorting," or "chasing the dragon") is becoming the preferred route for opiate users (Casriel, Rockwell, and Stepherson, 1988; Casriel, Des Jarlais, Rodriguez, Friedman, Stepherson, and Khuri, 1990; Strang, Griffiths, Powis, and Gossop, 1992). Typically this method involves heating the heroin until a vapor is given off, and then inhaling it through a tube. However, heroin is also increasingly being mixed with tobacco and smoked in cigarettes. Noting that this practice was becoming widespread in Britain during the last decade, Gossop (1988) attributed this change in part to the high oil content of increasingly available South Asian heroin. It also likely reflected attempts by heroin users, particularly new initiates to heroin, to reduce HIV exposure risk (Parker, Newcombe, and Bakx, 1987).

Given the increasingly high purity of heroin sold on the street, smoking, a less efficient but safer way of using the drug, becomes attractive. Heroin being sold on the street now is up to 64% pure in New York, 81% pure in Boston, and 38.7% pure nationally, compared to 3-4% purity 10 years ago (Treaster, August 1, 1993). The increased number of admissions seeking help at emergency rooms during late 1992 because of drug overdoses is likely a result (at least in part) of the increased purity and amount of street heroin available. In turn, heroin purity and availability is likely a result of both bumper crops of opium poppies over the past several years in growing regions, as well as increased marketing efforts on the part of distributors.

In 1988, Casriel, Rockwell, and Stepherson observed that at least half of the heroin addicts entering treatment had begun their heroin use by sniffing the drug. Some continued to use this route of administration, others moved on to injecting, and some dropped out of drug use. Casriel et al. (1988) also noted that regular sniffing of heroin was addicting, that a heroin habit and heroin craving were likely to result from sniffing, and that withdrawal symptoms were likely to result from discontinuation of use. While heroin might be initially used in a social or "party" context, such use was less likely to occur later in a sniffer's career, when seeking the drug is all that is of great concern. Casriel et al. (1988) concluded that the following differences existed between heroin sniffing and injecting: (a) an absence when sniffing, of the drug high or "rush" experienced by injectors, in contrast to a more gradual onset of the high; and (b) a rapid high while injecting thus requiring less heroin.

Describing the characteristics of heroin sniffers, Casriel et al. (1988) saw them as very diverse in their frequency of heroin use (from four times daily to a few times yearly), priding themselves in their being different from injectors (a distinction not often easily seen), being faced with the need to resist pressures to switch to injection (often accomplished by accentuating differences with injectors), and possessing ambivalence about entering treatment. Casriel et al. (1988) concluded that sniffers are a group of heroin users who may be reached and helped, but they represent a group on the brink of injecting. Thus, research is needed to provide appropriate interventions. There is a need to learn to identify those most likely to move on to injecting, and studying sniffers will help us further understand heroin addiction and improve treatment interventions.

In an attempt to learn more about British heroin users who take the drug by inhalation, Gossop (1988) interviewed both British injectors and noninjectors about their drug use. He found that chasing was not merely a preinjection phase—87% had been chasers for more than two years, and 27% more than five years, while injectors had begun using drugs intravenously within the first year of use. In addition, chasers were younger, injectors had started using heroin earlier, and males and females were equally represented in both groups. Cost did not appear to be an issue in moving from chasing to injecting. In a later paper, Casriel, Des Jarlais, Rodriguez, Friedman, Stepherson, and Khuri (1990) examined clinical issues which arose in the treatment of heroin sniffers at high risk for injecting drugs. Among those issues found were a generalized mistrust of authorities, denial of problems associated with noninjected drug use, and ambivalence about injecting. Both studies leave many unanswered questions concerning this population of heroin users. For example, Casriel et al. (1990) noted that friendship ties among the group they studied were formed easily, but did not extend to subjects convincing friends to participate in the study, raising the question as to how constructive group friendships could be reinforced in order to provide lasting support networks oriented away from drug injection.

Route of administration may also play a part in the severity of dependence which results from heroin use. (See Volume 1, Chapter 5, for a discussion of tolerance and dependence.) Gossop, Griffiths, Powis, and Strang (1992) found that heroin taken by injection produced a more severe dependence than did smoked heroin; while for cocaine, injection and smoking produced equally severe dependence, and use of cocaine by both of these routes produced more severe dependence than did intranasal use. Severity of dependence to amphetamines was not related to route of administration.

Gossop, Griffiths, Powis, and Strang (1992) also found that, among current users of more than one drug, more severe dependence was produced by heroin use than use of either cocaine or amphetamines, and that many users of these stimulant drugs experienced no dependency problems. Gossop et al. (1992) were not able to find any explanation accounting for why the route of administration should have a different effect for heroin, cocaine, and amphetamines. Severity of dependence was also found to be associated with dose and duration of drug use, although this association was more the case for heroin "chasers" (i.e., inhalers) than for heroin injectors. Previous attendance at a drug treatment agency was also found to be strongly associated with dose and duration of heroin use, although dependence problems were also found among those who had never received drug treatment. For stimulant users, however, reported severity was not related to having received treatment, reflecting either the greater emphasis on treatment of the opiate user in the British treatment system, or the experience of fewer and less severe dependence problems among stimulant users. With regard to this issue, Gossop et al. (1992) noted the similarity of their major finding to the report by Robins, Helzer, Hesselbrock, and Wish (1980) that American soldiers' use of heroin in Vietnam was more likely to lead to dependence than was use of cocaine.

Drug Use in the Homeless

Homelessness, while not a new problem in this country, has become a major national problem within the past decade, eliciting much discussion concerning its causes and interventions to address it (e.g., Jones, Levine, and Rosenberg, 1991;

Shinn and Weissman, 1990). Homelessness not only presents a problem in and of itself, but the homeless also present a major risk population for the interrelated problems of mental illness, substance abuse, sexually transmitted diseases, and HIV infection. While alcohol abuse is the primary substance abuse problem in this population, other substance abuse follows closely. Fischer (1989) has estimated the prevalences of alcohol and drug abuse problems to range respectively from 4% to 86% and from 1% to 70% for men and women combined, with both alcohol and drug abuse problems more common among males than females (alcohol problems—80% versus 63%; drug problems—61% versus 26%). Substance abuse has been found to be highest in the 16-19 years age group (Wright and Knight, 1987), although problems far exceed those in the general population at all ages, particularly in the age 35 years plus category (Fischer and Breakey, 1991). While opioids are much less likely to be the drug of choice, their level of use in one study was found to be equivalent to that of barbiturates and amphetamines (Toro and Wall, 1989). Mental illness is often a concurrent problem with substance abuse, constituting some 10% to 20% of the homeless population (Drake, Osher, and Wallach, 1991). Causality with respect to substance abuse and homelessness seems to be bi-directional; alcohol and drug abuse increases the likelihood of homelessness, and dislocation and loss of shelter lead to substance abuse (McCarty, Argeriou, Huebner, and Lubran, 1991).

Treatment interventions for the homeless population present significant problems, particularly given the multitude and complexity of substance abuse and mental disorders present. However, research and service advances on addressing this problem have been increasing (Dennis, Buckner, Lipton, and Levine, 1991), particularly with regard to those programs specifically directed at alcohol and drug abuse disorders (McCarty, Argeriou, Huebner, and Lubran, 1991). Among the intervention efforts demonstrating some success in addressing substance abuse problems among the homeless have been programs emphasizing (a) increasing access, both physical and psychological, to treatment; (b) low-demand service settings; (c) outreach efforts; (d) coordination of care; (e) addressing housing needs; and (f) skill training (e.g., Bonham, Hague, Abel, Cummings, and Deutsch, 1990; Comfort, Shipley, White, Griffith, and Shandler, 1990; Lubran, 1990; McCarty, Argeriou, Krakow, and Mulvey, 1990; Willenbring, Whelan, Dahlquist, and O'Neal, 1990).

With respect to the dually diagnosed homeless population, Drake et al. (1991) has listed a number of principles which should guide treatment: (a) integrated treatment for substance abuse and mental health problems; (b) intensive case management; (c) group treatment; (d) phasing of treatment (i.e., engagement, persuasion, active treatment, and relapse prevention); (e) the need for substitute activities; (f) the cultural relevance of both programs and program staff; (g) the ongoing training of clinicians; and (h) the need for outreach to the families of homeless individuals.

COST-EFFECTIVENESS AND FINANCING
OF DRUG ABUSE TREATMENT

The cost-consequences of drug abuse (see above) is not the only area to which attention has been paid regarding the economics of drug abuse. Increasing attention has also recently been focused on two other areas: the cost-effectiveness of drug abuse treatment, and the financing of drug abuse treatment—both of these areas present major issues for treatment planning, development, and implementation in an era of diminishing availability of fiscal resources for social problems. Apsler (1991), for instance, has raised questions about the cost-effectiveness of "typical" drug abuse treatment programs. He included among such programs those identified by the General Accounting Office for their failure to eliminate opiate use, offer appropriate services, or even know if referrals were utilized, as well as their clients' alcohol abuse (e.g., Shikles, 1989), *as opposed to* "model" treatment programs.

Furthermore, other evidence raises questions about the cost-efficacy of drug abuse treatment. Apsler (1991) noted, for example, that individuals on waiting lists for drug abuse treatment often show improvement without treatment (e.g., Brown, Hickey, Chung, Craig, and Jaffe, 1988), are often provided with smaller than necessary doses of methadone for eliminating clients' desire for opiates (e.g., the 1992 report by D'Aunno and Vaughn), and may be kept in treatment longer than needed (McGlothlin and Anglin, 1981).

Among those recent developments which have increased the cost-effectiveness of drug abuse treatment, noted Apsler (1991), were the possibility of slowing the spread of HIV through the reduction of intravenous drug use and needle sharing (e.g., Ball, Lange, Myers, and Friedman, 1988), effective matching of patients to treatments (e.g., McLellan, Woody, Luborsky, O'Brien and Druley, 1983), expansion of treatment programs for incarcerated drug users (e.g., Anglin and Hser, 1990), and provision of aftercare (e.g., McAuliffe, Ch'ien, Launer, Friedman, and Feldman, 1985). To this list can be added the general decreases in drug use (e.g., Hser, Anglin, and Chou, 1988; Hubbard et al.; 1989), and criminal behavior (e.g., Hunt, Lipton, and Spunt, 1984; McLellan, Luborsky, O'Brien, Woody, and Druley, 1982), as well as increases in employment (e.g., Harlow and Anglin, 1984; Hubbard et al., 1989) and program retention (Sells, 1979), which may be expected following drug abuse treatment.

Having noted a general absence of rigorous cost-effectiveness studies, and having elsewhere suggested the reasons for this unfortunate state of affairs (e.g., Apsler and Harding, 1991), Apsler (1991) has made a number of suggestions for encouraging research on the cost-effectiveness of drug abuse treatment. However, these implementations all require the investment of substantial resources by funding agencies. His suggestions include (a) broad and strong support from funding agencies; (b) sufficiently long project periods during which to collect posttreatment follow-up measures; (c) the use of objective outcome measures, regardless of cost; (d) encouragement by funding agencies of treatment programs; and (e) use of large samples from many programs.

The AIDS epidemic has substantially raised the stakes with respect to the demonstration of cost-effectiveness of drug abuse treatment. With injection drug users at high risk for contracting HIV with consequent costs for both the individual and society, effective drug abuse treatment is likely to slow the rate of progression of the disease among injection drug users. Lampinen (1991), after reviewing the cost-effectiveness of drug abuse treatment within the context of the AIDS epidemic, concluded that increases in expenditures for drug abuse treatment for the primary prevention of AIDS among injection drug users are justified.

After reviewing the results of a NIDA technical review on the economic aspects, cost-effectiveness, and financing of community-based drug treatment, Cartwright and Kaple (1991) reached the following conclusions: (a) an overarching goal of economic cost research in drug abuse treatment requires the capture of improved economic data to better inform treatment services research, and such surveys as the National Household Survey on Drug Abuse, the National Health Interview Survey, and the National Nutrition Examination Survey, as well as the Drug Abuse Warning Network, should be used for increased capture of economic data; (b) cost-effectiveness research on alternative approaches to drug abuse services is a critical research focus, including examinations of issues related to recruitment into and retention in treatment, as well as the impact of varying treatment goals; and (c) the need for, costs of, and sources of current drug abuse treatment services requires attention.

CONCLUSIONS

Heroin addiction continues to represent a major problem in the United States, accounting for significant costs to both the individual and society. Despite the rapid increase in cocaine use over the past decade, heroin use, as measured by a number of indicators, continues to exist, with most indicators placing opiates as the third most frequently abused category of drugs for most age groups. Most drug abusers today are also abusers of multiple drugs, making it increasingly likely that hard drug users will use heroin at some point. Further, injection drug use, which most heroin users are likely to engage in at some point in their addiction careers, carries with it not only the risk of increased mortality and medical complications (see Volume 1, pp. 80–102), but also the risk of contracting HIV infection. National resources expended on treating heroin addiction continue to remain at a high level. These expenses, together with the costs of associated criminal activity and law enforcement directed toward both interdicting heroin trade, and dealing, as well as heroin-related crime add to the social costs of this problem.

PART TWO

Advances in Conceptualizing and Understanding the Treatment Process

CHAPTER 2

Addiction Careers and Readiness for Treatment

Entry into treatment represents the single most important step a drug user may have to take in addressing his or her problem. Voluntary treatment entry represents a commitment for change, no matter how transitory or weak, as well as a possible turning point in an individual's addiction career. For some proportion of the addicted population, reaching this point may be involuntary in that there is a requirement to enter treatment in lieu of incarceration or as a condition of parole. For most addicts entering treatment, however, such entry occurs for reasons other than involuntary compulsion—the individual typically makes a commitment to change for any one of a variety of reasons. Yet, only relatively few heroin addicts enter treatment in any one year, and many may not enter treatment for 20 years after beginning regular use of heroin and other drugs. This delayed entry into treatment may at times be a function of external factors such as the lack of availability of treatment in a particular locale, or it may reflect internal factors on the part of the addict, such as the level of motivation and readiness for treatment. Since treatment obviously cannot have an impact upon drug use until it is entered, increasing emphasis has been placed recently on developing a greater understanding of the events and processes that underlie and determine entry into treatment. One such process is the extent to which the individual is ready to change.

READINESS FOR CHANGE: STAGES OF CHANGE

How people intentionally change addictive behaviors has not been well understood by behavioral scientists. Prochaska, DiClemente, and Norcross (1992), in a highly influential article for the addictions field, reviewed research on both self-initiated and professionally facilitated changes in addictive behavior seeking and the " ... basic, common principles that can reveal the structure of change with and without psychotherapy ... " (p. 1102). Such change, they observed, could be viewed as a progression through five stages operating in accord with a finite set of change processes governing progress through these stages. Employing a model derived from their original research on smoking cessation (Prochaska and DiClemente, 1982), Prochaska, DiClemente, and Norcross (1992) posited the following stages of change for addicted persons: (a) *precontemplation*, a stage at which there is no intention to change, often seen in individuals who are unaware that they have a problem (when treatment is entered, or change demonstrated at this stage, it is usually the result of pressure from others, and the behavioral changes taking place often dissipate when that pressure is removed); (b) *contemplation*, the stage at which a problem is recognized and change is considered by the individual, but a commitment to action has not yet taken place; (c) *preparation*, involving both intention to take action within the next month, and behavioral criteria, such as having undertaken unsuccessful attempts at change within the last year; (d) *action*, the stage at which individuals begin to modify their behavior in ways that require considerable commitment of time and energy, and do so for periods of one day to six months; and (e) *maintenance*, when gains attained during the action stage are consolidated, and attempts are made to avoid relapse. This latter stage, characterized by stabilizing behaviors and the avoidance of relapse, may last from six months to an indefinite period of time.

Examining how people actually move through the five stages of change, Prochaska, DiClemente, and Norcross (1992) posited that

the underlying structure of change is neither technique-oriented nor problem specific. The evidence supports a transtheoretical model entailing (a) a cyclical pattern of movement through specific stages of change, (b) a common set of processes of change, and (c) a systematic integration of the stages and processes of change. (p. 1110)

Prochaska, DiClemente, and Norcross (1992) concluded that, for most people, perhaps up to 85%, progression through the stages of their model of change is spiral in nature (i.e., forward progress with relapse), rather than linear (i.e., simple and discrete progress through each step). Yet, spiral change is positive, with lessons learned from mistakes, and new strategies undertaken with additional attempts. One implication of this pattern is that people in treatment may drop out because of their simply *not* being at the action stage of change. The figures cited by Prochaska, DiClemente, and Norcross (1992) suggest that for smokers, this problem may be present in up to 85–90% of cases, with 30–40% being at the contemplation stage, and 50–60% in the precontemplation stage. As a result, addiction professionals only employing programs appropriate for patients at the action stage may fail to significantly address the needs of the majority of their target populations, who may be at other stages. Additionally, progress made in treatment may be a function of their pretreatment stage of change (Prochaska and DiClemente, 1992) with patients who remain in treatment moving from the preparation for action stage to the taking action stage (Prochaska and Costa, 1989, cited in Prochaska, DiClemente, and Norcross, 1992). In treatment for weight loss, change in stage scores were second only to processes of change used early in therapy; these two variables surpassed age, socioeconomic status, problem severity and duration, goals and expectations, self-efficacy, and social support (Prochaska, Norcross, Fowler, Follick, and Abrams, 1992).

In one of the few application of the Stages of Change model to drug addicts (i.e., individuals dependent on opiates, amphetamines, or cocaine), Vollmer, Ferstl, and Ellgring (1992) evaluated an "individualized" behavior therapy treatment based on the Prochaska and DiClemente model with standard behavior therapy alone, and a humanistic approach. The results indicated better outcomes for the patients in the individualized treatment group. However, as Vollmer, Ferstl, and Ellgring (1992) observed, the results could also be explained on the basis of other variables operative in the treatment environment, such as the older ages of the patients in the individualized therapy condition, or the effect of introducing a new treatment element.

The model proposed by Prochaska, DiClemente, and Norcross (1992) has been developed primarily with smokers, and to date applied more to the problems of smoking (e.g., Glynn, Boyd, and Gruman, 1990), weight control (e.g., Prochaska, Norcross, Fowler, Follick, and Abrams, 1992), and alcoholism (e.g., Institute of Medicine, 1989) rather than to drug addiction. Yet, it holds great promise for application to drug addiction research and treatment through specifying a theoretical framework within which the patient's readiness for change can be assessed and interventions tailored accordingly.

An important clinical application of the Stages of Change model is *motivational interviewing* (Miller and Rollnick, 1991). This intervention is based on a view of motivation for change as a *state* of readiness or eagerness to change, rather than as a *personality trait* or problem on the part of the patient. This state is characterized by resistance, denial, and apparent noncompliance with therapy. Miller and Rollnick (1991) have defined motivation for change as " . . . the probability that a person will enter into, continue, and adhere to a specific change strategy" (p. 19). Using this definition, and with the focus of motivation defined as residing within the interpersonal context of the counselor-client interaction, motivation for change becomes the counselor's or therapist's responsibility. This implies that the counselor or therapist must not only provide advice about change, but must also be responsible for increasing the likelihood that the client will follow the appropriate regimen leading to change.

Briefly, motivational strategies suggested by Miller and Rollnick (1991) include (a) *giving advice*, a strategy identifying the problem or risk area, explaining why change is important, and advocating specific change; (b) *removing barriers*, primarily those relating to access to treatment; (c) *providing choice* among available alternatives; (d) *decreasing desirability* for maintaining the status quo, perhaps relating to the costs (risks) of changing behavior; (e) *practicing empathy* through accurately understanding the client's circumstances; (f) *providing feedback* about the client's current situation and related risks or consequences; (g) *clarifying goals* so that they are realistic and attainable; and (h) an *active helping* attitude toward the change process.

Motivational interviewing is seen by Miller and Rollnick (1991) as " . . . a particular way to help people recognize and do something about their present or potential problems . . . " (p. 52), including helping them to resolve ambivalence about changing and to begin the change process. It may be used as a brief motivational boost, or as a prelude to treatment. Specifically with respect to the treatment of heroin users, van Bilsen (1991) described the application of motivational interviewing to a Dutch heroin-dependent sample utilizing a program developed for this population (van Bilsen and van Emst, 1986, 1989), and Saunders, Wilkinson, and Allsop (1991) described an application of motivational interviewing with heroin users attending a methadone clinic.

MOTIVATION FOR CHANGE AND TREATMENT

Regardless of whether an addict ultimately becomes drug free as a result of any one attempt to quit addiction, many are ordinarily voluntarily or involuntarily abstinent a number of times during the course of their addiction (Crawford, Washington, and Senay, 1983). The length of such abstinence might well reflect the addict's degree of motivation to forsake drug use, as suggested by Mann, Charuvastra, and Murthy (1984). They posited three levels of motivation to become drug free: (a) *uninternalized motivation* (that is, coerced or otherwise externally enforced); (b) *ordinary internalized motivation* (which the authors described as somewhat like making a New Year's resolution); and (c) *very profound motivation*, such as having a spiritual experience or "bottoming out." Using a statistical model often employed to determine the time to failure of manufactured material, the authors analyzed the remission rates of 405 narcotic abusers in Baltimore, 88 methadone patients from a hospital methadone service, and some

5,000 abusers in Newark community drug treatment programs. Mann et al. (1984) found evidence that length of last prior abstention was a relatively reliable predictor of length of next abstention, and argued that the longevity of abstention implies an underlying level of motivation. Thus, addicts who resumed heroin use within a relatively brief period after detoxification were seen by the authors as having arguably uninternalized motivation, while those who remained abstinent for long periods were likely to have a more profound level of motivation. Mann, Charuvastra, and Murthy (1984) reasoned that these findings had implications for enhancing the efficacy of treatment for a broad range of addicts. They acknowledged that the motivation of an addict may be determined to a fair degree by factors that cannot be affected by treatment personnel. Therefore, they suggested that interventions should be aimed at intensifying the addict's experience of dysfunction and promoting the likelihood of the addict undergoing extraordinary or "profound" experiences. Based on interview data, they further suggested that such interventions should be made quite early in the treatment experience; that is, during detoxification. Their assumption was that the more profound an experience the addict underwent during detoxification, whether positive or negative, the deeper the level of motivation to remain abstinent. Further empirical evaluation of this provocative assumption is called for.

In a nonexperimental ethnographic study, Rosenbaum (1982) explored the types of motivation for, and obstacles to, obtaining treatment in a group of 100 female methadone maintenance patients. This study identified four predominant themes in the self-reported motivation to seek treatment: (a) the need to decrease the chaos associated with a drug abusing lifestyle; (b) having health concerns; (c) having concerns regarding the ability to parent (including being pregnant, or having children old enough to comment on their mother's drug use); and (d) undergoing identity crises. Obstacles to treatment were characterized by two themes: the fact that an addict must admit to, and is viewed by her peers as being a failure (either at being an addict, or at becoming drug free) if methadone treatment is sought; and practical aspects of receiving methadone treatment, such as location, cost, and waiting lists. Finally, Rosenbaum (1982) noted that for many of those addicts who sought treatment to reduce chaotic living situations and to remove themselves from heroin dominated lifestyles, methadone treatment was not sufficient. Subjects still found themselves enmeshed in the heroin culture at the maintenance clinic. Although the author did not address the issue of what might be done to ameliorate the myriad problems faced by the addict, many of these problems would appear to be amenable to change. For instance, the type of motivation that an addict presents could provide guidance in determining whether they should receive parenting training, psychotherapy oriented toward addressing identity issues, or more highly structured, non-drug-oriented social and work-related activities.

In a more controlled study of treatment motivation, among other variables,

Oppenheimer, Sheehan, and Taylor (1988) examined types of initial motivation for treatment in 150 drug abusers attending three drug treatment centers in London. Two questionnaires were utilized to tap into reasons for seeking treatment and fears regarding treatment, and factor analyses were used to delineate general types of motivation. The findings confirmed and expanded upon two other reports in which characteristics of drug misusers seeking treatment at London clinics in the 1980s were described and compared with those of drug misusers from the 1960s and 1970s (Sheehan, Oppenheimer, and Taylor, 1986, 1988). Six basic groups of motivational factors, and two factors relating to fears regarding treatment were obtained. As in Rosenbaum's (1982) sample, the chaotic nature of the addict's life (labeled "problems with personal decline"), and the realization that one was addicted (somewhat akin to an identity crisis) were common motivations. Oppenheimer et al. (1988) also investigated addicts' motivations to seek treatment. In this study, addicts reported difficulties in obtaining drugs, interpersonal crises (such as a friend's death through overdose), problems with loss of assets, and the physical inability to continue injection because of the lack of injectable veins. Oppenheimer et al. (1988) also drew a distinction between the frequency of reasons for seeking treatment in their sample, and the relative impact of such reasons. Most of the foregoing events had relatively high impact and frequency. High impact, low frequency motivations included court orders for treatment, need for immediate medical attention, and serious debts. The most common concern regarding entrance into treatment was a fear of failure, either through some personal weakness or through programmatic shortcomings. As in Rosenbaum's (1982) sample, being stigmatized as a failure was also an important concern for this group. The second fear factor identified by Oppenheimer et al. (1988) consisted of addicts' concern over having treatment program personnel and families in control of their lives. On the basis of these findings, Oppenheimer et al. (1988) concluded that treatment centers could take positive steps toward increasing the number of patients who seek treatment, and toward decreasing the salience of those concerns that impede entrance into treatment. For instance, they suggested that advertising by treatment facilities should address the specific issues and concerns that most drug abusers have at the start of treatment. They also noted that particular drug treatment programs might have special strengths in addressing certain concerns (e.g., health problems, employment, and financial assistance), and would benefit patients by emphasizing those capacities in publicity and educational efforts. In terms of actual services within existing treatment programs, it may be important for staff to address the fears that addicts express regarding failure and control issues, and to take pains to understand individual addicts' concerns and to communicate that understanding.

Murphy, Bentall, and Owens (1989), in a retrospective study, asked addicts about the reasons motivating them in their most recent attempt to withdraw "cold turkey" from heroin. Using factor analytic techniques, they identified two basic factors. The first, which they labelled *private affairs motivation*, reflected high loadings on concern for health and concern for close relationships, and was significantly associated with withdrawal success. The second, labeled *public affairs motivation*, reflected issues related to employment and concern over pending court cases, and was associated with withdrawal failure, although nonsignificantly. Another study of addicts' motivation to withdraw from heroin (Murphy and Bentall, 1992), without regard for method of withdrawal, revealed three factors: (a) *private affairs motivation*, accounting for 26.5% of the variance, and loading on such items as "I am worried about my state of health," "Withdrawal symptoms are worrying me," "I will not have a good future if I continue to use heroin," and "I want to have more meaningful relationships with people"; (b) *external constraints*, e.g., "I am afraid of getting into trouble with the police," and "I am letting my family down" (accounting for 7.2% of the variance); and (c) *negative effects of heroin use*, e.g., "Using heroin is dangerous" and "I no longer like using it" (accounting for 6.6% of the variance). Murphy and Bentall (1992) noted the relevance of knowledge of these motivations for planning successful treatment approaches on an individual basis.

De Leon and Jainchill (1986) attempted to define the dimensions of motivation for drug treatment, and operationalized them into a four-scale instrument labeled the CMRS (Circumstances, Motivation, Readiness for treatment, and Suitability of treatment program instrument). A modest correlation was found between scores on this scale and treatment tenure in a therapeutic community. Three additional scales, labeled Drug use problems, Desire for help, and Treatment readiness, and intended to represent progressive levels of change as described by Prochaska and DiClemente (1986), were later identified by Simpson and Joe (in press). Desire for help, together with indicators of social stability (e.g., marital status and fewer prior arrests), previous treatment experience, expectations for reducing future drug use, and higher methadone dose level all predicted treatment retention beyond 60 days.

"NATURAL RECOVERY" FROM ADDICTION

Most studies on the recovery process have utilized treatment samples. However, Biernacki and Waldorf conducted a series of studies on the recovery process among untreated addicts (Biernacki, 1986; Waldorf and Biernacki, 1981; Waldorf, 1983) using a snowball sampling procedure[1] and focused interviews. In this regard, they collected retrospective data on a sample of some two hundred ex-ad-

[1]This technique is a sampling strategy which has been developed in order to measure links among "natural" groupings of subjects within "fuzzy" populations such as drug users (Kaplan, Dorf, and Sterk, 1987). Based on the early work of Coleman (1958), Goodman (1961), and TenHouten, Stern, and TenHouten (1971) and typically employed in the social sciences to study sensitive topics, rare traits, personal networks, and social relationships, snowball sampling involves the development of

dicts, half of whom had drug treatment histories and half had not received treatment.

Among the findings of the Waldorf (1983) study were that opiate use began in both the treated and untreated subsamples at approximately age 20 and lasted for some 8.1 years (a finding very similar to the 8.6 years reported by Winick in 1965, although very different from the 15–20 years reported by Iguchi, Platt, French, Baxter, Kushner, et al. [1992], and likely reflective of an increasing length of addiction careers for a currently aging population of heroin addicts). The untreated addicts did, however, have shorter addiction careers (6.2 years) than did the treated sample (9.9 years). Otherwise, the two subsamples were found not to differ on such variables as religion, education, employment, and drug use. Three addict lifestyles were identified: (a) the *street addict*; (b) the *middle-class counterculture addict*; and (c) the *situational addict*. Each lifestyle reflected a different set of background, motivational, and lifestyle variables. *Street addicts* typically were working class youths who had been reared in areas associated with high drug use and who had begun their drug use at an early age. *Middle-class counterculture addicts*, seen as possessing an intellectual approach to drug use, supported themselves primarily through drug sales or hustling, and typically were so traumatized by incarcerations that the fear of future incarcerations served to deter them from maintaining a daily drug-use lifestyle. *Situational addicts* displayed use specific to situations of high drug availability, but generally did not adopt the drug-use lifestyle. Examples of situational addicts are the Vietnam veterans who ceased drug use upon their return home, and sex partners of addicts who only use drugs when living with addicts.

Patterns of recovery from drug use identified by Waldorf (1983) tended to be related to the conditions and consequences of the addict lifestyle as well as environmental influences. Such patterns included (a) maturation; (b) religious, spiritual, or ideological conversion; (c) behavioral change brought about by the environment; (d) cessation of drug use while otherwise maintaining the addict lifestyle; (e) alcohol substitution or mental illness; and (f) drifting into the societal mainstream.

With respect to self-reported rationales for stopping drug use, Waldorf and Biernacki (1981) cited the feeling of many addicts that they had reached "rock bottom," a point in their lives where personal crises and negative experiences had resulted in a state characterized by despair or existential crisis. Another feeling reported by addicts as related to quitting drugs was the sense of a dysfunctional lifestyle characterized by street hassles, police involvement, and similar problems. Resolutions to stop using opiates generally fell into three categories: (a) stopping drug use without a firm decision to do so (about 4–5% of those quit-

---

samples on the basis of "insider" knowledge and referral chains among individuals who possess some common quality or trait of research interest. Kaplan et al. (1987) provided an illustration of the application of this useful technique in studying the social contexts of heroin-using populations.

ting opiates); (b) quitting as the result of a rationally developed and explicitly stated idea (about 2/3 of those quitting); and (c) having reached rock bottom or having experienced an existential crisis, and where a decision to quit generally arose out of a "highly dramatic, emotionally loaded life situation" (about 1/4 to 1/3 of those quitting; p. 43).

Noting the difficulty of the course of natural recovery from addiction, Biernacki (1986) stated the opinion that, since the 1960s, the emphasis on research efforts to identify how people become addicted, the incidence of addiction, and how addicts might best be treated has turned research efforts away from developing a fuller understanding of the natural course of addiction through its termination. Biernacki (1986) observed that existing theories of addiction were absolute, deterministic, and pessimistic in their belief that " . . . without major social reform or dramatic therapeutic intervention, drug addiction is an unalterable affliction" (p. 18), a view, noted Biernacki, similar to that held by Alcoholics Anonymous, in which both alcohol and opiate addictions are unlikely to change if they are allowed to follow their "natural course."

Biernacki (1986) viewed an adaptable, process-based social identity as the key to his symbolic-interactional perspective of human behavior. In such a view, self-concept and role-taking were central concepts of the "script" the addict evolved for thinking and acting with regard to others. In effect, he stated that addicts recover through transforming their identities by

. . . *reverting to an old identity* that has not been damaged too badly as a result of the addiction. Or they can *extend an identity* that was present during the addiction and has somehow remained intact. Or they can engage an *emergent* identity that was not present before or during the addiction (p. 179).

Identity materials included social roles and vocabularies that derived from social settings and relationships, which could provide the substance needed in order to construct a nonaddict identity and positive self-concept. Eventually, according to Biernacki (1986), the addict's self-identity and perspective *as an addict* became so distant that they became virtually nonexistent.

Biernacki's and Waldorf's work has clearly made an important explanatory contribution to a fuller understanding of the recovery process, particularly when it takes place outside of treatment. Despite his perspective, it should be noted that Biernacki (1986) never ruled out the importance of professional intervention in assisting recovery for many addicts, noting that addicts differed greatly in personal and social resources.

The findings of Joe, Chastain, and Simpson (1990b) regarding the following most important reasons for quitting daily opioid use were consistent with those obtained by Waldorf and Biernacki (1981): (a) having become tired of the "hustle" (83%); (b) needing a lifestyle change or "hitting bottom" (82%); (c) special events such as getting married (66%); (d) fear of being jailed (57%); and (e) family responsibilities (57%). Noting that reasons for quitting addiction were usually concerned with the negative consequences of drug use, they concluded that this finding was inconsistent with the "maturing out" hypothesis (Winick, 1962). Joe, Chastain, and Simpson (1990b) also drew conclusions concerning the role of various aspects of the availability of drugs in quitting drug use. Examining the importance of nonavailability of opioids, bad quality of the drug available, high cost of the drug, and having no available money with which to purchase the drug, the cost of drugs was found to be more important as a reason for quitting when compared with other factors. However, being cited by only 40% of the sample, it ranked behind the other reasons cited above. Further, this reason was most frequently noted among those persons who had cited intrapersonal reasons (i.e., seeking euphoria and anxiety reduction) as major influences in starting daily drug use.

European scientists, in particular, have been concerned with motivational factors within the context of studying the "autoremission thesis," the concept of spontaneous remission or natural recovery from substance abuse. They have considered such reversibility of substance abuse as not only possible, but likely to be a more common event than previously thought. Klingemann (1991), for example, saw the autoremission thesis as a view which " . . . contrasted sharply with the deterministic views of the disease concept and the notion of the irreversibility of deviant careers" (p. 727). Noting the attention being paid to this concept in the alcohol research field (e.g., Stockwell, 1988), Klingemann (1991) also saw this hypothesis as challenging " . . . the widely held belief that comprehensive and early detection of addiction behaviour as well as more therapy for everything and everybody represents a desirable policy" (e.g., Peele, 1989; p. 727). In a Swiss study, which Klingemann (1991) identified as the first comparative examination of autoremission in alcohol and heroin user groups, 60 subjects were recruited who had demonstrated a "significant improvement" in their consumption of alcohol or heroin (as primary drugs of abuse) " . . . without any considerable intervention of professional or trained therapists or self-help groups and [whose remission had] lasted at least one year before the time of the interview" (p. 728). Of the 60 "practically treatment-free remitters" (p. 727), 30 of whom had been heroin users and 30 had been alcohol users, all but 2 of the heroin users stopped their consumption entirely as did 14 of the 30 alcohol users. Among the motivational factors leading to autoremission identified by Klingemann (1991) were (a) "hitting rock bottom"; (b) wanting to drop out before reaching the absolute rock bottom point, which he labels "cross-roads cases"; (c) those for whom social pressure plays a role; and (d) the familiar "maturing out." Interestingly, 86% of the heroin remitters resolved their problems before age 30, a finding which Klingemann interpreted as supporting the "maturing out" hypothesis, although he saw his findings as supporting a much broader range of reasons for autoremission. Klingemann's (1991) findings also suggested that abstinence was the usual solution to the drug use problem for the heroin users in his study; controlled drinking or "functional abstinence" was more frequent for the alcoholics.

When cognitive elements of the autoremission process were examined, Klingemann (1991) found that almost all of the autoremitters could name a key element contributing to their remission, and that between one-third and one-half experienced the natural recovery process as gradual or planned, and were capable of presenting it within the framework of a complex life-course drawing. Additionally, social pressures were more evident among the heroin remitters than among the alcohol remitters, with such pressures being most evident in the year prior to the spontaneous remission. Klingemann (1991) interpreted these findings within the theoretical framework provided by Prochaska and DiClemente (1986), and suggested that these pressures may have contributed to a general consciousness raising and facilitated entry into the serious contemplation stage.

Finally, it should be noted that Kreutzer, Römer-Klees, and Schneider (1992) made the point that addiction careers were not inevitable. They observed that many regular heroin users never become addicted, and that other users constantly shifted their use of drugs in order not to become physically dependent. Patterns of discontinuance of drug use involved both spontaneous remission as well as tapering.

"CRAVING" AND RECOVERY

An important element in relapse is "drug hunger" or *craving*. According to Wise (1988), subjective craving for a drug is consonant with the compulsive nature of drug administration and " . . . reflects the subjective reports of addicts regarding their attempts to abstain from drug use and the state of their minds at the point at which those attempts fail" (p. 118).

Craving was considered by Dole and Nyswander (1967) as the primary cause of relapse to drug use (see Volume 1, pp. 307–308). Ludwig, Wikler, and Stark (1974), in an early paper on craving in alcoholism, described craving as a cognitive representation of an increased motivation to seek a drug in order to terminate withdrawal. Craving was seen by Dole and Nyswander (1967) as resulting in a persistent derangement of the endogenous ligand-narcotic receptor system, which, in turn, resulted from chronic use of opioids. Thus, to Dole and Nyswander (1967), reduction of craving was a key justification for the use of methadone maintenance.

Wise (1988) attempted to define craving, a subjective term, in quantifiable terms. Drawing on recent studies on the neurobiology of drug reinforcement, Wise (1988) concluded that (a) drug cravings resulted from both a previous history of positive reinforcement (explaining both initial addiction and relapse), and a current condition conferring negative reinforcing potential on the drug; (b) one common pathway is likely to exist for the reinforcing effects of different drugs (e.g., opiates and cocaine), probably a nervous system positive reinforcement system; (c) stimulation of the common neural circuitry involved in this pathway can be triggered by use of any substance having such qualities, including possibly nicotine, caffeine, and alcohol, and placing the ex-addict at risk; and (d) given that positive reinforcement and memory for reinforcement are both biological events, there is a need for the clinician " . . . to distinguish the biologically based 'cravings' that involve the positive reinforcement substrate from the biologically based cravings that involve negative reinforcement substrates" (p. 125). While Wise (1988) defined craving as possessing a biological basis, he also saw pharmacological approaches to addiction as less than totally effective in treatment as long as they only treated the withdrawal symptoms associated with detoxification.

The meaning of craving has perhaps been "stretched" by its increasing use over the last decade to cover a broad array of drug- related phenomena interfering with the use of the term as a scientific construct (Kozlowski and Wilkinson, 1987). Noting that craving was little understood with respect to its role in drug abuse and its treatment, a conference was held at the Addiction Research Center in Baltimore with the aim of reaching a consensus on its definition and measurement. Pickens and Johanson (1992) reported that a consensus was reached among the conferees that craving was " . . . a subjective state in humans that is associated with drug dependence" (p. 128), and that it was a significant factor in the continuation of drug use, as well as in relapse. Among the problems cited with respect to the study of craving were those of imprecise measurement and a lack of correspondence between laboratory- and clinically-based reports. General conclusions reached were that (a) two likely causes of craving were the presence of acute drug deprivation and drug-related stimuli; (b) craving was neither a sufficient nor a necessary determinant of drug abuse; and (c) it was unlikely that a single factor such as craving could account for continued drug abuse and relapse. Nonetheless, it was concluded that craving likely played a role in such behaviors, probably in the form of a dynamic state which was influenced by environmental factors.

Biernacki (1986) described the feelings associated with craving to be similar to those associated with being high on the drug or similar to the "rush" reported after having used an opiate. For some addicts, the experience of craving even included nausea following the highs. Such feelings could frequently be localized to a part of the body (e.g., the throat, the abdomen, or in particular, the stomach). Craving has recently been subjected to experimental investigation, both in the laboratory (e.g., Childress, McLellan, Ehrman, and O'Brien, 1988; Sherman, Zinser, Sideroff, and Baker, 1989) and in naturalistic settings (e.g., Kaplan, 1992; Kampe and Kunz, 1992).

Examining factors influencing relapse and treatment dropout within the context of German therapeutic communities, Kampe and Kunz (1992) observed that craving appeared to have been the most important variable in the processes that ultimately led to relapse. Craving was characterized by three components: (a) "coercive negative drug desires" (drug seeking); (b) conditioned withdrawal symptoms; and (c) conditioned drug effects. Kampe and Kunz (1992) noted that these three factors were most frequently cited as reasons for relapse in their sample of German addicts. Positive-effect expectations, anger, or frustration, while also mentioned, were not seen as having great importance in relapse, while temptations assumed somewhat greater importance. Otherwise unexplainable craving "attacks" which arose in the absence of external stimuli were interpreted as having been triggered by drug-related thinking and negative emotional states, while conditioning accounted for the craving response in social temptation situations.

Investigating the subjective effects of craving, Sherman, Zinser, Sideroff, and Baker (1989) had 35 male addicts rate their affect, craving, and withdrawal in response to boring, anxiety eliciting, and heroin stimuli. They observed that (a) heroin cues were most effective in eliciting self-reports for craving; (b) but that craving was not associated with any particular affective state, but rather with a variety of negative affective states, including anxiety, depression, fatigue, and anger; and (c) while craving was reported without withdrawal sickness, addicts virtually never reported withdrawal sickness without craving. Sherman et al. (1989) concluded that " . . . the potential for negative reinforcement subserved stimulus elicited craving and that craving involved cognitive appraisal processes (attributions, expectations)" (p. 611).

Craving has characteristics of a conditioned phenomenon, as originally proposed by Wikler (e.g., Wikler, 1948; Wikler and Pescor, 1967) in his conception of environmental stimuli having the ability to elicit "counter adaptive" interoceptive responses. Recent work by Meyer (1988) demonstrates a relationship between the availability of heroin, the subjective experience of craving, and the occurrence of heroin acquisition and self-administration behaviors. In addition, O'Brien, Childress, McLellan, Ehrman, and Ternes (1988a,b) demonstrated a role for opponent process conditioning during the development of tolerance to morphine effects, supporting this conception. Meyer (1988) reported that craving for heroin increased just prior to heroin having been made available, while for subjects on naltrexone, craving decreased when heroin injections failed to produce anticipated physiological and subjective effects. This finding led to the proposal that craving resulted when the addict felt that heroin was "available." Thus, the drug-free addict, when in a setting where heroin was available, experienced a dysphoric response (craving) that might include classically conditioned abstinence symptoms, as well as the almost certain presence of anxiety and tension arising from an approach-avoidance conflict resulting from past "highs" associated with heroin use, as well as the consequences and guilt associated with drug use.

The study of craving as a psychological phenomenon in addiction has been greatly facilitated by the development of experience sampling methodology (ESM) for the study of daily activities and experiences in both normal behavior and psychopathology (e.g., see reviews by Csikszentmihalyi and Larson [1987] and deVries [1992]). Similar in concept to data collection via the Holter monitor used in cardiology, ESM involves the repeated sampling of experiences by the subject in his or her natural environment. Experience sampling questionnaires elicit quality of thoughts, mood and other subjective states such as anxiety, motivation, physical states and discomforts, social contact, and use of drugs. Questionnaires are completed some 10 times daily, at preselected, but random moments, when the subject is prompted to do so by an electronic signaling instrument. Typically, a sampling trial lasts for six days, allowing collection of some 60 descriptions (deVries, Kaplan, Dijkman-Caes, and Blanche, 1990). A full description of the technique can be found in the volume by deVries, 1992, while Kaplan (1992) specifically discussed its application to the operational measurement of craving in heroin addicts. Of particular value to understanding craving would appear to be the application of this technique to the study of situational determinants of addictive behavior, as described by Kaplan (1992). Among his findings was support for the view that craving is both constituted by purely symbolic cues such as money, as well as by physiological symptoms such as restlessness.

WHY ADDICTS QUIT ADDICTION: OTHER DATA

Jorquez (1983) reviewed and classified a number of theoretical frameworks concerned with the termination of narcotic use. These included (a) theories emphasizing more of a rational decision-making process involving both the cognitive and affective experiences of "hitting bottom," and the attractions of the desirable aspects of conventional life (e.g., Brill and Leiberman, 1972; Waldorf, 1973; McAuliffe and Gordon, 1980; Greaves, 1980), a view for which Jorquez (ibid) provided some empirical support; (b) theories emphasizing the concept of pleasure and emotional fixation, with drug addiction being characterized as a "chemical love" (e.g., Bejerot, 1980); (c) learning theories emphasizing the concepts of reinforcement and classical conditioning (e.g., Wikler, 1980; Goodwin, 1980; Frederick, 1980); and (d) social psychological theories emphasizing the influence of roles and subcultural influences (e.g., Winick, 1980; Johnson, 1980; Milkman and Frosch, 1980).

Evidence regarding how and why addicts quit addiction has been provided by a longitudinal study of addiction careers in Britain by Stimson and Oppenheimer (1982). These authors followed heroin addicts receiving prescriptions for heroin for 10 years. They found that approximately 38% of the original sample became abstinent from opiates during this time and went on to lead reasonably normal lives free from drugs. Another 38% were still attending clinics and receiving prescriptions, while 15% had died, and 9% were of equivocal status or were not accounted for. When the patterns of quitting drug use were examined for those who had successfully done so, along with the triggers and incidents contributing to successful outcomes, several were found: (a) a gradual reduction of daily dose over a period of time; (b) changing personal circumstances leading to a reduction in dose, often involving an added trigger for the final stage (e.g., suicide of a friend, death of another patient in the clinic, a final rejection by a significant other, arrest with the threat of imprisonment, a bad drug experience, or a sudden deterioration in health); and (c) the presence of external pressure, such as imprisonment or coercion by others. When those addicts in the original group were divided on the basis of their having led "stable" lives (i.e., being employed, avoiding other addicts, crime and health problems) versus "chaotic" (i.e., frequent overdoses, hospitalizations, and imprisonment) the stable group was found to have more frequently stayed addicted and to have remained on heroin maintenance without interruption over time. Specific reasons addicts gave for coming off drugs included (a) disappointment with drug effects; (b) disappointment with the addict lifestyle, including boredom with the clinic routine; (c) seeing themselves as being too old for the addict lifestyle; (d) bad drug experiences and health fears; (e) problems relating to arrest and imprisonment; and (f) interference with doing other things they wanted to do or with leading a normal life.

Examining the reasons addicts gave for their having quit heroin use, from the viewpoint of attribution theory, Coggans and Davies (1988) observed that such explanations had functional utility in the service of self-esteem. In a sample of heroin users, they found explanations for quitting to be consistently related to level or pattern of heroin use in a manner which enhanced or preserved self-esteem. For example, the addicts in the Coggans and Davies (1988) study explained the behavior of other drug users by saying that they had stayed off drugs when things got better, and had resumed use when things got worse. On the other hand, their own use was explained in terms of their own "good" (positive) reasons, their having quit heroin under conditions of stress. Not surprisingly, the assessments of others by addicts was probably more accurate than self-assessments, if one considers the addiction literature which indicates that stressful life events (including interpersonal conflict and negative emotions) precede relapse in general (e.g., Chaney, Roszell, and Cummings, 1982; Grey, Osborn, and Reznikoff, 1986; Marlatt and Gordon, 1980), and heroin addiction in particular (e.g., Krueger, 1981).

With respect to the role of stress in continuing drug use, data from Stimson and Oppenheimer (1982) have suggested that stress, at least that inferred to result from chaotic life events, did not result in continued drug use. Similarly, Hall, Havassy, and Wasserman (1990) found the effects of acute stress (i.e., negative moods, life events, hassles, and symptoms) less important than level of commitment to abstinence in precipitating return to drug use in groups of treated alcoholics, opiate users, and cigarette smokers. Gorman and Brown (1992), after reviewing the research literature on the contribution of stressful life events to the development of addictive disorders (primarily alcohol addiction), found little empirical support for these assertions. They concluded that not only was the available research sparse, but that researchers in this area have neglected recent methodological refinements, particularly as related to the measurement of the meaning of life events. Thus, this area of research remains relatively unexplored.

With respect to factors predicting length of addiction careers, Joe, Chastain, and Simpson (1990a) reported that *sociodemographic background variables* were the strongest, with those addicts with longer careers not only having begun their addictions at an earlier age, but also having had less education, being African American, and having lower parental socioeconomic status. Long-term addicts also tended to have more interactions with the law over time. *Intraindividual variables* (e.g., satisfaction with life, arrests, employment, sensation-seeking, etc.), next in order of significance, tended to assume more importance over time, being most influential later in the addiction career and in terms of overall career length. *Interpersonal variables* were of only limited importance in predicting career length, but most strongly represented by satisfaction with family involvement (e.g., leisure time with family, fighting with parents, etc.). Less important in the interpersonal sphere were such factors as deviancy problems on the part of peers and impressing peers. Although important in beginning addiction, peer-related issues were not related to opioid use in later phases of an addiction career. *Environmental factors* important in predicting career length included availability of drugs, probation and parole considerations, and peer group influence. Joe, Chastain, and Simpson (1990a) concluded that their results provided strong support for those theories which emphasized *intrapersonal* factors as reasons for the termination of daily opioid use, although they also saw theories which emphasized *interpersonal* relationships as being relevant.

TREATMENT AVAILABILITY AND TREATMENT ENTRY

It is generally agreed that, particularly in the age of AIDS, treatment should be available for injection drug users on demand (Public Health Service, 1988; Turner, Miller, and Moses, 1989). In fact, increasing the number of addicts in treatment is a major priority in combatting the AIDS epidemic (Ball, Lange, Myers, and Friedman, 1988; Hubbard, Marsden, Cavanaugh, Rachal, and Ginzburg, 1988). As Watters (1988) has pointed out, however, simply increasing treatment capacity will not necessarily result in increased motivation on the part of drug users to enter treatment. One barrier preventing greater rates of entry into treatment in some locales in addition to the lack of sufficient treatment facilities for all those wishing it, is the cost of such treatment to the patient. Treatment participation can be increased by reducing such barriers, by expanding the availability of free treatment, or by otherwise increasing access to it.

An innovative approach to increasing access to treatment for street addicts was introduced by the New Jersey Department of Health. Coupons redeemable for free 21-day methadone detoxification were distributed in areas of New Jersey with high rates of street addicts by trained ex-addict community health educators (Jackson, Rotkiewicz, Quinones, and Passannante, 1989). Evaluation results indicated an 84% rate of coupon redemption for the 970 coupons which were distributed. Of those redeeming coupons, 45% had no prior drug treatment experience, and men tended to redeem the coupons at a higher rate than did women. Most important, a significant number (28%) of coupon recipients remained in methadone maintenance treatment following the 21-day detoxification, primarily those who were older, female, and of non-Hispanic origin. Similar programs have been introduced in Tacoma and Seattle, Washington, San Mateo and San Francisco, California (cited by Sorensen, Constantini, Wall, and Gibson, 1993), and Newark and Jersey City, New Jersey (Bux, Iguchi, Lidz, Baxter, and Platt, 1993).

Attempting to determine if coupon distribution programs actually reached drug users at risk of HIV infection, as well as the treatment outcomes of those recruited, Sorensen et al. (1993) examined the characteristics of addicts recruited into outpatient detoxification treatment by free coupons in San Francisco. Their results indicated that coupon users, in contrast to those recruited through other treatment channels, were less likely to have had prior drug treatment experience (28% versus 13%), were older, more likely to be male, members of ethnic minority groups, and more likely to have shared needles in the previous 30 days. Sorensen et al. (1993) concluded that the coupon program reached a higher risk clientele, based on the higher prevalence of HIV among ethnic minority users and those who share needles. Bux et al. (1993) noted that many addicts may prefer detoxification rather than methadone treatment, yet may be unwilling to enter short-term detoxification because of beliefs of the difficulties it presents. Accordingly, long-term detoxification, allowing a greater degree of patient engagement and a more gradual detoxification process, may strike an appropriate balance. To test this hypothesis, Bux et al. (1993) distributed coupons for free treatment to 4,840 injection drug users reporting current heroin use who had not been in treatment for six months and randomly assigned patients to either 21- or 90-days of detoxification treatment. Of the 4,390 treatment coupons distributed, 56.9% of the 21-day and 59.9% of the 90-day coupons were redeemed. Among those who redeemed coupons, a significant number had never received prior treatment for drug abuse (43.6%) or were HIV seropositive (44.9%). Some 23 variables were each found to significantly and independently predict redemption of coupons: frequent drug use, prior detoxification, frequent drug injection, cleaning needles with bleach, non-African American race, Hispanic ethnicity, no recent homosexual activity, and Newark residence. Variables negatively associated with coupon redemption included: being a homosexual/bisexual IDU, being African American, being an IDU and never having been in treatment, and being a less frequent injector of heroin. Bux et al. (1993) concluded that both this study and Jackson et al.'s (1989) study clearly demonstrated the effectiveness of a coupon distribution program in engaging IDUs in treatment. The lower rate of redemption in the Bux et al. (1993) study may be reflective of the fact that in this study, the coupon could only be redeemed by the person to whom it was issued, thus eliminating the possibility of the coupons being given away or sold, as well as the fact that in the Jackson et al. (1989) study only those persons who had expressed interest in receiving treatment were likely to be given coupons by street outreach workers. Finally, the fact that the Bux et al. (1993) study paid participants $15 for participating in a research interview may have selectively recruited addicts who were only interested in receiving the money.

TREATMENT SELECTION FACTORS

An issue related to level of motivation for treatment is patient treatment preference. Raymond and Hurwitz (1981) interviewed 136 addicts upon intake into a treatment program and assessed preferences as to the type of treatment the patient desired. They then assessed length of stay, comparing whether the patient actually had received the desired treatment, or had been placed in a different treatment modality. Program assignments were made by intake staff. The results indicated that length of stay was significantly related to congruence between patient preference and actual treatment program. Raymond and Hurwitz (1981) suggested that assessment of patient factors helps in understanding retention in treatment programs, and they argued that a good "person-environment fit" (p. 438) was likely to assist patients in accepting and utilizing a particular treatment modality.

One aspect of the previously described study by Oppenheimer, Sheehan, and Taylor (1988) (other results from which can be found in Sheehan, Oppenheimer, and Taylor, 1988) focused on the similarities and differences among drug abusers attending three clinics in London. Although many characteristics of these 150 subjects were shared, there were a number of statistically significant differences across treatment settings. Those drug abusers attending a drug treatment clinic (which consisted of inpatient and outpatient services) were more likely to be living with parents and to have had less drug and alcohol involved parents than did addicts attending a therapeutic community (intended to provide long-term residential treatment), or addicts attending a 21-day residential detoxification program. The drug treatment clinic patients were also less likely to have been aware of different drug treatment services and were less motivated for treatment than addicts in the other two programs. Drug abusers in the therapeutic community tended to have had higher levels of high risk drug use (e.g., injection of heroin), longer histories of drug abuse, more drug-related health problems, and more criminal convictions than did the other two groups. They were also "agency and treatment wise, compared with the patients at other agencies ... [and] were in a more distressed life situation, but also more impelled to seek treatment" (Oppenheimer et al., 1988, p. 646). Detoxification subjects were involved in less drug and crime than were the therapeutic community members, though they tended to be more like therapeutic community members than clinic patients. They also had fewer previous contacts with treatment programs and were more likely to report financial difficulty as a reason for seeking detoxification services. Oppenheimer et al. (1988) argued that these differences between groups can be used to stimulate further research regarding differing methods of recruitment, referral, and selection of drug abusers seeking treatment, as well as for exploring the impact of matching patients to treatments. Although these findings may not be generalizable to other programs, they nonetheless imply that some distinctions can be drawn between patient characteristics in different types of programs, and that these distinctions might prove useful in tailoring treatment services to fit more closely the needs of help-seeking addicts.

ADDICTION CAREERS AND MATURING OUT

Ball and Ross (1991), in a review of the life histories of the 617 male methadone patients they studied in their evaluation of the effectiveness of methadone maintenance treatment, found that most had become enmeshed in a drug-oriented peer group subculture at an early age. A similar finding was reported by Dinwiddie, Reich, and Cloninger (1992a) who found that "any history of [intravenous drug use] ... indicated substantial lifetime use of illicit drugs and early onset of psychoactive substance use" (p. 1), and that the mean age of onset of intravenous drug use was 18.5 years, following initiation of alcohol use at age 14, and cannabis use at age 16, findings relatively consistent with those reported in earlier studies (see Volume 1, pp. 192–196). In another study, Dinwiddie, Reich, and Cloninger (1992c) reported that lifetime intravenous drug users were more likely than hospitalized alcoholics, felons, or control subjects to have had numerous behavioral and social difficulties relating to conduct, early initiation of drug use, and disrupted living situations before age 15, as well as to have demonstrated conduct problems, in comparison with other drug users. The presence of greater numbers of such problems was associated with increased risk for injection drug use.

Describing their sample of young drug users and their subcultural environment, Ball and Ross (1991) observed that they had

... glorified drug abuse and the exciting way of life it denoted, that their daily use of opiates and other drugs continued during their adult years, and that their preoccupation with obtaining and using drugs was associated with an ever-present network of friends and associates who supported this way of life. These young, inner-city males became confirmed addicts who found it difficult to extricate themselves from the daily demands of drug use and criminal behavior (p. 52).

Noting that 94% of the 617 patients in methadone maintenance they studied had previously been enrolled in drug treatment programs, and 72% in methadone maintenance treatment, Ball and Ross (1991) concluded that this history of treatment attempts established a lack of naïvete about treatment on the part of these patients. Ball and Ross (1991) then asked the question of whether this history of past failures in treatment was due to treatment inadequacies or patient deficiencies, and concluded that it was due to " ... some combination of the two ... " (p. 52).

Ball and Ross (1991) made three points about opiate addiction, which while generally known to those working in the field, deserves restatement. They noted that (a) most addicts seeking treatment have a history of ten years or more of regular drug use, suggesting that rehabilitation requires a long-term effort; (b) successful rehabilitation requires a major change in the addict's lifestyle, including his values, attitudes, habits, behavior, friends, how he spends money, etc.; and (c) the likelihood of success is mitigated by the fact that many addicts do not remain in treatment until they are rehabilitated. They concluded that "although the task of treating contemporary opiate addicts is clearly formidable, it is feasible if realistic expectations of success are maintained" (p. 54).

Studies flowing from the Drug Abuse Reporting Program (DARP) have made important contributions to our overall understanding of factors that influence the course and length of addictive careers. Data collected from a 12-year follow-up of 490 addicts, who had been interviewed six years following entrance into treatment, have confirmed that there are multiple pathways and factors involved in the initiation, maintenance, and cessation of drug abuse (Simpson, Joe, and Lehman, 1986). Subjects in this study reported that the factors most likely to influence initiation of daily heroin use were euphoria, anxiety reduction, availability of heroin, and to a lesser extent, interpersonal pressure (e.g., emulating or impressing others and being pressured by peers). The most common reasons given for cessation of drug abuse were being "tired of the hustle," "hitting bottom," fear of jail, family responsibilities, and other personal events (p. 20). Interestingly, some of the reasons for initiation of heroin addiction were correlated with the addicts' motivation throughout their careers: If an addict gave anxiety reduction or interpersonal pressures as reasons for initiation of heroin use, these reasons tended to be consistent with reasons given for the initiation, continuation, relapse, and cessation of heroin use.

Of equal importance, the DARP data have revealed limitations in the ability to predict long-term outcomes (as opposed to career lengths or motivation) past a certain point, and to delineate those factors that are the strongest predictors of such outcomes. Outcomes in these studies had been measured by opioid and nonopioid use, criminal activity, and employment. All told, the range of variables used to predict 12-year outcome accounted for only between 25% and 30% of the variance. However, Simpson, Joe, and Lehman (1986) found only small proportions of predicted variance in the outcomes to be associated with variables measured prior to the 6-year follow-up interview. Additionally, baseline measures of behavior upon intake and treatment type were not meaningfully predictive of long-term outcomes.

A more sophisticated path model of DARP results, developed to describe the degree and chronological relationship of factors related to long-term outcome, confirms the limitations on such long-term predictions (Lehman, Joe, and Simpson, 1990). Essentially, while pretreatment factors contribute significantly to the prediction of initial outcomes, the influence of these factors wanes as time elapses. For instance, although background influences accounted for almost 27% of the variance in initiation and baseline behaviors upon intake, about 24% of treatment history during the six years following intake, and about 17% in outcome measures in the sixth year following intake, they were not significantly related to psychological dysfunction and overall outcome at year 12. Lehman, Joe, and Simpson (1990) concluded that the most powerful predictors were those temporally close to the criterion measures. In part, this explains the tendency for DARP longitudinal or cross-sectional measures of behavior following treatment to have been more strongly predictive of behaviors and psychological states that were closer in time (Lehman and Joe, 1987). However, even using contiguous predictors, some two-thirds of the variance in long-term outcome was not accounted for by any of the dozens of variables collected in the DARP study. Regarding this point, Simpson, Joe, and Lehman (1986) suggested that other predictor domains needed to be measured for the development of a comprehensive model to predict behavioral outcomes in opioid addicts.

DARP data regarding addiction career length were also analyzed using regression analyses. Simpson, Joe, and Lehman (1986) found that the strongest predictors of addiction career length, accounting for 21.5% of the variance, were demographic characteristics (e.g., era of initial addiction, education level, race, and parental socioeconomic status). Thus, addicts in this sample who initiated heroin use prior to 1964, who were less educated, were African American, and whose parents had lower socioeconomic status were more likely to have longer addiction careers. Less influential (though still statistically significant) factors included environmental variables (such as drug availability, which accounted for 7.6% of the variance, and legal restrictions, which accounted for 2.4% of the variance), intraindividual variables (such as satisfaction with life, which accounted for 4.2% of the variance), interpersonal/familial relationships, and interpersonal/peer relationships. Overall, 21 such variables accounted for 47.9% of the variance in the length of addictive career. One subset of addicts, who appeared to have had a different pattern of addiction length than most, were those who were legitimately employed during a substantial portion of their drug use. Though these addicts had better overall outcomes, their careers tended to be longer than most of the addicts in this study. A second subgroup of subjects who had been highly criminally active prior to addiction also demonstrated longer careers.

Logically, maturation would seem also to have an influence on the length of the addiction career. Research findings have begun to delineate the conditions under which Winnick's (1965) maturing out hypothesis seem to hold. Anglin, Brecht, Woodward, and Bonett (1986) conducted a retrospective study of factors which interacted with the process of maturing out of heroin addiction. They interviewed 406 males who had been admitted to the California Civil Addict Program (CAP) between 1962 and 1964. The mean time between entrance into treatment and follow-up was 11 years. Anglin et al. (1986) hypothesized that four factors would interact to facilitate or impede the process of maturing out of heroin addiction. These factors included age, length of addiction, degree of involvement with drug dealing, and degree of involvement with more serious crime. Not surprisingly, results suggested that older addicts were more likely to cease heroin use (75%) than were younger addicts (50%). It is important to note, however, that when addicts were heavily involved with drug dealing or serious criminal activity, the relationship between age and heroin addiction did not hold. Further, age and length of addiction showed different relationships to drug dealing and serious criminal activity. While age interacted with involvement in drug dealing and criminal activity, length of addiction did not. Instead, it appears that the longer the addiction, the more likely it was that an addict would mature out. Thus, the results of this study suggested that older addicts were more likely to mature out of addiction to the extent that they were less involved with drug dealing or serious criminal activity. However, the longer the period of addiction (as distinct from the absolute age of the addict), the more likely it was that maturing out would result, criminal activity or drug dealing notwithstanding. On the basis of such results, Anglin et al. (1986) suggested that heroin addicts who were involved with drug dealing or serious criminal activity may have required more specialized training which had a particular focus on finding suitable economic alternatives to antisocial behavior. In addition, it should be noted that older addicts who were relatively uninvolved with the above-mentioned activities, and long-term addicts in general, might have been more successful candidates for less cost-, and labor-intensive treatment programs.

Finally, an increased understanding of factors relating to outcome has been provided by a treatment outcome study conducted by Kosten, Rounsaville, and Kleber (1987a). These investigators found, in a 2.5 year follow-up of 150 opiate addicts, substantial improvement in many areas of functioning, with the area of greatest improvement being drug abuse, and with alcohol abuse showing the least improvement. These findings were substantially similar to those obtained by others (e.g., Simpson, 1981; Hubbard, Allison, Bray, Craddock, Rachal, and Ginzberg, 1983; see above). Attempting to predict outcome at a 2.5 year follow-up point, Kosten, Rounsaville, and Kleber (1987b) found outcome (a) to be multi-dimensional, and not dependent on a single dimension, such as drug abuse—one factor loaded on employment, medical, psychological, family, and alcohol scales of the Addiction Severity Index (ASI); while a second loaded primarily on drug and legal problems; (b) at the same time, abstainers showed more improvement than nonabstainers, particularly in the drug abuse and legal areas, with most non-drug improvement not accounted for simply by abstinence; and (c) clinician ratings at intake to be, at the best, weak predictors of outcome at follow-up. Kosten, Rounsaville, and Kleber (1987b) concluded that

... a unidimensional view focusing on abstinence described an important part of drug abuse treatment outcome, but a psychosocial factor, that did not include drug abuse, accounted for a large part of outcome variance (p. 3).

It should be emphasized that heroin addiction is a chronic, relapsing disorder. Hser, Anglin, and Powers (1993), examining rates of, and factors related to, abstinence in their 24-year follow-up of addicts admitted to the California Civil Addict Program during 1962–1964 (see Chapter 1), found that some 18.9% of the original sample of 581 male narcotics addicts had reported complete abstinence for at least three years prior to their 1985–1986 interview, while 36.5% reported no daily use. Mean years of abstinence for the 354 addicts interviewed in 1985–1986 was 3.8 years; while it was 6.8 years for 145 inactive addicts. Those addicts who had become inactive users by 1985–1986 had indicated at the time of the 1974–1975 interview that they had been less involved with the criminal justice system, were employed more, smoked fewer cigarettes, and had experienced more drinking problems than had active addicts. The major finding, however, was that overall patterns of narcotics use remained stable during the final 10 years of the 24-year follow-up, with the only major change in addiction status being due to death. Hser et al. (1993) observed that these findings confirmed the cyclical pattern of addiction, abstinence, and relapse as part of the natural history of addiction noted by other writers (e.g., Simpson, Joe, Lehman, and Sells, 1986; Vaillant, 1973). Another report on the same sample by Hser, Anglin, and Hsieh (1993) confirmed this finding. At the 1985–1986 follow-up point they found that 16.7% of the original sample had ceased drug abuse and criminal activity for a period of three years and 13.0% had not been involved with narcotics and crime for at least one, but less than, three years. Some 41.2% of the original sample had not ceased narcotics use, but had not been incarcerated during the past year, while 29.1% had been incarcerated during the same period. Drug and alcohol use other than opiates was high among all groups at the follow-up point, leading the authors to conclude that " . . . eventual cessation of narcotics addiction is not common among addicts . . . a more common pattern is a predilection for a drug-using lifestyle involving multiple substances" (p. 1).

Finally, it should be noted that many addicts are reluctant to enter or remain in treatment. This reluctance may be due to the demands made by treatment, including the imposition of controls and the need for a great deal of work to overcome social and psychological deficits.

CONCLUSIONS

Recruitment and entry into treatment has become a natural area of increasing research interest over the last decade as treatment interventions have improved over this time. As will be seen, evidence presented in Volume 3 indicates strongly that treatment for addiction to heroin and other drugs is effective. A major problem, therefore, is to both attract the drug-abusing individual into treatment and to retain him or her there. Several major advances have taken place during the past decade with respect to increasing our understanding of factors underlying entry into treatment, readiness for change, and treatment retention:

- The most important development in the areas covered by this chapter is the beginning of an understanding of those variables underlying the process of change on the part of the patient. Entry into treatment, retention in treatment, and change in treatment are of course complex, multidetermined events reflecting the operation of a number of internal and situational variables. The work of Prochaska and DiClemente (1986; Prochaska, DiClemente, and Norcross, 1992) has begun to provide a theoretical framework for developing a full understanding of *how* people change addictive behaviors. Their theoretical model of the change process with respect to addictive behaviors has already led to an applied technology, *motivational interviewing*, which is at the same time both an applied application in the form of a treatment intervention system, and a system having theoretical aspects of its own. Perhaps one of the most important elements of this approach has been the definition of motivation for change as being in the realm of the responsibility of the therapist or counselor, and the spelling out of specific strategies for employment by the change agent. Motivational change strategies (e.g., Miller and Rollnick, 1991) provide a specific set of guidelines for application of the stages of change model by clinicians.

Yet, applications of the readiness for change model have been sparse with respect to the problem of drug addiction, when compared to the problems of alcoholism, smoking, and obesity. However, it is likely that such work will make a significant contribution towards improving the treatment of heroin addiction.

• An increased understanding of the motivations for change in addictive behaviors has also come from work by other workers in the field. For instance, a number of studies have examined the nature of motivations for, and obstacles preventing, treatment entry and identified processes underlying addicts' motivation for change (e.g., De Leon and Jainchill, 1986; Hall et al., 1990; Jorquez, 1983; Mann et al., 1984; Murphy et al., 1989; Oppenheimer, Sheehan, and Taylor, 1988; Rosenbaum, 1982; Sheehan, Oppenheimer, and Taylor, 1986, 1988). The primary contribution of these studies is an understanding of the specific positive and negative beliefs and motivations toward treatment on the part of addicts. From these have come specific suggestions concerning how treatment programs can begin to identify and address such issues.

• The ethnographic studies of patterns of natural recovery from opiate addiction by Biernacki and Waldorf (Biernacki, 1986; Waldorf and Biernacki, 1981; Waldorf, 1983), and the studies of autoremission by Klingemann (1991), have been most valuable in the development of an understanding of the dynamic nature of the natural history of heroin addiction, and of the variables related to, and influencing, such recovery. This work has contributed substantially to our understanding about with whom, how, and the points at which, intervention will be most effective, and would appear to complement the work of Prochaska, DiClemente, and their associates. Yet, such an application has yet to be implemented. An understanding of those variables which influence the course and duration of addict careers has also emerged from cross-sectional studies of addicts in treatment, such as those of methadone maintenance treatment by Ball and Ross (1991), by Simpson and associates (Joe, Chastain, and Simpson, 1990a,b; Simpson, Joe, and Lehman, 1986), and by Hubbard and associates (e.g., Hubbard et al., 1989) with respect to other treatments in addition to methadone maintenance. Large scale and long-term follow-up studies such as those conducted by these investigators will undoubtedly significantly contribute to our knowledge of the careers of heroin users.

• Central to any understanding of internal processes is a fuller understanding of drug hunger or "craving," a process identified by Dole and Nyswander (1967) as being the primary cause of relapse. This process appears to play an important role in both motivating addicts' drug-seeking behaviors as well as relapse after abstinence. Here again, major efforts have been directed toward developing an understanding of this process on both theoretical (e.g., Wise, 1988) and empirical levels, both in naturalistic (e.g., Kaplan, 1992; Kampe and Kunz, 1992) and laboratory settings (e.g., Childress et al., 1988; Sherman et al., 1989). Important steps in developing such an understanding appear to have been taken with recent work on defining the phenomenon (e.g., Pickens and Johanson, 1992; Wise, 1988), and on the measurement of techniques for nonintrusive measurement of addicts' subjective states (e.g., experience sampling, Csikszentmihalyi and Larson, 1987; deVries, 1992).

• The availability of treatment clearly has an important effect on rates of treatment entry. Treatment for the addictions has never been fully accessible, particularly in high population density areas, and increasing demands are being heard for the availability of treatment on demand (e.g., Public Health Service, 1988; Turner, Miller, and Moses, 1989). Effective means of increasing rates of treatment entry by such means as street outreach and coupon programs (e.g., Jackson et al., 1989; Bux et al., 1993) have contributed to the ability to attract and enroll difficult to reach patients into treatment.

• Finally, studies of addiction careers confirm the view that addicts become involved in drug use at an early age, often through emeshment in a drug-oriented peer group (e.g., Ball and Ross, 1991; Dinwiddie et al., 1992a), and that drug careers may be decades in length (Iguchi et al., 1992). These and other recent findings (e.g., Hser, Anglin, and Powers, 1993; Hser, Anglin, and Hsieh, 1993) confirm the nature of drug abuse as a chronic, relapsing disease, with shifts in patterns, but not necessarily termination of, drug use. At the same time that our understanding of addiction careers has increased, however, the ability to predict long-term outcomes for addicts has not shown dramatic improvement (e.g., Simpson, Joe, and Lehman, 1986), although our ability to do so in the short term has continued to develop (e.g., Hubbard et al., 1983; Kosten, Rounsaville, and Kleber, 1987b).

CHAPTER 3

Improving Treatment Outcome and Preventing Relapse

MATCHING PATIENTS TO TREATMENTS

In order to improve treatment outcomes, Miller and Hester (1986) proposed treatment matching in the field of addictions treatment. This concept encompasses matching patients, on the basis of their identified needs and pretreatment characteristics, with the requirements and benefits of specific therapies. Finney and Moos (1986) have noted, however, that the conceptual basis for matching patients with optimal treatments is limited, and suggested three conceptual issues requiring attention if such matching was to be successfully accomplished: (a) selection of effective matching variables; (b) specification of the end results that matching is to enhance; and (c) determination of the treatment stage(s) at which matching decisions are to be made. McLellan and Alterman (1991) observed that while the idea of patient-treatment matching is not new, it has recently become increasingly attractive for several reasons: (a) the expansion, over the past decade, in numbers of substance abuse treatment programs, and access to such programs through increased insurance coverage; (b) increasing pressures for limiting length of inpatient stays, which has resulted in a greater variety of rehabilitation modalities; and (c) the recent increase in cocaine use, which has also increased the number and variety of treatment approaches to substance abuse. Thus, financial and political pressures for optimal efficiency and decreased costs have added to those already felt by clinicians and researchers.

A study conducted with alcoholics (Kadden, Cooney, Getter, and Litt, 1989) attempted to accomplish such matching. The specific hypothesis tested was that subjects (alcoholics recruited from a 21-day inpatient unit) with higher levels of sociopathy, psychopathology, and neuropsychological impairment would have better outcomes when assigned to coping skills training (e.g., highly structured groups focusing on skill acquisition, including problem solving, interpersonal skills training, relaxation, and skills for coping with negative moods and drinking urges), while those with less impairment in these areas would benefit more from interactional treatment (e.g., psychotherapeutic groups based upon Yalom's model of focusing on "here and now" group interactions [Brown and Yalom, 1977]). Following random assignment to the two conditions, the results indicated that while patients in both conditions improved with respect to number of nondrinking days in the last month and Addiction Severity Index Psychiatric severity and Social behavior scales (but not ASI Employment), coping skill training was more effective for patients with higher levels of sociopathy or psychopathology, while interactional training was more effective for patients lower in sociopathy. While both treatments appeared to be equally effective for Ss lower in psychopathology, neuropsychologically impaired patients did better after interactional therapy. A replication of this study with drug abusers would be of value in determining the effectiveness of treatment matching across addicted groups.

RETENTION IN TREATMENT AND TREATMENT OUTCOME

A consistent and important finding of research on addiction treatment over the past decade has been the relationship between length of time in treatment and good treatment outcome (e.g., Simpson, 1981). The evidence from the Drug Abuse Reporting Program (DARP; Simpson and Sells, 1982a,b) and the Treatment Outcome Prospective Study (TOPS; Hubbard et al., 1989), two major studies of treatment outcome, indicated that favorable outcomes in drug abuse treatment were a direct function of the amount of time patients had spent in treatment. For example, Simpson and Sells (1982) found a direct, linear relationship between time spent in treatment (methadone maintenance, therapeutic communities, or drug-free treatment) and positive outcome. Likewise, Hubbard, et al. (1984, 1989) found time spent in treatment, along with pretreatment drug abuse pattern (regardless of treatment modality), to be the most important predictors of posttreatment heroin use. Similar findings have been reported by other investigators (e.g., McLellan, Luborsky, O'Brien, Barr, and Evans, 1986; Riordan, Mezritz, Slobetz, and Kleber, 1976).

While posttreatment heroin use has been shown to be a function of length of time in treatment, differences have been found to exist across modalities with respect to the minimum time necessary to produce this outcome. For instance, the results of the DARP study indicated that treatment episodes of less than 90 days did not produce any different outcomes than detoxification alone, but for patients who remained in treatment more than 90 days, treatment outcome was directly related to length of treatment stay, regardless of modality (i.e., methadone maintenance, therapeutic community, or drug free; Simpson and Sells, 1982a,b). In the TOPS study, Hubbard et al. (1989) found that a minimum of one year of treatment in outpatient methadone maintenance or residential treatment was necessary for a significant reduction in posttreatment regular heroin use. On the other hand, similar conclusions could not be drawn for outpatient drug-free treatment, in large part because of the smaller number of heroin users in such treatment.

A similar time in treatment associated with positive outcome effect has also been reported for patients in therapeutic communities (De Leon, 1986, 1991), and for addicts participating in the California Civil Addict Program (CAP). CAP addicts spent more time in treatment than did those in a comparison group who were discharged from treatment on procedural grounds, with subsequent minimum program exposure, and had consequent reductions in illicit drug use and criminal behavior (Anglin, 1988a,c). Thus, the finding of an association between greater length of time in treatment and better treatment outcome has been found to exist across a number of treatment settings and populations.

Condelli and Dunteman (1993) assessed the impact upon outcome of varying exposure to methadone maintenance treatment. Utilizing data collected on 526 patients in the Treatment Outcome Prospective Study (TOPS), 40% (207) of whom had received methadone maintenance treatment, the authors found that there was no difference in heroin use rates among those patients who had dropped out of methadone maintenance treatment after being exposed to it for varying lengths of time. Patients were then, however, assigned to one of three methadone maintenance exposure groups: (a) *short-term exposure* (less than three months) during treatment and follow-up; (b) *long-term exposure* (3 months to 40 weeks); and (c) *continuous exposure* (never left TOPS methadone programs or left and went to other methadone programs for a total of more than 40 weeks during the follow-up year). Although all patients had been heroin users prior to treatment entrance, heroin use dropped to 39% and 40% respectively for those exposed to either long or short periods of methadone maintenance. For those patients who had been continuously exposed to methadone treatment, only 17% were heroin users during the follow-up year. Thus, a marked decline in heroin use existed regardless of pattern of exposure to methadone maintenance (i.e., short-term versus long-term). On the basis of these data, Condelli and Dunteman (1993) concluded that continuous versus short- or long-term exposure to methadone programs was a key issue with respect to preventing resumption of heroin use. These divergent findings suggest the possible existence of more subtle relationships between length of time in treatment and outcome than previously believed.

Assessing the effect of long-term methadone maintenance treatment upon reducing intravenous drug use while still in treatment, Ball, Lange, Myers, and Friedman (1988) found that of 388 methadone maintenance patients who had remained in treatment for one year or more, 71% had ceased intravenous drug use, while 82% of those who had left treatment relapsed rapidly. On the other hand, Ball and Ross (1991) did not find a close association between length of stay in treatment and treatment outcome for their in-treatment sample. They suggested two reasons for this finding. First, long length of stay in treatment (usually several years, and typical of most of the patients they studied at the initial point of the study), may have attenuated the influence of length of stay at the point when outcome was evaluated. Second, there may have been a threshold point beyond which length of stay had only a small effect on outcome.

Several studies have identified key variables predicting retention in treatment. Simpson and Joe (in press) found the following variables to predict retention in methadone maintenance treatment beyond 60 days: (a) social stability (marital status, employment, and fewer arrests); (b) previous treatment experience; (c) expectations for reducing future drug use; (d) higher methadone dose level; and (e) higher motivation. Among the variables found to be related to retention in TOPS methadone maintenance programs in a study by Condelli and Dunteman (1993) were the following: (a) positive patient ratings of the quality of the social services they received during their first month in TOPS treatment programs; (b) ease of access to the program; and (c) patients being informed about dose level.

DROPOUT FROM TREATMENT

Failure to complete drug abuse treatment remains a persistent problem. This failure is particularly problematic given the association between length of treatment and outcome and the high rates of attrition in treatment programs. Pickens and Fletcher (1991), citing the results of several studies, noted that 12-month treatment retention rates ranged from 34% to 85% for outpatients in methadone maintenance treatment and 4% to 21% for patients in therapeutic communities, with most addicts relapsing within a few days or weeks of leaving treatment. With respect to reasons for patients having left methadone maintenance treatment, Ball and Ross (1991) reported that 32% of patients in the eight methadone maintenance treatment programs they studied had dropped out voluntarily. Other reasons for leaving treatment included (a) treatment completed (detoxified), 21.9%; (b) transfer to another treatment, 15.2%; (c) arrest and incarceration, 10.5%; and (d) discharged by program for disciplinary infractions or noncompliance with program procedures, 20.0%.

Craig (1985a) presented a review and analysis of 40 research articles which have addressed dropout in drug abuse, alcohol, and psychiatric treatment programs, expressing the view that premature treatment termination was of "epidemic" proportions in drug abuse programs. Noting that staff attitudes can have a significant effect upon patient behavior, particularly when dropout is viewed as "a patient problem," Craig (1985b) described a program he developed for reducing patient dropout from 70% to 20% through changing staff attitudes so that the staff came to view premature termination as "their" problem.

A major reason for failure to complete treatment is drug use while still in treatment. Greenfield, Weiss, and Griffin (1992) examined drug use leading to premature discharge while on an inpatient substance abuse treatment unit. They found that those patients with a history of heroin and methadone use before treatment, as well as a diagnosis of antisocial personality, to be most at risk for drug use while in treatment. Further, such use tended to occur among clusters of patients, reflecting the possible stimulation of craving on the part of other patients.

Failure to complete treatment has also been of particular interest to European researchers. Küfner, Denis, Roch, and Bohmer (1992) examined dropout during the first 90 days of residential treatment for a group of German polydrug users, predominantly opioid-using addicts. Overall, some 74% of the study sample terminated treatment prematurely, with about 60% dropping out within the first 90 days. Among the findings of factors influencing dropout were the following: (a) for both men and women, the introduction of crisis therapists in the treatment programs had a significant effect on reducing dropout during the first 90 days of treatment, with a stronger effect for men; (b) when the impact of crisis therapists upon dropout within the first 90 days was examined by age and sex, both younger and older men showed a decrease in dropout rates (47.6% to 29.7% and 43.0% to 24.5% respectively), but the largest change came in the case of the older women (38.3% to 20.7%) while the younger women showed no change (43.7% to 44.5%); (c) unemployment was higher among early dropouts, while (unexpectedly), dropouts were more likely to have stable partners; and (d) early dropouts took cocaine and other illegal drugs besides opiates less frequently than those staying in treatment longer. Examining factors influencing dropout from drug abuse treatment programs in the Küfner et al. (1992) study, Denis, Küfner, Roch, and Bohmer (1992) found social interpersonal relationships to be dominant among the reasons cited for dropping out (accounting for 61.3% of the sample), in contrast to drug-related factors, which accounted for 35.2% of dropouts. Among interpersonal relationships, external relationships unconnected with drug or disciplinary factors were more important for women (23.8%) than for men (8.5%). Within the treatment facility, nonsexual relationships with other patients were more important for men (28.2%) than for women (9.5%), while sexual relationships within the facility were more important for women (38.8%) than for men (19.4%) with respect to being listed as reasons for dropping out. Among drug-related factors for dropping out, relapse (14.8%) and craving (7.0%) were the most frequently cited categories. The authors concluded that these findings suggested that in understanding the dropout process, special attention towards the relationships between the patient and other patients, the therapist, and those in his or her social network is necessary.

Seeking variables with which to predict premature termination from treatment, Vollmer, Ellgring, and Ferstl (1992) found successful variables to be both program- and time-specific. Seeking predictors of dropout and relapse in a multicenter study, Herbst (1992) found only one highly significant variable, self-assessed improvement in the psychological status of patients during treatment. Further, those patients who had low self-assessed improvement scores after 60 days of treatment were at a very high risk of dropout. Thus, perceptions of self-efficacy appear to be related to risk of dropout.

Examining the basis of therapeutic accessibility of addicts during treatment in therapeutic communities, Kunz (1992) identified the ability of patients to produce adequate explanations for their behavior to be an important factor in determining dropout. Earlier research (Kampe and Kunz, 1981) had demonstrated that "succeeders" in therapeutic communities, in contrast to dropouts, produced more adequate means-ends statements on the Means-Ends Problem-Solving Procedure (Platt and Spivack, 1977), while the opposite was true of early dropouts (i.e., the production of more inadequate than adequate means-ends statements). Thus, this study identified a cognitive variable underlying performance in treatment programs. In other studies, the analysis of 148 written life reports of drug addicts indicated the dominance of drug-related thinking content among dropouts, while treatment succeeders cognitively emphasized school and general educational problems rather than drug problems (Kampe, Kunz, and Kremp, 1986; Kunz and Kampe, 1985). Such cognitive dominance of drug-related contents has also been found to persist with dropouts over the years. This dominance appears to correspond to the drug use histories of the patients, and to be highly resistant to change (Kampe and Kunz, 1984). Kunz (1988, 1992) presented a model employing path-analysis using these variables that predicted 43% of the variance associated with the course and duration of treatment. When reactions to personal or rule conflicts in the therapeutic community were examined, Kunz (1992) found that succeeders reacted by attempting to find an adequate solution to the problem, while dropouts reacted with denial or defensiveness. Further, these differences existed independently of confrontation themes in groups and did not appear with respect to the resolution of emotional themes. Kunz (1992) concluded that these results suggested the need to structure therapeutic programs to maximize therapeutic accessibility. This structuring requires that both the treatment philosophy and the therapeutic process must take into account the differing abilities of patients.

Some studies have attempted to understand the determinants of program retention. These studies aimed at seeking predictors of patient retention in therapeutic communities. For example, Condelli and De Leon (1993) examined the relative value of "dynamic" (i.e., changeable variables, such as psychological status) and "fixed" variables (i.e., demographic characteristics). While both dynamic and fixed variables were found to predict retention in treatment, two dynamic variables, i.e., ex-addict interviewers' predictions of success in treatment and predrug experience with large groups of persons (versus solitary experience), were found to be the strongest predictors. Sorensen, Gibson, Bernal, and Deitch (1985) aimed at determining the impact on program retention of requiring methadone maintenance applicants to have a non-drug-using friend or family member sponsor involved in their treatment. These authors predicted that the existence of a sponsor requirement was likely to increase attrition for some groups of applicants. Data for 242 program applicants were compared for the six months prior to requiring a sponsor, with the six months following the implementation of this requirement. The existence of this requirement only slightly decreased the likelihood of program entry, with single addicts and younger addicts having recent drug histories being most likely to be affected. The implication of this study was that family involvement did not seriously compromise addict entrance into methadone maintenance. Sorensen et al. (1985) noted that these findings were encouraging in light of the potentially positive impact that family and community involvement could have in the rehabilitation of heroin addicts.

CASE MANAGEMENT

Case management, as a coordinating mechanism in providing services for persons with multiple and complex needs, as is often seen in addicted individuals, is a relatively new concept in its application to opiate addicts as the target population. Deriving from social casework (Schilling, Schinke, and Weatherly, 1988), and having been extensively applied previously to mental health, welfare, homeless, and medically disabled populations, case management is a means of providing accessibility to, and coordination of, care services provided by multiple agencies over time. Ridgely and Willenbring (1992) observed that part of the current interest in case management reflected the increasing emphasis on accountability and cost reduction on the parts of both public and private payers, particularly if it resulted in (a) the substitution of less expensive forms of treatment and (b) the substitution of drug abuse treatment for incarceration or hospital care.

Case management, according to Johnson and Rubin (1983; quoted by Ridgely and Willenbring, 1992), typically involves (a) the development of new linkage systems to meet the patient's needs; (b) the establishment of initial linkages between people and resource systems; (c) the establishment of linkages between resource systems themselves; (d) the facilitation of interactions between people in resource systems to make them more effective and humane; and (e) assisting patients themselves to develop their own problem-solving and coping abilities. Further, case management typically includes both increasing the individual's self-reliance and independence and coordinating care. Each of these aims are accomplished through creation, implementation, and monitoring of a case management plan (Leiby, 1978, cited by Ridgely and Willenbring, 1992). The reader is referred to Ridgely and Willenbring (1992) for an overview of case management models, as well as issues related to the effective implementation of case management.

Models of Case Management for Addicts

Recently, largely as a result of funding by the National Institute on Drug Abuse, both through its regular mechanisms and the National AIDS Demonstration Research (NADR) initiative (Brown, 1992), research has resulted in the development and evaluation of a number of case management models for the addiction treatment field. Some of these are reported in a NIDA monograph (Ashery, 1992a). Among the specific proposals made, Rapp, Siegal, and Fisher (1992) suggested the adoption of a mental health model emphasizing intensive case management/advocacy (CM/A) strategies approach based upon the patient's strengths and assets. This model was literally based on the question "What is healthy about you [the patient] and how can you use these assets to secure the resources you need?"

Lidz, Bux, Platt, and Iguchi (1992) proposed a specialized case management program, which they called "transitional case management," (TCM), designed to operate as an integral component of an AIDS outreach program. Based on the realities of implementation in an urban environment in which the available resources could not meet the need of the 1,000 or more clients seen by their project each year, approximately half of whom were HIV positive, Lidz et al. (1992) proposed and evaluated a time-limited case management model designed to make a quick, effective intervention in the lives of clients. With an emphasis on the brokerage element of case management—the attempt to place clients with agencies that can meet their needs—clients transferred relatively rapidly to other agencies.

Other models of case management for opiate and other addicts have been presented by Dennis, Karuntzos, and Rachal (1992), who focused on meeting the needs of methadone maintenance patients; Bokos, Mejta, Mickenberg, and Monks (1992), who used a model amalgamating several social work and mental health models, and Levy, Gallmeier, Weddington, and Wiebel (1992), who utilized a community-based service (CBS) model incorporating peer-support techniques designed to reduce both HIV- and drug abuse-risk through addressing the demands and meeting the needs of living drug-free in the community. Also emphasizing case management models addressing both drug use and AIDS, Falck, Siegal, and Carlson (1992) proposed a modified service broker model nested within an educational program designed to reduce AIDS risk; McCoy, Dodds, Rivers, and McCoy (1992), a model serving HIV-positive injection drug users; while McCarthy, Feldman and Lewis (1992) emphasized interagency cooperation and integration as a means of bringing primary health services and addiction treatment to substance abusers.

With respect to addressing specialized addicted populations, Inciardi, Isenberg, Lockwood, Martin, and Scarpitti (1992) described a program, Assertive Community Treatment (ACT), which had as its goal the reduction of recidivism for prison releasees. Unfortunately, more recent outcome data (Martin and Scarpitti, 1992) demonstrated little difference between parolees completing the ACT program and a comparison group. Perl and Jacobs (1992) described 13 demonstration programs funded by NIDA to establish treatment programs for homeless persons, noting that each of these programs conceptualized the structure and intensity of its case management model differently, in part due to organizational philosophy and in part due to the availability of local resources. Perl and Jacobs (1992) also provided a useful overview of the dimensions along which case management models differ, both with respect to structure and implementation. A similar approach was taken by Willenbring (1992), who discussed the importance of integrating both qualitative and quantitative approaches to case management while evaluating the effectiveness of differing levels of intensity of case management. Case management services for pregnant, homeless, or addicted women were the focus of a number of reports (Rahdert, 1992; Alemi, Stephens, and Butts, 1992; McMillan and Cheney, 1992), as were services for chemically abusing and emotionally disturbed youth (Evans and Dollard, 1992).

MANAGED CARE

Managed care is an increasingly used system of treatment regulation accomplished through the determination of payment for treatment based upon assessment of the appropriateness (i.e., need for, and effectiveness) of the services provided, and involving negotiation between insurers and treatment providers. Needless to say, for those familiar with the contemporary American health care system, this increasingly popular (on the part of payers for health care, including governments at all levels) model is not viewed positively by many care providers. Managed care may be both a boon for addiction treatment (in that it is likely to require increasing efforts in evaluating the efficacy and cost-effectiveness of addiction treatment) and a serious problem for service providers who cannot demonstrate the effectiveness of the services they provide.

Managed care may involve regulation of (a) service utilization by beneficiaries or (b) the supply of such services by providers, and may be accomplished in a number of ways. These may include (a) certification or preadmission reviews (PARs) of hospital stays; (b) utilization reviews of services during or after provision; (c) the use of preferred provider organizations (PPOs) or individuals; as well as (d) specialized management of high-cost cases (Institute of Medicine [Gerstein and Harwood], 1990). Woodward (1992) questions the clarity of this definition, noting that, among other ambiguities,

[this] definition does not distinguish prepaid financing mechanisms such as health maintenance organizations (HMOs) and preferred provider organizations (PPOs) from the more loosely structured managed care providers. It does not distinguish "financial case management" and "clinical case management." ... It is unclear from the definition whether managed care is a type of treatment, a form of financing, an approach to cost management, or a combination of these. Finally, the definition ignores differences between public- and private-sector managed care of drug treatment (p. 35).

Woodward (1992) has provided a useful overview of issues related to the implementation of managed care principles in managed care and substance abuse treatment. He noted two important issues in managed care that are of particular relevance to the case management of drug abuse treatment: (a) the lack of explicit and widely agreed-upon criteria for managed care and (b) the lack of demonstrated cost savings attributable to managed care. This last point is confirmed by Dennis, Karuntzos, and Rachal's (1992) failure to identify *any* published evaluations of case management in methadone maintenance treatment and Chamberlain and Rapp's (1991) inability to identify more than six methodologically sound studies of case management in the field of mental health. After reviewing the work that had been published on case management in addiction treatment, Dennis et al. (1992) noted that "although the need for case management in addiction treatment has been recognized for more than a decade, there is little consensus about what it is or who should provide it" (p. 57).

SOCIODEMOGRAPHIC CONTEXT

A number of commentaries on problems associated with treatment have focused on the broader context within which treatment services are delivered. Brown (1985), reflecting on the development and implementation of federal drug abuse policy, has pointed out that the federal government's dual role of law enforcer and treatment provider had contributed to its being perceived by treatment recipients as having an ambiguous stance regarding drug abuse. That is, during the 1970s the government expressed a commitment (albeit ambivalent) to the rehabilitation of drug abusers, yet linked such efforts to fighting crime. Coupled with the prevailing community view that the Nixon administration had, at best, an attitude of neglect toward minorities, this gave rise to serious and long-term problems in the provision and utilization of treatment facilities for inner-city populations.

Also related to minority group relations, Brown (1985) observed that drug treatment graduates who went on to staff community programs were often supervised by nonminority professionals who were earning considerably more income in the same treatment system. Adding to this problem, methadone maintenance has been viewed by some communities as a political means of supervising and controlling minority citizens, rather than as the provision of an effective treatment modality. Hence, Brown (1985) argued that the political and social context within which drug treatments were developed during the 1970s had a powerful impact on the acceptability, usefulness, and, probably, the outcome of such treatments. He suggested that there continued to be a pressing need to understand and address the special needs of minority group populations in the effort to deal with drug addiction. In keeping with this view of drug addiction as a social and political issue, Brunswick (1985–86) conducted a series of 20 interviews with community leaders in four high drug use areas in New York City, and summarized the social aspects of heroin use as described by those leaders. In particular, the community leaders viewed heroin use as highly interrelated with unemployment, poor housing, and limited education. There was general agreement that child abuse and neglect, conditions of poverty, materialistic values, and hopelessness among the youth in these communities were also important contributors to the high level of addiction. The absence of avenues of opportunity and the existence of financial inducements for young people to become involved in the drug trade were seen as reasons for its intransigence. The community leaders interviewed in this study also pointed to the ambivalent implementation of drug control policies in their communities, and voiced the opinion that law enforcement agencies permitted the continued drug trafficking by organized crime. Treatment services were viewed as inadequate, in part because of the relative lack of drug-free programs, and in part because of an overreliance on methadone maintenance, an avenue of treatment viewed with suspicion and distrust among these community leaders. Respondents recommended a number of interventions which they believed would decrease the high levels of drug abuse in their communities. These interventions included increased law enforcement, more preventive approaches to drug abuse that included the family, coordination of drug-abuse related agencies, community participation, increased treatment evaluation, development of alternative treatment modalities, and improvement of economic conditions in the community. Brunswick (1985–86) reached the conclusion that it was important, when considering drug-abuse treatment policy, to view the issue in its wider ecological context. Indeed, as Brown (1985) has suggested, it seems necessary to understand the social and political issues that have an impact on the delivery and effectiveness of treatment services so that their acceptability and efficacy can be maximized.

The need for socioeconomic avenues of opportunity was suggested by data reported in Platt and Metzger (1987a) as a necessary component in the treatment of heroin addicts. Heroin addicts who had been recently incarcerated in a facility for youthful offenders were interviewed and asked to estimate the number of property crimes they had committed during their life- times. The number of such crimes was found to be positively related to interpersonal problem-solving levels, suggesting that those who were better problem solvers were also more effective at avoiding arrest (and staying out of institutions). In another study (Platt, Labate, and Wicks, 1977a), levels of problem-solving skills at discharge were found to be positively related to the length of time subjects were able to maintain a satisfactory parole status. Controlling for differences in length of time on parole, the relationship between frequency of criminal acts and level of interpersonal cognitive problem-solving (ICPS) skills upon discharge was also examined. Paradoxically, those subjects who had higher ICPS scores had engaged in more property-related crimes than had those who had left the institution with lower ICPS skill levels. It may be that the high problem-solving parole failures identified here had fewer legitimate routes available in which they could apply their new skills. This analysis lends support to the arguments by Brown (1985), Brunswick (1985–86), and Platt (1986), to the effect that treatment alone may not be sufficient to foster socioeconomic advancement. Developing the means by which addicts can obtain such advancement, in addition to providing necessary skills training, appears to be an important dimension of any system of treatment.

VOCATIONAL REHABILITATION OF HEROIN ADDICTS

Employment rates among drug abusers in treatment are usually quite low, ranging from about 15% to 35% (Platt, 1994; see also Volume 1, pp. 182–183). Among methadone maintenance patients, this rate is between 25% and 35% (CODA AP, 1985; Flaherty, Kotranski, and Fox, 1984; Hubbard, Rachal, Craddock, and Cavanaugh, 1984; Singh, Joe, Lehman, Garland, and Sells, 1982). In addition, as discussed in Volume 1 (pp. 289–290), evaluations of the differences between employed and unemployed methadone maintenance patients have suggested that personal characteristics of employed patients are closely related to employment status. For example, Metzger, Platt, and Morton-Bey (1986) compared the psychological symptomatology of employed and unemployed methadone maintenance patients and hypothesized that employed patients would show significantly fewer symptoms of distress than would those who were unemployed and that level of symptomatology would decrease as length of employment increased. Upon entrance into one of five methadone maintenance clinics in the Philadelphia area, 398 patients completed demographic questionnaires and the Symptom Checklist-90 (SCL-90). One hundred and twenty-two patients were employed and 276 were unemployed. Results showed that on each of the nine subscales of the SCL-90, the unemployed methadone patients were significantly more symptomatic than the employed patients. There were, however, no significant correlations between length of employment and severity of symptomatology. These results were interpreted as suggesting that while employed methadone patients were less symptomatic, this relative lack of psychological symptoms may have enabled these patients to find and maintain employment rather than resulting from the employment experience itself. Such findings are consistent with those of Caplovitz (1976) and others, who have suggested that employed methadone maintenance patients are not as distant from the dominant culture as are most heroin addicts.

In a study of the relative contributions of background demographic, vocational, and clinical characteristics in differentiating chronically unemployed methadone patients from those regularly or intermittently employed over a three-year period, Hermalin, Steer, Platt, and Metzger (1990) identified risk variables significantly related to unemployment. Patients who had "ever" received job training were more than twice as likely to be employed as those who had never received such training. Further, "not knowing how to look for work" or "lacking the desire to work" resulted in unemployment at a rate three times as great as those not citing such problems. Of the 47 variables examined, the three most important variables predicting (working) employment status were (a) having ever collected unemployment compensation; (b) knowing how to look for work; and (c) race (African Americans were three times less likely to be employed over the three-year period). When considered simultaneously, nine variables retained significance. These included (a) race (being white); (b) receipt of a high school diploma; (c) currently collecting welfare; (d) heroin use during the past month; (e) having ever been in a job training program; (f) having ever been fired; (g) having ever collected unemployment compensation; (h) lack of a desire to work; and (i) not knowing how to look for a job. Noting that none of the scales on the measure of psychopathology employed in the study, the SCL-90, related to employment over the three-year period studied, Hermalin et al. (1990) advanced three possible explanations: (a) that skill level and capability were more important than psychopathology in obtaining a job; (b) that mental health status can be falsified, hidden, or denied during a job interview; and (c) that current psychopathology scores are not reflective of one's mental health status over the entire three-year period. Participation in methadone treatment does not necessarily result in improved employment rates (Hermalin et al., 1990), a finding perhaps reflective of the fact that relatively few methadone maintenance treatment programs offer vocational services (Brewington, Arella, Deren, and Randell, 1987).

Patterns of employment were described for a sample of 479 methadone patients from clinics in the Philadelphia area by Platt and Metzger (1987b). Upon intake, 69.2% of subjects were found to be unemployed, with over half of unemployed patients reporting that they were seeking work. An evaluation of employment status at four assessment points over a 15-month study revealed that the most common pattern was consistent unemployment (46.3%). The next most frequent pattern was being employed at only one assessment point (19.4%). Thirteen percent of patients were employed at three of the four assessment points, and 12.7% were continuously employed. The smallest proportion consisted of patients who had inconsistent employment patterns (8.0%).

The impact of drug abuse treatment on employment status was not found to be strong in the TOPS study (Hubbard et al., 1989). Methadone maintenance treatment, residential, and drug-free treatment modalities all resulted in increased rates of employment in the percentage of patients employed full time, when the year before treatment was compared with the year following treatment. With respect to the relative amount of change, the increase for patients in methadone maintenance treatment was less than that for drug-free and residential treatment. The employment rates for patients in methadone maintenance treatment was 24.2% in the year before treatment, remained relatively stable during treatment, declined slightly after treatment, and increased to 29.3% by the second year following treatment. By three years after treatment, however, the percentage employed had dropped to 17.7%, the rate prior to treatment entry.

Interventions to Increase Employment

Employment is an important factor in the rehabilitation of drug addicts (Platt, 1994). Given the relative lack of treatment effects on employment as described above, it is surprising that programs specifically designed to increase employment rates for methadone patients have not been more common. Further, most of those implemented before 1980 have either not been evaluated or did not describe their effectiveness (Hubbard, 1981; NIDA, 1981). Nonetheless, there have been several studies evaluating the impact of vocational programs on addicts' abilities to obtain and maintain employment which suggest the beneficial effects of such interventions. Vocational interventions for drug abusers can be divided into three categories: (a) supported work interventions; (b) job seeking and placement interventions; and (c) personal competency and skill building interventions. Reviews of these programs can be found in Hall (1984b) and Platt (1994).

Supported Work Programs

These programs involved job-site training and intervention, as well as ongoing assessments, as part of large scale supportive work environment demonstration projects. Three examples of such programs have been conducted with drug abusers: the "Wildcat Experiment"; the National Supported Work Demonstration Program; and the Manpower Demonstration Supported Work Project.

The Wildcat Experiment was instituted in New York City in 1972, lasted four years (Friedman, 1978), and was designed to increase employment in ex-offenders and ex-addicts (primarily methadone patients). Over 4,000 subjects participated in this project, the premise of which was that the transition from unemployment to employment would be facilitated by providing a work environment in which unemployed addicts could receive personal support and have their particular rehabilitative needs addressed. This environment was created by assigning three to seven subjects to a "crew," and designating one subject as a crew chief who in turn was supervised by persons concerned with production and rehabilitation requirements. The program succeeded in eliciting and maintaining the participation of subjects in the supportive work settings (most of which were either clerical, paraprofessional, or maintenance positions). However, subjects in the experimental work groups were no more successful at obtaining independent employment than were controls.

Dickinson and Maynard (1981) reported on another large project, the National Supported Work Demonstration Project, wherein roughly 13% of the subjects were ex-addicts ($N = 8,696$). Like the Wildcat Experiment, few differences between experimental and control groups were found upon completion of this 18-month program. There were, though, differences (48% employment for experimental subjects and 31.6% for controls) at the 36-month follow-up.

The third program, the Manpower Demonstration Supported Work Project (Board of Directors, Manpower Demonstration Research Corporation, 1980) was a major undertaking involving some 1,200 ex-addicts, mostly drawn from methadone maintenance treatment programs (of a total of 10,043 participants) which provided 12 months of supported work, followed by assistance in finding employment. Results indicated a higher employment rate and more hours employed for experimental subjects, but only for earlier, rather than later entrants. However, the results of this study are attenuated by design and implementation problems (cf., Hall, 1984b).

Job Seeking and Placement Programs

The first intervention program in this category, entitled Training, Rehabilitation, and Employment for Addicts in Treatment (TREAT; Bass and Woodward, 1978, cited by Hall, 1984b) recruited clients from large multimodality programs, randomly assigning them to either vocational training or a control condition. Outcomes were mixed, with decreases in drug use and better treatment outcomes for experimental subjects, but no better outcomes for experimentals with respect to treatment retention or criminal behavior. A second job seeking/placement program, Employment Specialists (NIDA, 1982), provided placement services to patients in methadone, residential drug-free, and outpatient programs. No significant differences in employment rates were found as a result of this intervention, although significant improvements in treatment retention and reduction in drug use were found in the experimental group. The third program in this area, JOBS for Rehabilitated Drug Users (Double and Koenigsberg, 1977), provided screening and counseling intended to obtain jobs for ex-drug users, appropriate placements, as well as furnishing follow-up information to employers and workers regarding job problems. The results indicated a significant rate of employment among participants, with almost 79% of employers having rated the ex-drug abuser as the same or better than other employees. Attitudes towards the job, ability to relate to co-workers, and desire to succeed were rated very high when compared with co-workers, while only for punctuality and absenteeism did negative ratings exceed 20%. Unfortunately, data relating to job retention, a key outcome variable, was only fragmentary. At one year postintervention, about 25% of program-placed participants had retained their jobs for one year or longer.

Personal Competency/Skill-Building Programs

The third major approach to increasing employment in drug abusers consists of interventions which were designed to provide those skills necessary to successfully seek and obtain employment. Hall and her associates (Hall, Loeb, Coyne, and Cooper, 1981; Hall, Loeb, LeVois, and Cooper, 1981; Hall, Loeb, Norton, and Yang, 1977) developed the Job Seekers' Workshop, a training program based on the Job Club model introduced by Azrin and his associates (Azrin, Flores, and Kaplan, 1975; Azrin and Besalel, 1982). The Job Seekers' Workshop consisted of 12 sessions wherein job search and job interview skills were taught. Hall et al. (1981a,b) experimentally evaluated the impact of employment skills training on employment level among methadone patients. The intervention consisted of a 12-hour manual-based program specifically designed to address behavioral problems urban drug addicts demonstrated with respect to job seeking. In an initial study, Hall, Loeb, Norton, and Yang (1977) found that at three months following the intervention, 50% of experimentals, versus 14% of the controls, had found employment or placement in a job-training program. In a second study (Hall, Loeb, LeVois, and Cooper, 1981), 30 randomly chosen volunteers from four San Francisco clinics were assigned to the training, and 30 were assigned to the control condition in which a one-hour job resource orientation was given. Experimental subjects had a somewhat greater likelihood of obtaining employment (50% versus 30%), but this difference was not statistically significant. As the authors noted, this lack of statistical significance might have been due to the small sample size, or to the fact that, regardless of the presence or absence of skill training, having a job within five years prior to entering methadone maintenance treatment was significantly related to job acquisition during the experiment. A third study (Hall, Loeb, Coyne, and Cooper, 1981), involving 55 probationers and parolees with heroin abuse histories, resulted in 86% of the experimentals, versus 54% of controls, having found employment by three months post study. One important aspect of the Job Seekers' Workshop studies was the evaluation of three methods of disseminating information about this intervention to drug treatment programs in six states by Sorensen, Hall, Loeb, Allen, Glaser, and Greenberg (1988). Targeting individual treatment programs, Sorensen et al. (1988) found the highest adoption rate for the intervention by programs that had been site-visited (28%), followed by those that had participated in a conference (19%), those that had only received printed materials about the program (19%), and the control condition (no intervention; 0%).

The most recent personal competency/skill-building program, the Employment Readiness Skill Intervention (Platt, Husband, Hermalin, Cater, and Metzger, 1993), was based on interpersonal cognitive problem-solving training (Platt, Prout, and Metzger, 1986; Platt, Taube, Metzger, and Duome, 1988). This intervention was designed to assist methadone maintenance patients in identifying and overcoming their own personal barriers to employment, thus readying them for work. Platt et al. (1993) evaluated the effectiveness of an intervention consisting of 10 training sessions that focused on clarifying work motivation, work barriers, employment-related resources and skills, goal setting and problem-solving thinking. Unemployed patients were randomly assigned to the training group or to a control group which consisted of treatment as usual. When the experimental group was compared to the control group following the 10-week training, there were no statistically significant differences in employment rates (the experimental group had increased its employment by 15.9% and the control group had increased its employment by 19%). At the six-month follow-up, however, rates of employment for the experimental group went from 13.4% to 26.9% while control group employment remained essentially static (11.1% to 9.5%), with African American subjects showing greater improvement. At the one-year follow-up, the differences between the experimental and control groups were no longer detectable. Additionally, overall, members of the experimental group were found to have acquired significantly more jobs than had controls during the 12 months following the intervention. Platt et al. (1993) concluded that (a) the intervention was better at helping patients find work than in assisting them in maintaining it; (b) ethnic differences in treatment effectiveness may have meant that unemployment within the African American subject pool was a different phenomenon than it was with white subjects; and (c) the types of jobs acquired (83% were unskilled or semiskilled positions) might not have provided sufficient financial and personal incentives to maintain employment, particularly in the face of losses in basic services (e.g., Medicaid) due to taking a job.

Deren and Randell (1988) reported on a three year study—the Venus Project—that attempted to identify the obstacles to utilization of vocational services by methadone maintenance patients and to evaluate interventions designed to address these obstacles. Based on a literature review (see Brewington, Arella, Deren, and Randell, 1987) and interviews with program staff and patients (Arella, Deren, Randell, and Brewington, 1986; Arella, Deren, and Randell, 1988; Brewington, Deren, Arella, and Randell, 1990), an expert panel selected two obstacles considered to be the most important and most amenable to change: (a) program level disincentives to utilize vocational services, such as methadone programs receiving more income for services from unemployed patients on Medicaid than from employed patients without Medicaid, and (b) a failure to integrate vocational services into treatment programs. Based on these identified obstacles, the investigators developed two interventions. Funding for employed patients was provided to close the gap between program income from unemployed Medicaid patients and employed patients, and a "vocational integrator" was provided to enhance the program coordination and delivery of the then-available vocational services. The effectiveness of these interventions was assessed by comparing the monthly employment status and related employment activities of methadone patients in four New York City clinics. One of these clinics served as a control, one received only a vocational integrater, one received only the additional funding, and one received both interventions. Results showed greater patient involvement in activities with the addition of a vocational integrator, but no differences in employment rates were detected. The authors suggested that (a) there might not have been sufficient time in the assessment phase (which lasted one year) to detect existing differences; (b) the addition of a vocational counselor to provide direct services might be necessary to increase and maintain employment rates; and (c) programmatic incentives to increase vocational services should be provided to increase employment, rather than merely to reduce program disincentives.

Reviewing the literature concerning the vocational rehabilitation of drug abusers, Platt (1994) concluded that (a) over the past twenty years, there has been an increasing awareness of the importance of employment and employment-related issues in drug abuse treatment, together with a number of efforts to develop employment-related interventions; (b) yet, relatively few interventions exist, and of those that do, many have defects which either limit their generalizability, have not been demonstrated to work with drug addicts, or otherwise raise questions about whether their use would represent a wise investment of scarce resources; and (c) there is an absence, in the employment literature, of a comprehensive theory which can guide research. Platt (1994) concluded this overview with a listing of factors associated with employment that needed further exploration. These included the roles played by cognition, parental modeling, and the special needs of women and minorities. Additionally, other factors requiring further exploration included the characteristics of appropriate interventions for increasing employment among addicts, such as the identification of personal barriers to employment, and the mechanisms to assist in maintenance of effective employment-related behaviors.

RELAPSE AND RELAPSE PREVENTION

As McAuliffe, Feldman, Friedman, Launer, Magnuson, et al. (1986) have noted, relapse is one of the central defining characteristics of heroin addiction. In two major studies of treatment outcome, relapse to some opiate use among methadone maintenance patients was found to be 57% in the year following treatment (Drug Abuse Reporting Program (DARP); Savage and Simpson, 1980), while among methadone maintenance patients who had used opiates at least weekly prior to treatment, some 43% had relapsed to weekly or more often opiate use in the year following treatment (Treatment Outcome Prospective Study; Hubbard et al., 1984). Such relapse is highly likely to occur within the first three months following treatment. Joe, Chastain, Marsh, and Simpson (1990) for example, found that 27% of DARP patients had relapsed to daily opiate use following treatment after three months, 44% within 36 months, while 71% had relapsed one or more times within 12 years. Hubbard and Marsden (1986) found that some two-thirds of those subjects in the TOPS study with a history of drug use had relapsed to regular use within three months and 51% had relapsed within one year.

It is also evident that relapse is present in all addictions. As Catalano, Howard, Hawkins, and Wells (1988) commented with respect to treatment outcome in the opioid, alcohol, and tobacco dependence fields,

... reviews ... suggest that clinical interventions are often successful in producing short-term cessation of drug use but that maintenance of treatment gains is more difficult to achieve (p. 1).

Thus, it is not surprising that strategies intended to prevent relapse have been both implicitly and explicitly incorporated into research which has been done relating to improvement of treatment outcome. Additionally, there has been an increasing interest in, and research focus on, relapse as a phenomenon in its own right, and as a feature of addiction that deserves special attention in treatment programs. However, as Wesson, Havassy, and Smith (1986) have pointed out in their review of theories of relapse and recovery, relapse, or drug use occurring after a period of abstinence, has been variously defined as either a discrete event (i.e., the single use of a drug) reflecting either return to the primary drug or abuse or return to use of any psychoactive drug, or a process developing over time. The latter may in turn reflect (a) daily drug use for a period of time; (b) return to drug use at or above pretreatment levels; (c) readmission to treatment as a result of drug use; (d) a psychometrically defined event; or (e) a return to use at or beyond specified levels of use, in terms of either quantity or duration of use. The addictions research field can only benefit from the development and usage of common definitions of relapse.

Relapse Among Heroin Addicts

The classic studies in this area by Hunt and his associates (Hunt, Barnett, and Branch, 1971; Hunt and Bespalec, 1974), carried out in the early 1970s, demonstrated a remarkable similarity of relapse curves for patients discharged from treatment programs for opiate, alcohol, and tobacco dependence programs. Literature reviews on factors influencing relapse following opioid treatment can be found in Volume 1 (pp. 211–218); Catalano, Howard, Hawkins, and Wells (1988); and Maddux and Desmond (1986).

Typical of the findings of recent studies of relapse among opioid users are those of Simpson and Marsh (1986) who, as part of the larger Drug Abuse Reporting Program (DARP) study, analyzed the relapse rates of addicts at 6 years following treatment and at 12 years following treatment. They found that almost regardless of treatment modality, some 36% of their sample had relapsed at least once by the 6-year follow-up interview. At year 12, some 65% had relapsed at least once. While this latter figure appears particularly discouraging, it should be noted that over 60% of the sample had not used opiates for the three years prior to follow-up, and over 75% had not used opiates within the year prior to follow-up. The 65% relapse rate, however, confirms and highlights the need to more fully understand the process of relapse.

Posttreatment follow-up data for the 490 addicts in the DARP study yielded survival curves indicating that relapse was most likely during the first three months following treatment, when 27% had reverted to daily opiate use. Forty-four percent had relapsed by 36 months, and 72% had relapsed one or more times by the time of the 12-year follow-up. Yet, only 25% were still addicted by year 12, and 63% had not been addicted for three years or more. When factors contributing to relapse among DARP participants at the 12-year follow-up were examined, those persons at greatest risk of relapse were found to have (a) had an age of less than 28 at admission; (b) had less than a high school education; (c) begun their career at younger ages; (d) been more likely to have been involved in illegal activities as a means of support; (e) been *more* satisfied with their lives at the time of addiction; (f) used drugs for sensation-seeking; and (g) had a longer history of legal deviance. Joe, Chastain, Marsh, and Simpson (1990) concluded that these results " . . . suggested an underlying concept reflecting degree of socialization into a supportive network and to a conventional lifestyle as being significant in predicting later recidivism to opioid addiction" (p. 121).

Catalano et al. (1988), reviewing the literature on relapse in the addictions, concluded that a number of variables were related to relapse to opiate addiction. For example, among *background* factors were the following: (a) pretreatment severity of drug use; (b) degree of neuropsychological and psychiatric impairment; (c) level of pretreatment criminality; and (d) extent of prior treatment; while demographic variables were not clearly related. Likewise, the following *treatment* factors had been found to be related to relapse among opiate users: (a) length of time in treatment; (b) treatment completion; (c) use of drugs or involvement in crime during treatment; (d) expectations of treatment outcome; and (e) modality of treatment. Among *posttreatment* factors were (a) absence of a strong prosocial interpersonal network, including the presence or absence of family networks and family supports and familial discord; (b) peer and social network factors, including peer pressure to use drugs and social isolation; (c) lack of involvement in productive roles, such as work and/or school, and employment; (d) lack of involvement in active leisure and recreational activities; (e) negative emotional states, including depression and other negative affects; (f) negative physical states, including chronic pain; (g) deficits in social, coping, and problem-solving skills; (h) negative life events, including death, major illnesses, and other life transitions; and (i) lack of needed services.

Maddux and Desmond (1986), after reviewing the literature on relapse among opioid and other drug users, identified the following common themes as being present: (a) a special *vulnerability* for the use of psychoactive substances, genetic or acquired; (b) a *high-risk environment* with respect to familial and social factors, and availability of drugs; (c) a *wide variation* in the duration and severity of addiction careers; (d) substance substitution; (e) *high mortality* rates; (f) *frequent and rapid relapse*, usually within one year; (g) *increasing abstinence* with the passage of years; and (h) the association of a period of three years of a recovery process with good outcomes.

An important contribution to the understanding of relapse comes from Vaillant's series of longitudinal studies (Vaillant, 1966a,b,c,d; 1988) describing the lives of a cohort of heroin addicts treated at the U.S. Public Health Service Hospital at Lexington, Kentucky in 1952. This cohort consisted of 100 male first admissions from New York City, with an average age of 25 years and two years of addiction to heroin at admission. Seventy-five percent had been voluntary admissions and 95% required methadone during withdrawal (Vaillant, 1966a). Vaillant (1988) saw the addict as having begun a drug-seeking career because of a lack of opportunity to engage in other competing forms of independent behavior. For such individuals, where " . . . daily life is unpatterned by a job, addiction imposes a very definite and gratifying, if rather stereotyped, pattern of behaviour" (p. 1150).

The existence of substitute prosocial behavioral patterns, which evolve in addiction in the absence of patterned social behavior, lead to a high likelihood of relapse. Examining characteristics which differentiated good from poor outcomes, Vaillant (1988) observed that, for the 100 heroin addicts he studied, "external interventions that restructured the patient's life in the community . . . often were associated with sustained abstinence" (p. 1153). This conclusion is reflected in the relative efficacy of four different modes of treatment for his sample, in terms of percentage of the sample for which the treatment was followed by one year of abstinence: (a) hospital detoxification (3%); (b) short imprisonment (3%); (c) prison plus one year's parole (71%); and (d) methadone maintenance (67%). Vaillant (1983) also found four factors, other than treatment, to have been associated with relapse prevention in treated abstinent heroin addicts: (a) *compulsory supervision*, or having experienced an aversive physical problem associated with substance use (e.g., use of disulfiram or a painful ulcer), present in 47% of cases; (b) having found a *substitute dependency*, such as meditation, overeating, compulsive gambling, etc. (60% of cases); (c) the presence of *new social supports* (e.g., a grateful employer, a new marriage), 63%; and (d) *inspirational group membership*, 20%. On the basis of these data, Vaillant (1988) concluded that " . . . it was the premorbid capacity for sustained structured behaviour and the discovery of competing sources of gratification that distinguished the best from the worst outcomes . . . " (p. 1152).

Marsh, Joe, Simpson, and Lehman (1990) examined the relationship between treatment experiences and long-term outcome as part of Simpson and Sells's (1990) 12-year study of drug abuse treatment outcome in 490 former opiate addicts. Most important among the findings were that addicts whose treatment had been received primarily in therapeutic communities and other drug-free treatment programs tended to have had fewer admissions to treatment in their addiction careers and to have had shorter drug-use careers than did those addicts who had had their treatment experiences in methadone maintenance and detoxification programs. Additionally, more of those in the therapeutic community and drug-free groups reported their treatment experiences to have been positive than did those in the methadone maintenance and detoxification groups.

With respect to long-term outcome, Marsh et al. (1990) found few differences between the four modalities with respect to behavioral outcome—with the exception of employment, which was higher at follow-up for the therapeutic community and drug-free groups than for the methadone maintenance and detoxification groups. Marsh et al. (1990) suggested that, among other reasons, this difference was likely reflective of a stronger desire to terminate drug use on the part of therapeutic community and drug-free patients; as well as a generalized drug-free orientation resulting from incorporation of their program philosophies on the part of these patients. However, when treatment *exposure*, rather than treatment *entry*, was considered, more differences emerged. Overall, addicts with *any* therapeutic community experience had (in contrast to the groups having had drug-free, methadone maintenance, and detoxification treatment experience) (a) lower opioid, alcohol, and marijuana use; (b) lower criminality; and (c) higher employment. A similar positive finding was obtained for those addicts who reported having had helpful treatment experiences. Those who had such a "helpful" experience in a therapeutic community had better outcomes with respect to opioid use and employment than had those who had been in detoxification and methadone maintenance treatment. Similarly, those who had had positive experiences in the drug-free group had shorter drug careers, number of treatments entered, and positive perceptions of the efficacy of drug-free treatment. However, exposure to methadone maintenance did not result in outcomes as positive as those shown by addicts exposed to therapeutic communities.

Fortunately, relapse is not the only outcome to be expected after treatment. In a study described by the authors as the first systematic British investigation of outcomes for opiate addicts following treatment, Gossop, Green, Phillips, and Bradley (1987) followed 50 opiate addicts for six months after discharge from inpatient treatment during which they had been withdrawn from opiates. At follow-up, Gossop et al. (1987) found, after excluding hospitalized and incarcerated subjects, that some 47% of those living in the community were not taking opiates. When "nonaddicted" subjects (e.g., those using opiates less than once a day, and thus considered by the authors not to be physically addicted), were added to this number, some " . . . 68% of the sample were not addicted to opiates six months after finishing treatment . . . " (p. 1379). Gossop et al. (1987) interpreted their findings as "both surprising and gratifying" (p. 1379), although they noted that a very high proportion of subjects had used opiates immediately following discharge, 18 within the first week. Examining the data more closely, women tended to have had poorer outcomes, both with respect to having remained abstinent less often and having used opiates more frequently.

Further, a first relapse to opiates in this study did not necessarily mean a full relapse into addiction. Sampling their subjects at two-month intervals after discharge, the proportion of those using drugs occasionally fell over subsequent sampling points, the proportion of those abstinent grew, and the proportion of daily users remained constant. Another finding of this study was that the substitution of alcohol use or other drugs for opiates did not appear to have occurred in this sample, a finding similar to that obtained by Stimson and Oppenheimer (1982). The Gossop et al. (1987) study presents some provocative findings which can only be generalized to the American scene with caution. Yet, the conclusions drawn warrant attention, and the following point is well worth heeding:

In view of the considerable costs of treating addicts it is imperative that the hard won gains of inpatient care should not be allowed to disappear through lack of attention being paid to this critical phase of treatment. The results also confirm that one lapse need not lead to a full blown relapse . . . Many people took opiates soon after discharge but did not subsequently become daily users (p. 1379).

Explanations of Relapse

Explanations of relapse are as diverse as are theories regarding the entire cycle of addiction. For example, Wesson, Havassy, and Smith (1986) described seven approaches to relapse, including genetic, metabolic, classical conditioning, social learning, psychopathology, stress, and social support theories. Wesson et al. (1986) observed that theoretical approaches themselves determined to some extent the type of relapse-related variables explored, the nature of treatments chosen, and the outcome variables measured. These diverse theories could also be viewed as addressing different levels of analysis and understanding, and as providing information regarding important pieces to the complex puzzle of relapse. As such, at least some of these approaches may be complimentary rather than exclusive.

Maddux and Desmond (1986) noted the following problems as handicapping a full understanding of the phenomenon of relapse to drug (primarily opiates) and alcohol use: (a) an absence of *generally accepted criteria*; (b) a need to clarify and better measure *etiological factors*, both individual and environmental; (c) more precise analysis and measurement of *motivation for recovery*; (d) a better understanding of *social or controlled drinking*; (e) a better understanding of *treatment effects* on addiction careers; and (f) continued study of the validity of *addict self-reports*.

One aspect of the newly developing research on relapse, relapse prevention, and recovery focuses upon treatment variables and addict characteristics. For instance, in a preliminary study, McAuliffe, Feldman, Friedman, Launer, Magnuson, et al. (1986) reported on the frequency of, and variables related to, relapse among 184 opiate addicts recruited at the point of treatment completion. They found that psychological craving for addictive substances accounted for some 30% of the variance in relapse at 6- and 12-month follow-ups. Factors related to craving included the degree of recent drug abuse, physical addiction, depression, anxiety, withdrawal sickness, and euphoria seeking. Not surprisingly, addicts who were sufficiently motivated to complete long-term drug-free treatment demonstrated less craving at follow-up points. On the basis of these and earlier findings, McAuliffe et al. (1986) suggested that addicts "in treatment and aftercare programs should be educated regarding the course of their disease and the prospects for recovery when certain events, such as a 'slip' or 'lapse' occur" (p. 153). It might also be useful to address depression and anxiety through supportive/expressive or cognitive psychotherapy, and to utilize extinction techniques to address conditioned withdrawal symptoms and physical dependence.

As a means of addressing the increasingly prevalent phenomenon of polydrug abuse, and in an attempt to make use of previously observed similarities between various substances of abuse (e.g., Hunt, Barnett, and Branch, 1971; Marlatt and Gordon, 1980), relapse research has also incorporated a broader cross-drug research perspective. Though these comparisons do have substantial limitations (Rounsaville, 1986), they may be helpful in shedding some light on the general parameters of relapse. For example, Hubbard and Marsden (1986) analyzed data from pre- and posttreatment interviews with 2,280 drug abusers who had participated in the Treatment Outcome Prospective Study (TOPS) during 1979 and 1980. They assessed the abuse of four general types of illicit drugs (including heroin, other narcotics, cocaine, and nonnarcotics) and found that in the year following treatment, some 40% of narcotics abusers had shifted their drug use patterns to nonnarcotics use. However, about one-third of the heroin and other narcotic abusers had resumed their pretreatment patterns of narcotic use. Perhaps not unexpectedly, the most frequent posttreatment relapse phenomenon was the return to pretreatment patterns and levels of abuse. Regardless of the type of substance abused, for those patients who had resumed drug abuse, some two-thirds did so within three months following treatment. The highest levels of continued abstinence were found in nonnarcotic substance users (59%). Hubbard and Marsden (1986) concluded, among other things, that " . . . more emphasis on aftercare and postdischarge counseling that focuses on prevention of relapse might help reduce relapse rates and increase periods of remission for relapsing clients" (p. 164).

Hall and Havassy (1986) investigated similarities in relapse factors across tobacco, alcohol, and opiate dependent subjects. These subjects were assessed along five independent measures once weekly for 12 weeks following termination of treatment. The dependent measure consisted of time to relapse. Among other things, their preliminary findings on 77 of 230 subjects indicated that regardless of abused substance, those subjects who had endorsed more restrictive goals (i.e., complete and final abstinence, versus controlled use), were more likely to remain abstinent for longer periods. Interestingly, the perceived degree of difficulty in terminating dependence did not uniformly predict length of time before relapse across substance type. While smokers who predicted high levels of difficulty in smoking cessation were more likely to have had shorter periods until relapse, similar predictions in alcoholics were unrelated to length of abstinence, and opiate addicts who predicted greater difficulty in abstention had had longer periods following treatment during which they had maintained a drug-free state. Hall and Havassy (1986) also found that the groups differed overall in terms of time to relapse, with addicts showing the briefest mean drug-free period (6.11 weeks), and smokers showing the longest (10.37 weeks). Though preliminary in nature, the authors' conclusion was that substance abusers' commitment to abstinence was a potentially important factor warranting further attention in research on relapse prevention and recovery, a finding confirmed in a subsequent report (Hall, Havassy, and Wasserman, 1990).

A number of writers have called for more research into factors related to relapse and strategies for decreasing relapse (Hall and Havassy, 1986; Leukefeld and Tims, 1986; Rounsaville, 1986). Leukefeld and Tims (1986), in their summary of conclusions flowing from a conference on relapse and recovery, discussed a number of directions for future investigation. They suggested that studies should focus on the natural history of addiction careers, addict characteristics related to relapse, physiological factors, the role of stimulus control, and the role of individual and familial psychopathology.

Conditioned reactions to both environmental and internal stimuli (cues) may play an important part in triggering relapse to drug use in general, and to opioid and cocaine use in particular, and a significant body of research has emerged in this area (Rohsenow, Niaura, Childress, Abrams, and Monti, 1990–91). To a great extent, this work is founded in the conditioned withdrawal model of relapse proposed by Wikler (1965, 1980; see Volume 1, pp. 106–112), as well as in more recent (although quite different) formulations by Siegel (1983), Stewart, deWit, and Eikelboom (1984), and Wise (1988). Studies by Chaney, Roszell, and Cummings (1982) and Childress, McLellan, and O'Brien (1986a,b) have indicated that such stimuli as negative mood states and scenes associated with drug use (e.g., seeing drugs being used, seeing drug paraphernalia or even money) were likely to trigger relapses to drug use. Chaney and Roszell (1985) identified four such clusters of situations: (a) withdrawal-related stimuli; (b) interpersonal cues, positive emotional states, or positive social pressure to use drugs; (c) negative emotional states; and (d) negative physical states other than withdrawal.

Childress and her associates (e.g., Childress, McLellan, Ehrman, and O'Brien, 1988; Childress, McLellan, and O'Brien, 1984; O'Brien, Childress, and McLellan, 1991) have been concerned with conditioned responses associated with chronic opioid use (and more recently, cocaine use) and their role in triggering relapse to drug use in the abstinent patient. The strategy employed by Childress and her co-workers has been straightforward: (a) identification of the kinds of conditioned responses experienced by drug users which appear to be related to relapse to drug use; (b) identification of those stimuli which reliably elicit these responses; (c) development of extinction procedures, such as non-reinforced exposures, to reduce or eliminate these responses; and (d) comparison of clinical outcomes for patients who have experienced reduction of conditioned responses with controls in order to determine the extent to which these responses contribute to relapse (Childress et al., 1988). Targeting responses with theoretical and face significance, such as conditioned withdrawal and conditioned craving, which might contribute to relapse, Childress and her associates have employed such measurements of arousal and withdrawal as patients' subjective ratings of withdrawal, observational checklists of withdrawal-associated signs and symptoms, and physiological reactivity measures (including heart rate, respiration, skin resistance, and peripheral skin temperature). Collecting data in the laboratory, the clinical setting (usually the methadone clinic), and the patients' natural environment, Childress, O'Brien, McLellan, and their associates have identified a wide variety of apparent conditioned responses upon exposure to drug-related stimuli (e.g., injection equipment, such as syringes, cookers, etc., and color slides and audiotapes of drug-buying locations, drug purchases, and drug use), including subjective reports of "highs," craving, and withdrawal, as well as physiological arousal and decreased peripheral skin temperature. Such responses differed from those obtained from neutral stimuli (Childress, McLellan, and O'Brien, 1984; 1985). Other findings include: (a) the presence of such responses in abstinent former opioid-dependent patients for at least 30 days immediately following detoxification, suggesting a high vulnerability to relapse following discharge (Childress, McLellan, and O'Brien, 1986b; Childress, McLellan, Ehrman, and O'Brien, 1987); (b) a higher incidence of drug-related conditioned responses in the addict's natural environment (Childress, McLellan, and O'Brien, 1986a,b); (c) the usefulness of extinction procedures in reducing the response to drug-related stimuli (Childress et al., 1984; Childress, McLellan, and O'Brien, 1985); and (d) the significant impact of mood state (e.g., depression and anxiety) upon the nature and intensity of conditioned responses to external stimuli (Childress, McLellan, Natale, and O'Brien, 1987).

Having demonstrated that conditioned responses occurring in connection with drug use could be readily elicited for study, and that conditioned craving occurred in response to drug-related stimuli independently of other conditioned withdrawal responses, Childress et al. (1988) concluded that

current extinction protocols are effective in reducing the conditioned responses to both opioid and cocaine-related test stimuli. How well this extinction training generalizes to the "real world," is, of course, the crucial clinical question (p. 40).

Increasing evidence exists relating to the effectiveness of cue exposure in the treatment of opiate addicts. In one such study, Childress, McLellan, Ehrman, and O'Brien (1988) provided outpatient methadone patients with a standard set of drug-related stimuli, including the patient's own imagery; audiotapes of drug-related situations; color slides of preparing and using opiates; and actual handling of drug paraphernalia, in that order. After up to 35 exposure sessions to these cues, followed by psychotherapy and relaxation training, craving, but not withdrawal symptoms, declined. This cue exposure group, and a control group receiving psychotherapy, both showed significant improvement at outcome in comparison with an attention-control group which received only extra drug counseling without psychotherapy. Disappointingly, however, there were no differences between the two groups in drug use as determined by positive urines.

Finally, O'Brien, Childress, and McLellan (1991) have provided a review of recent research into conditioning factors in relapse to drug abuse. Commenting on the presence of subjective and physiological responses to drug related stimuli, they observed that

patients who already have been treated in the traditional manner may continue to show dramatic responses to drug-related stimuli despite a strong conscious motivation to avoid drug use in the future (p. 309).

Moring and Strang (1989), noting the importance of cue exposure as a treatment technique, observed that it had been largely overlooked as an assessment technique of cue vulnerability in planning for relapse prevention. Cue exposure was seen as particularly important in environments where drugs, and therefore cues triggering their use, were readily available. One question persisting with respect to relapse after opiate withdrawal is whether cues which have formerly been associated with opiate use could themselves elicit withdrawal symptoms, which in turn led to renewed use of drugs, as hypothesized by Wikler (1973), or whether the motivational properties of these cues were a direct result of the reinforcing properties of opiates (Bozarth and Wise, 1981). In an attempt to answer this question, Legarda, Bradley, and Sartory (1990) investigated the relationships among responses to drug-related stimuli as a function of drug status. Current heroin users, methadone users, detoxified heroin users, and controls were shown a videotape of drug administration and their psychophysiological responses recorded. If conditioned withdrawal had taken place, drug-related cues should have elicited a negative shift in mood and increase in heart rate in the heroin user and detoxified addict groups; if, however, drug-related cues had elicited opiate-like effects, a positive shift in mood would have occurred in these two groups, while heart rate should have decreased in drug users and increased in detoxified users. The results were inconclusive in that none of the user groups differed from controls. Detoxified users showed an elevated heart rate prior to the presentation of the stimulus; current users showed an increased heart rate and controls showed slowing of heart rate during the video presentation; while detoxified users showed increased skin conductance. A tendency towards a positive shift in mood was shown by current heroin users, and a negative shift by methadone users and detoxified users.

Noting that the hypothesis that drug cues could actively serve to keep addicts on continuous and compulsive drug use is an old one, but that the application of such principles to the clinical management of long-term habituation is recent and at a preliminary stage of development, Tobeña, Fernández-Teruel, Escorihuela, Nuñez, Zapata, Ferré, and Sánchez (1993) discussed the application of exposure techniques to managing long-term dishabituation. They noted that cue exposure treatments have limited effectiveness in preventing relapse to drug use because extinction and habituation of responses to drug cues (or aftereffects) are unstable and strongly dependent upon context. Tobeña et al. (1993) then suggested several strategies to improve the stability of extinction and habituation in preventing relapse to drug use: (a) both warning patients about the episodic resurgence of unexpected urges or cravings precipitated by contextual cues and exposing them to such contexts; (b) maximally recreating the original learning context (i.e., all possible cues) during extinction; and (c) incorporating into cue exposure treatment the behavioral chains involved in self-administration (without, of course, the permitting consummatory responses) in order to decrease their signal value as drug-taking cues.

Powell, Bradley, and Gray (1992) observed that the "classical conditioning" (i.e., Wikler's [1965]) view that craving is elicited in detoxified addicts by conditioned responses to stimuli associated with the onset of drug effects and the "cognitive" (e.g., Marlatt and Gordon, 1985) view that craving derives directly from positive outcome expectancies concerning drug use models generate different predictions concerning the correlates of subjective craving. Powell et al. (1992) then tested the two models by analyzing the correlations between craving responses and each model's hypothesized outcome. Fifty-six detoxified opiate addicts participated in a Craving Test requiring ratings by them of craving, physical state, and emotions during the presentation of neutral and drug-related stimuli. The findings indicated that a large number of subjects failed to report changes in craving, symptomatology, or dysphoria to cues. While some of the predictions derived from the classical conditioning model were borne out, the cognitive model received more consistent support.

Relapse Prevention Interventions

Rounsaville (1986) has offered a number of recommendations as to how, even with the present state of knowledge, relapse prevention might be increased in current treatment programs. First, he suggested that programs should explicitly acknowledge the potential for relapse, and should attempt to facilitate newly readdicted patients' re-entry into treatment. Second, he proposed that skill training in constructive responses to relapse should be included in treatment programs. Third, he suggested that social support between addicts and via addict families should be encouraged and be included as an integral part of treatment programs. Fourth, he recommended aftercare programs that focused upon less intensive treatment (e.g., once weekly counseling, phone contacts) throughout the first year following termination of the formal treatment program. Fifth and finally, Rounsaville recommended that drug programs address the issue of multidrug abuse and drug substitution, either through subprogram components or through patient participation in multiple treatment programs.

Strategies for preventing relapse have become an extremely active area of clinical research interest. Catalano, Howard, Hawkins, and Wells (1988) organized such strategies into the following categories, and provided a number of examples of each: (a) *skill-training strategies* most notably reflected in the work of Marlatt and Gordon (1980, 1985; also see Volume 3, Chapter 1), but applied more to alcohol than to drug treatment (see also Platt and Hermalin, 1989); (b) *active-leisure focused strategies*, reflecting attempts to increase the social participation of patients beyond work or treatment, primarily by involvement in self-help groups (e.g., Catalano and Hawkins, 1985; Hawkins and Catalano, 1985; McAuliffe et al., 1985; Nurco, Wegner, Stephenson, Makofsky, and Shaffer, 1983; (see also Volume 3, Chapter 1); (c) *negative emotional state strategies*, including service provision to ameliorate such states as depression, anxiety, or anger, either through traditional interventions such as counseling or psychopharmacological interventions (see Volume 3, Chapters 1, 3, and 5), stress management training, relaxation, or meditation (e.g., Charlesworth and Dempsey, 1982; Marlatt and Gordon, 1985), or through such techniques as assertiveness training (Warren and McLellan, 1982), stress inoculation (Novaco, 1977), and coping skill training (Hawkins, Catalano, and Wells, 1986; Hawkins, Catalano, Gillmore, and Wells, 1989); (d) *negative physical state strategies*, through acute or chronic pain management (e.g., Keefe, Gil, and Rose, 1986; Turner and Romano, 1984) or reduction in opioid withdrawal symptoms through the use of clonidine (e.g., Gold, Dackis, and Washton, 1984); (e) *pharmacological interventions*, through employment of such medications as naltrexone, buprenorphine, or clonidine (see Volume 3, Chapter 5); (f) *social support strategies*, including services to families and strengthening existing or creating new social networks via involvement in such self-help groups as Al-Anon, Nar-Anon, and Families Anonymous (Ashery, 1979; Emrick, 1987) that involve the families of addicts in their treatment (Stanton, 1980; Sorensen, 1990), and involvement in either traditional self-help programs such as Alcoholics Anonymous and Narcotics Anonymous, or professionally run groups such as those described by McAuliffe and his associates (e.g., McAuliffe, 1990; McAuliffe and Ch'ien, 1986); and (g) *vocational strategies*, including supported work (Manpower Research Corporation, 1980), job training (Bass and Woodward, 1978), job seeking and interview skills (Hall, Loeb, and LeVois, 1985), and employment readiness training (Platt, Husband, Hermalin, Cater, and Metzger, 1993; see also Platt, 1994).

CONCLUSIONS

The studies reviewed in this chapter reflect an increasing attention to improvement in treatment outcome in the addictions in general, and specifically to the recovery process, which has emerged in the drug abuse treatment field over the past decade. As has been observed by McAuliffe et al. (1986), relapse is a central defining characteristic of addiction. Attention to treatment improvement not only reflects an increasing emphasis on making treatment more effective, but also the increasing effort towards reducing the revolving door nature of drug abuse treatment, in which the patient repeats a cycle of addiction, treatment, and re-addiction. Attention to the recovery process reflects both the recognition of the importance of this process, and the impetus given to the development of relapse prevention techniques stimulated by the pioneering theoretical advances of Marlatt and his associates with respect to alcoholism treatment. Specific advances in our understanding of the recovery process, relapse, and treatment outcome include the following:

- The matching of patients, based upon their needs and characteristics, to appropriate treatments has become an important area of investigation (e.g., Kadden et al., 1989), as well as of methodological attention (e.g., Finney and Moos, 1986; McLellan and Alterman, 1991). Matching of patients to appropriate treatment has been implemented both with respect to alcoholism (e.g., Miller and Hester, 1986) and drug abuse treatment (e.g., Luborsky, McLellan, Woody, O'Brien, and Auerbach, 1985; Woody et al., 1984, 1985, 1988; also see Chapter 5). This line of research is likely to yield improvement in both effective utilization of treatment resources and treatment outcome at a time of diminishing availability of treatment resources.
- The relationship between time in treatment and treatment outcome (e.g., Simpson, 1981; Simpson and Sells, 1982a,b; McLellan, Luborsky, O'Brien et al., 1986) continues to be confirmed across modalities (Anglin, 1988c; De Leon, 1986, 1991; Hubbard et al., 1989), although attempts to quantify this relationship through identification of the minimal time needed for this effect suggests that it may be modality specific (e.g., Ball and Ross, 1981; Hubbard et al., 1989).
- Treatment dropout, a major problem in substance abuse treatment, has increasingly been addressed and work on this issue has been the subject of several reviews (e.g., Craig, 1985a; Pickens and Fletcher, 1991), and of a number of research studies (Denis et al., 1992; Greenfield et. al, 1992; Küfner et al., 1992; Kunz, 1988, 1992; Vollmer, Ellgring, and Ferstl, 1992), although broadly applicable solutions for this problem remain to be devised.
- With the advent of managed care and greater emphasis on issues of accountability, issues such as those related to case management have assumed their appropriate importance (e.g., Ashery, 1992a). Given the multiple needs of many drug abusers, case management would appear to be a necessary element in effectively treating drug abuse, particularly in high-risk populations. Both case management and managed care are relatively new concepts to the drug-abuse treatment field and will require the development of both conceptual models and methodologically sound research (e.g., Chamberlain and Rapp, 1991; Dennis et al., 1992).

- A specific need of heroin addicts, as identified by a number of studies, is vocational rehabilitation, or as is often appropriately the case, vocational habilitation (see reviews by Hall, 1984b; and Platt, 1994). Often, treatment does not address this issue (Platt, 1994), although unemployment is frequently considered a contributing variable to initiation and continuation of drug use (e.g., Faupel, 1988). Interventions to increase employment have been relatively few in number, and many of them are limited with respect to generalizability (Platt, 1994).

- Relapse to drug use is of course one of the major problems facing the treatment field (e.g., Catalano et al., 1988; Maddux and Desmond, 1986; Wesson et al., 1986). An understanding is now emerging, however, of variables influencing relapse to opioid addiction. In general, severity of impairment with respect to drug use, psychiatric status, and criminality have all been found to be predictors of relapse (e.g., Catalano et al., 1988; Maddux and Desmond, 1986; Wesson et al., 1986). Other factors found to predict relapse are the extent and intensity of treatment experience, posttreatment factors such as the existence of an interpersonal network and other family factors, and personal variables such as social competencies and problem-solving skills, among others (Catalano et al., 1988; Vaillant, 1988). These findings give clear guidance as to the direction of interventions for reducing relapse to drug abuse (perhaps as well suggesting how to prevent the initial development of drug abuse).

- An understanding of the external dimensions associated with successful long-term outcome for opiate users has emerged, in terms of findings concerning the relative effectiveness of different interventions. Vaillant's (1983) identification of compulsory supervision, substitute dependency, the establishment of new social supports, and inspirational leadership as elements contributing to successful long-term outcomes in recovery provides an increased understanding of the variables important for successful relapse prevention.

- The relapse process is being increasingly studied, and as a result, is becoming more precisely defined by such researchers as Gossop et al. (1987) who examined relapse to drug use as a function of level of drug use as well as time. More precise definition allows for the specification of better theories as well as more precise research questions (e.g., Hall and Havassy, 1986; McAuliffe et al., 1986; Wesson et al., 1986) and research into what constitutes more effective interventions (e.g., see Catalano et al., 1988).

- Conditioned cues which elicit craving and relapse to drug-taking behaviors have been closely studied in the laboratory (e.g., Childress et al., 1988; O'Brien, Childress and McLellan, 1991), and have provided an important contribution to an understanding of how environmental factors can trigger craving and drug-seeking. Yet, clinically meaningful generalization of extinction procedures in the laboratory to the "real world" remains to be firmly established. Moring and Strang's (1989) observation that cue exposure has been largely overlooked as an intervention technique is a cogent one that awaits an appropriate experimental test.

• Many treatment programs have not adequately addressed relapse prevention, in part because of the absence of sophistication in the techniques needed for implementation on the part of line staff, and in part because of misconceptions concerning the relapse process; yet, line staff are often in the best position to provide such interventions. A range of such procedures now exists (e.g., Catalano et al., 1988) and Rounsaville (1986) has provided several recommendations for the implementation of relapse prevention procedures in treatment programs.

• Perhaps the most established finding with respect to treatment outcome is the relationship between length of time in treatment and treatment outcome, regardless of treatment modality. This finding clearly indicates that drug abuse treatment has a favorable impact on decreasing drug abuse. The relevant problem now is how to identify the specific elements in treatment services which produce this effect and to increase the efficiency of treatment.

• Dropout from treatment remains a major problem in treating drug abuse. Initial studies of dropout have identified characteristics of patients who fail to complete treatment, a second stage of description following determination of dropout rates. Studies have now begun on prediction of dropout (e.g., Vollmer, Ellgring, and Ferstl, 1992). Given the relatively high level of work in this area, it is likely that advances in findings will move rapidly.

PART THREE

Advances in Understanding the Heroin Addict

CHAPTER 4

Addict Characteristics and Behavioral Patterns

It may well be that addicts may not all be treatable in the same manner with the existing treatment armamentarium. Further, the increasing precision in substance abuse treatment evaluation studies has brought with it a recognition of the existence of more complexity, rather than simply having provided answers to the questions surrounding treatment outcome. Yet, it continues to be difficult to attract and retain heroin addicts in treatment, and to sustain abstinence once treatment has been completed. Moreover, it is clear that the "classic" heroin addict, who had a single drug preference and/or dependency, no longer exists. Even those addicts whose primary drug of abuse is heroin use many substances of abuse, thus somewhat blurring the distinction between the classic heroin addict and other substance abusers, and requiring more broadly applicable treatment approaches.

Parallel with advances in research and treatment methodology, there has also been an increasing appreciation of the implications of the diversity that exists among heroin addicts. This appreciation should help to refine our knowledge of the treatment needs of a given subgroup of patients, thus increasing the likelihood of efficient and effective treatment for those who can be reached. While research methodology continues to be a problem because of the extraordinary difficulties that exist when attempting research on such a complexly determined phenomenon as heroin addiction, there is a slow but steady movement toward the goal of delineating the most efficacious treatments and improving the manner in which such treatments are delivered. The purpose of this chapter is to describe recent research findings concerning the characteristics of addicts and the implications that these hold for treatment. Such characteristics include demographic characteristics, drug use patterns, patterns of criminal involvement, addict typologies, and the impact of genetic factors and early experience.

ADDICT CHARACTERISTICS: IMPLICATIONS FOR TREATMENT

Gender Differences

Differences and similarities between male and female heroin addicts continue to be of interest to investigators, particularly as both the number of female drug users increases and greater awareness of the specific treatment needs of women emerges. Such gender differences exist from the point of initiation into drug use. Examining sex differences on variables related to the onset of drug use in a sample of over 500 Anglo and Chicano heroin addicts admitted to treatment to methadone programs in Southern California, Anglin and his associates (Anglin, Hser, and McGlothlin, 1987; Hser, Anglin, and McGlothlin, 1987) found dissimilar patterns for males and females. Initial use in female addicts was strongly influenced by male sex partners, many of whom were addicts. Initial use in males, however, was strongly influenced by male friends. On the other hand, both males and females reported that both curiosity and peer acceptance were primary reasons for initiating drug use, and that involvement in multiple drug use and dealing preceded initiation into heroin use.

Moise, Reed, and Ryan (1982) investigated similarities and differences between women ($N = 156$) and men ($N = 177$) entering methadone maintenance treatment and therapeutic communities. The factors they assessed included circumstances of initial drug use, patterns of drug use, interpersonal relationships, criminality, and social and economic resources and responsibilities. Results suggested, among other things, that women addicts had more difficulty than men in almost every area of living. Addicted women had fewer economic resources, less job experience, and more family disturbance. They more frequently had substance abusers as partners, had more medical problems, and were more likely to be responsible for children. It would seem, therefore, that any treatment program serving women addicts would need to build in components that addressed the specialized employment, childcare and familial needs of this group.

Kail and Lukoff (1984a, 1984b) assessed gender-based differences within a population of African American heroin addicts who had entered a methadone maintenance program, the majority of whom were retained for one year. The sample included 104 women and 104 men. They investigated retention in treatment, missed medication, heroin use, crime rates and employment rates. Results showed that women in this sample had more difficulty finding employment while on methadone maintenance, with 16% of the women being employed at some time during treatment as opposed to 39% of the men. There were no statistically significant gender-based differences on any of the other variables studied.

In an effort to obtain a more refined picture of this population, Kail and Lukoff (1984a, 1984b) divided the female population into three groups: (a) those women who were heads of households; (b) those living with a stable partner with no children; and (c) those not living with family of procreation. These distinctions were based on the hypothesis that familial configurations might reflect pervasive differences in lifestyle. Results indicated that those women not living with family were more likely to be involved with property crimes and violent crimes, that women living with partners were more likely to miss medications and somewhat more likely to be employed, and that women living with children were more likely to be unemployed and have opiate-positive urines during treatment. In a similar, though not identical, breakdown of the male sample, results were consistent with those found within the female population. Though offering appropriate warnings regarding the retrospective and correlational nature of their study, the authors suggested that the most important aspect of these findings was the relative similarity between males and females in this sample. On this basis, they concluded that single gender treatment programs, at least for this treatment population, were not warranted. As Kail and Lukoff (1984a, 1984b) have noted, however, the greater need for career and employment opportunities for African American women in this sample should not be ignored.

In the course of a retrospective study of the effectiveness of methadone maintenance among 720 white and Latino heroin addicts, Hser, Anglin, and Chou (1988) found numerous pretreatment differences between males and females. For example, women reported significantly fewer criminal justice involvements and significantly greater levels of difficulty with parents. Women also used alcohol and marijuana less, were less involved in drug dealing, and were less likely to have been under legal supervision. Further, women addicts had a greater likelihood than men of being on welfare. After becoming addicted, women entered treatment more quickly than men. Interestingly, however, Hser, Anglin, and

Chou found that the overall effectiveness of methadone maintenance (i.e., in terms of decreasing heroin use and property crime) was consistent across gender. Nevertheless, attempts to address the differing personal, social, and economic needs of male and female addicts might have enhanced the capacity of methadone maintenance to attract patients and to produce positive outcomes.

In a longitudinal study of the impact of stress and social support on the heroin use of 49 methadone maintenance patients, Rhoads (1983) found that men and women differed along three variables. First, she noted that the women in her sample seemed to be more susceptible to stressful events. Second, it appeared that addicted women relied more on social support systems to cope with stress than did male addicts. Third, addicted women also became more depressed in the face of stressful life events, while men appeared to become somewhat more anxious. Rhoads (1983) suggested that these differences might have been due to a perceived lack of control over life events on the part of addicted women. She further suggested that a fruitful avenue of intervention with such patients might be to teach women addicts skills in stress management, to assist them in the development of a positive social support system, and to provide them with training in specific social skills that influence the ability to maintain and utilize social support.

Brunswick and Messeri (1986) used an event-history analysis in studying, among other things, the differential impact of treatment on African American male and female heroin users. This technique permitted an analysis of the probability of an event (here, abstinence from heroin) and its relationship to a number of potentially explanatory factors (such as treatment). From a considerably larger study population, the investigators evaluated the heroin use patterns of 43 male and 26 female subjects who had used heroin on more than an experimental basis. Their analysis revealed that treatment episodes had a significantly greater impact upon the likelihood of abstinence in young African American women than on the likelihood of abstinence in young African American men. That is, African American women in their sample relied more heavily on treatment to become abstinent. The authors argued that men who seek treatment may be those for whom independent achievement of abstinence is more difficult (see, e.g., Graeven and Graeven, 1983), and on this basis, cautioned against concluding that treatment is unnecessary or ineffective for the males in their sample. Brunswick and Messeri (1986) suggested that the more crucial role of treatment for women may have been due to gender differences in psychosocial supports, social expectations, and the nature of interpersonal networks of male versus female heroin users.

Clearly, pregnant addicts have additional needs that could be met by modifying the usual coeducational program. Finnegan, Kaltenbach, Ehrlich, and Regan (1990), as part of a descriptive retrospective study of pregnant addicts, had 178 subjects complete a questionnaire on life-time experiences of violence and sexual abuse. They found that 19% reported being severely beaten as children and 69% had been beaten as adults. Twenty-eight percent reported an experience of childhood molestation. Fifteen percent of this sample also had been childhood victims of rape and 21% had been raped in adulthood. Finnegan et al. (1990) pointed out the importance of investigating the possibility of physical abuse histories in the lives of women addicts, and suggested that such victimization may have been a motivating factor for substance abuse among some of these women. They also noted that this type of history can in turn affect a woman's parenting skills and ability. In the context of drug treatment programs, individual or group therapy oriented specifically toward the experience of physical and sexual victimization might be a useful addition to the usual treatment routine. For pregnant addicts, or addicts with children, parenting skills training might be offered. Empirical evaluations of the efficacy of such program augmentations could be an integral part of their implementation. (See Volume 3, Chapter 2 for a discussion of interventions for pregnant women and mothers.)

Ethnic Differences

Ethnically based distinctions among addicts might shed some light on specific population needs, treatment adequacy and outcome; but, correctly interpreting such distinctions are also fraught with difficulty. In studies where economic factors are not statistically or experimentally controlled, ethnic distinctions carry with them the potential for masking more pervasive socioeconomic disadvantages that differentially affect ethnic groups, possibly resulting in erroneous identification of racial factors as the basis for differential group responses. Even where socioeconomic status is controlled for, assessment instruments that have been normed on a predominantly white middle-class population, finding that some ethnic groups are "lacking" on these measures may be misleading and invalid in that context (Jones, 1988). Despite the increasing sophistication of researchers regarding group norms and racial comparisons, distinctions on the basis of race and ethnic origin must be viewed with caution.

An example of the "masking effects" of ethnicity is well described in a study by Iguchi, Stitzer, Bigelow, and Liebson (1988), which analyzed the demographic and environmental variables related to illicit drug use among 71 addicts during a 90-day outpatient methadone detoxification program. A multiple regression analysis revealed that gender, race, dollar value of opiate use upon intake, and length of opiate use prior to treatment were significant independent predictors of illicit drug use during the program. The lowest levels of illicit drug use were found in white female abusers having initially lower heroin costs and longer opiate abuse histories. However, when Iguchi et al. (1988) eliminated race and gender from the analysis, they found that three additional variables also accounted for a significant amount of variance. Greater numbers of different sources of heroin during the baseline period prior to intake, frequency of weekly opiate-related exposures during treatment, and weekly opiate use during the baseline period were all related to greater frequency in illicit substance abuse during the treatment process. Iguchi et al. (1988) suggested that the effects of racial and gender variables could obscure the impact of environmental factors, and that these external factors may be useful in increasing the ability to focus treatment resources.

Moise, Reed, and Ryan (1982) conducted an investigation wherein economic and cultural differences (rather than racial differences per se) were also identified in the course of examining differences between African American and white male and female addicts. In addition to the gender-based differences mentioned in the previous section, they found that African American women addicts had fewer family problems than white women, were more frequently associated with partners who were not substance abusers, and suffered significantly more economic hardships (including lack of job opportunity), more social isolation, and greater child care responsibilities than did white women. On the basis of these findings, the authors argued that African American women addicts needed a more pragmatic, problem-centered approach than white women addicts, with a focus on career options, housing, and child-care services, among other things. The investigators also noted that the greater childcare responsibilities of African American women addicts may have explained some of this group's reluctance to utilize therapeutic communities; these women may have been reluctant to leave their children to enter treatment. This possibility further argues for the incorporation of childcare into addiction treatment programming, and perhaps modification of traditional restrictions on contact with noncommunity members.

Results from a study by Platt, Steer, Ranieri, and Metzger (1989) also might suggest that treatment outcome research could benefit by shifting focus in accord with differences in addict ethnicity. In this study of 900 methadone maintenance patients, Platt et al. (1989) found that, on the SCL-90, white addicts showed higher levels of obsessive-compulsive and depressive symptomatology than African Americans. Though this finding alone does not rule out the importance, regardless of ethnicity, for the careful assessment of and provision for methadone patients' treatment needs, it does suggest that white patients might have a greater need for psychotherapeutic interventions directed toward depressive and obsessive-compulsive symptoms. A similar finding emerged in an employment skills intervention study, in which African Americans were found to have profited more from the intervention than whites, possibly because of a greater readiness or ability to profit from the intervention than whites due to the presence of less psychopathology (Platt, Husband, Hermalin, Cater, and Metzger, 1993).

In addition to evidence regarding the similarities and differences between African American and white heroin addicts, there is also a growing understanding of the factors related to addiction among Latinos. In a review of such research, Desmond and Maddux (1984) drew a number of conclusions regarding the distinctive features of this population. They suggested that Latino addicts in their study, who were overwhelmingly male, suffered from more severe educational and occupational deficits than did their African American and white counterparts. Further, this group tended to have used fewer types of illicit drugs, to have used opiates at an earlier age, to have delayed entrance into treatment longer, and to have had more frequent unsuccessful terminations from treatment than other ethnic groups. Although Latino heroin addicts are arrested more frequently, spend more years in prison than do other ethnic groups and probably have a higher degree of life-long alcohol dependence, they also spend more time voluntarily abstinent, and tend to have higher employment rates. It is important to note that this group is very unlikely to engage in group psychotherapy or to enter therapeutic communities, but may benefit significantly from affiliation with a religious group. Finally, Desmond and Maddux (1984) emphasized that Latino heroin addicts also differ substantially from other addicts of Hispanic origin.

Hser, Anglin, and Chou (1988) studied the impact of methadone maintenance on 720 white and Latino heroin addicts. Demographically, the Latino addicts in the Hser et al. (1988) sample were older than white addicts at the time of initial addiction, upon entry into treatment, and at the interview point. They were also representative of the larger Latino culture in that their backgrounds evidenced lower socioeconomic status and education than white addicts. Latino addicts in this sample were also incarcerated for longer periods prior to methadone maintenance, were more likely to have had family problems and earlier arrests, and were more involved with property crimes than their white counterparts. When level of treatment was accounted for, Hispanic and white addicts demonstrated substantially similar outcomes, although male Hispanic addicts who obtained moderate levels of treatment (as opposed to considerable levels of treatment) were employed to a lesser extent than white male addicts. This finding, on face value, seems to contradict the above mentioned results summarized by Desmond and Maddux (1984) who appear, for example, to have not distinguished between Latinos and white addicts on the basis of treatment level. Similar outcomes notwithstanding, Hser et al. (1988) noted that Latino patients "overall seem to respond to [methadone maintenance] treatment less well [than whites], for they were more likely to relapse to narcotics use, to deal drugs, and to commit crimes when off treatment" (p. 568). The investigators attributed these differences to initial socioeconomic and educational discrepancies between Latino and white addicts, and suggested that lower levels of occupational skills decrease legal economic opportunities.

Jorquez (1984) also noted differences between Latinos and other addicts. In a descriptive study of 18 Latino ex-addicts, he observed a culturally unique means by which addiction is characterized in that community. In the "tecato," or Latino addict subculture he investigated, the metaphor of an indestructible worm living in one's viscera, that is, a "gusano," is used to explain the recurring need for heroin. When one becomes abstinent, one "puts the tecato gusano to sleep." Jorquez commented that this metaphor aptly described a learning theory model of addiction. Jorquez suggested that the metaphor be used with this population to communicate various means of coping with drug craving and the difficulties encountered in maintaining abstinence. Jorquez (1984) also observed and described a set of processes that appear to be generalizable beyond the Latino culture. He noted that, in the process of becoming abstinent, addicts must extract themselves from the addict subculture (in this case, the tecato subculture), and then find a means of accommodating to the larger, nonaddict society. Though this set of hypotheses was not tested within the context of a controlled experimental design, it provides a potentially helpful model with which to view the tasks of treatment, and emphasizes that the differences between addict subtype and response to treatment may be more a manner of *how* extraction and accommodation take place, rather than of essential differences in the treatment process itself. Put another way, the differences within the heroin addict population suggested important ways in which treatment must be tailored, although the tasks and potential underlying processes of treatment are likely to be the same.

Psychological Characteristics

The debate regarding the importance of personality factors in heroin addiction (see Volume 1, pp. 158–164) has continued. For instance, Sutker and Allain (1988) have argued that the discussion regarding the addictive personality has been clouded by distortions and oversimplifications of the theoretical underpinnings and findings regarding personality factors. They also noted that some personality factors, such as antisocial behavior and depression, have been related to drug and alcohol addiction. They suggested the need for a greater scope of inquiry into multifactorial interactions between person and environment. On the other hand, Nathan (1988) has asserted that personality factors, as traditionally defined, have done little to elucidate the etiology of substance abuse, distinguish substance abusers from nonabusers, and identify those subtypes of abusers who would best benefit from treatment. Nathan (1988) further argued that those factors most often associated with substance abuse (i.e., antisocial behavior and depression), are not descriptive of internal personality characteristics. Rather, he suggested that these are behavioral and social descriptions of persons. He concluded that the role of personality variables in addictive behavior has not been established.

Despite the continuing controversy regarding its value, the psychological aspects of addiction continue to receive empirical scrutiny. While it also continues to be difficult to draw firm conclusions from a fair portion of this research (see, e.g., Craig, 1982; Volume 1, pp. 158–164), some findings still may be useful in aid-ing determinations of treatment focus. For instance, Steer (1982) investigated the differences in psychological symptoms evidenced by heroin addicts attending outpatient detoxification, and addicts involved in a methadone maintenance program. Using the revised Symptom Check List-90 (SCL-90-R), he found that the outpatient detoxification patients complained more of depression than did methadone maintenance patients, and that methadone maintenance patients evidenced more interpersonal sensitivity than detoxification patients. Steer (1982) concluded that different types of patients seek different kinds of treatment. These results also suggested that treatment modalities attracting patients with different psychological characteristics might attempt to focus on the more salient psychological symptoms presented by their patient populations. Hence, methadone maintenance programs might increase treatment efficacy by offering social skills training, whereas an emphasis on the treatment of depression might be more relevant for outpatient detoxification programs.

The possibility of an abstinence phobia also may influence the entrance into and efficacy of treatment. Hall (1984a) has argued that investigations into anxiety and drug abuse have been plagued by problems in measurement and definition, and more important, have not considered that anxiety might be a result, rather than a cause, of drug abuse. Drawing upon the literature on opiate abuse, smoking, alcohol abuse, and eating disturbances, Hall (1984a) proposed that abusers may develop a range of anxieties and phobias related to the elimination of their dependency. She posited a minimum of two avenues through which early withdrawal symptoms induce fears: first, via a classical conditioning model, early withdrawal symptoms evoke fears associated with the aversive experience of full blown withdrawal; and second, via instrumental conditioning these symptoms elicit anticipatory anxiety related to the need to use skills and behaviors that the abuser perceives he or she is lacking, such as employment skills, interpersonal skills, or childrearing skills. Hall (1984a) noted that there are a number of aspects of this hypothesis that call for empirical investigation. She suggested an assessment of the frequency of abstinence phobias, studies of whether phobias interfere with detoxification and recovery, and investigations into psychosocial characteristics of those substance abusers who exhibit these phobias. Assuming that abstinence phobias are a factor for some specified group or groups of substance abusers, Hall (1984a) suggested that this model had implications for treatment. These implications included a need to provide accurate information regarding the process of withdrawal, the use of anxiety reduction techniques, and training in interpersonal coping skills.

Social problem solving is another psychological dimension that appears to be related to treatment, abstinence, and relapse. Platt and Labate (1977) reported a prospective study of the relationship of interpersonal cognitive problem-solving (ICPS) skills, a social problem-solving construct, to the behavior of heroin addicts on parole. In a group of 191 addicts who completed a treatment program in a New Jersey reformatory, detailed parole reports on all subjects were examined every six months for two years. Results showed that narcotics use on parole was inversely associated with higher scores on the ICPS instruments, and that subjects with the ability to produce more relevant means to solve problems were less likely to be arrested on parole, as were those who had higher alternative thinking scores. No significant relationships were found between number of arrests on parole or the use of force in an offense and means-ends or alternative thinking scores. Intelligence test scores were also unrelated to parole outcome measures. Platt and Labate (1977) concluded that social problem-solving skills played an important role in mediating the ability of an addict to remain abstinent. It is interesting to note that social skill constructs have been identified as relevant to the rehabilitation process in a number of the recent studies mentioned above (e.g., Hall, 1984b; Kosten, Rounsaville, and Kleber, 1983; Rhoades, 1983; Steer, 1982). Reviews of social skills interventions for substance abusers may be found in Platt and Hermalin (1989) and Platt and Husband (1993).

Other Nontreatment Characteristics

Noting that many pretreatment demographic characteristics often predict treatment outcome better than do treatment modalities, Westermeyer (1989) reviewed nontreatment factors that affected outcome in substance abuse. Although Westermeyer (1989) was more concerned with alcoholism treatment, his classification is useful in understanding the relationship of such variables to treatment outcome. Employing the following categorization of variables: (a) self-help and social affiliations (e.g., attendance at Alcoholics Anonymous for alcoholics); (b) community reinforcements (e.g., social competency training, joining nondrinking clubs, etc.); (c) life events and residence changes; (d) demographic variables (e.g., employment, marital status, living with others, socioeconomic status; (e) coercion, both legal and nonlegal; (f) compliance; and (g) monitoring of recovery, Westermeyer (1989) concluded that researchers should view nontreatment "treatment predictors" as therapeutic opportunities within a process-oriented, change-oriented dynamic approach.

Ball and Ross (1991) found patient characteristics at baseline (as measured by such variables as race, age of onset of heroin use, history of cocaine use, and criminal behavior) to be related to successful outcome in methadone maintenance treatment; they had, however, less impact on outcome than did characteristics of the treatment programs (e.g., rehabilitation and long-term maintenance orientation, delivery of more counseling services, more effective directors) and what was experienced by the patient after admission. Those programs delivering more services were more effective than those with better staffing, facilities, and management, but which delivered fewer services.

DRUG USE PATTERNS: IMPLICATIONS FOR TREATMENT

Heroin Use Patterns

Crawford, Washington, and Senay (1983) compared the characteristics of heroin addicts and light, moderate, and heavy heroin experimenters. The results of personal history-taking interviews with a sample of 147 African American male heroin users showed that heavy experimenters and addicts were more likely to be involved in illegal activities, both during and after high school, than were light and moderate experimenters. Heavy experimenters and addicts were also more likely to have tried a host of other substances, including barbiturates, amphetamines, and codeine. Crawford et al. (1983) also found differences between the user groups studied in terms of their subjective reports of the effects of heroin. Heavy experimenters and addicts were more likely to "get high" during first heroin use than were moderate and light experimenters, and the latter group was also more likely to experience negative side effects than were the heavy experimenters and addict groups. Interestingly, the features of the heroin "high" that these groups reported as pleasurable were also different. Addicts and heavy experimenters more frequently reported that they enjoyed the "nod," freedom from worry, and relaxation, while moderate and light experimenters reported that increased relaxation and sociability were the most enjoyable aspects of the drug experience. Light experimenters reported that they discontinued heroin use primarily because they did not like the high, or preferred a different drug. Of those who continued on to heavy heroin use or addiction, a large majority (75% and 84%, respectively) began "chipping" (i.e., occasional use) within one month of their first heroin experience. Though use continued over a number of years, there were frequent voluntary and involuntary heroin abstinences for those with heavier use patterns. On the basis of these findings, the authors concluded that there were a variety of ways in which heroin was used. They argued that intervention into initial use patterns of those most at risk, that is, heavy experimenters and addicts, would be problematic given the relatively short time between introduction to heroin and the beginning of habitual use. These findings might also provide a basis for distinguishing those heroin users who require more intensive treatment efforts once they do seek intervention, as well as arguing for accurately assessing the level of heroin use in those users who seek treatment. Successful treatment for heroin users who have a stable pattern of thrice weekly use is likely to have different requirements than for those users who use heroin thrice daily.

Newman (1983) has argued that reports of a variety of heroin use patterns, such as those described above, call into question the usual notions that addiction is an inevitable and irreversible result of heroin use. Suggesting that the existence of various levels and types of heroin users requires that present concepts of addiction be redefined, Newman (1983) proposed that

... narcotic addiction be viewed as an atypical response to exposure to opiates, characterized by a tendency toward progressively greater consumption of the drug and a persistent disposition to relapse to drug use when abstinence has been achieved and physical dependence reversed (p. 1098).

This definition is broad enough to include those addicts who are currently in remission, and to exclude those narcotics users who, as described in the research above, have maintained long periods of occasional heroin use without becoming addicted.

In addition to assessing a number of social and personal characteristics of addicts as compared to nonphysically dependent heroin users, Flaherty, Kotranski, and Fox (1984) also investigated the degree to which heroin addicts engaged in the use of other substances. They trained nine staff members to conduct "street" interviews (i.e., interviews in bars, in subjects' homes, cars, and so on) with 300 subjects, and had treatment interviewers conduct the remaining 93 evaluations. There were 316 male and 77 female subjects in the study, all from the city of Philadelphia. Results showed that roughly two-thirds of the subjects used heroin once a day or more, and approximately one-third used heroin less frequently (ranging from more often than once a week to no heroin use within the prior month). Regardless of frequency of heroin use, all subjects frequently used drugs other than heroin, but those who used heroin daily did so more often than the nonaddict heroin users. Tranquilizers, stimulants, sedatives, and opiates other than heroin were used by 75% of each group within a month before the interview. Roughly a quarter of addicts, as well as nonaddicted heroin users, used opiates other than heroin, tranquilizers, or stimulants on a daily basis. Flaherty et al. (1984) concluded that "there is no longer a 'pure' heroin user" (p. 313). Rather, the findings seemed to imply that in addition to differences in the amount of heroin use, there were numerous other drugs that were abused on a daily basis, particularly among those who were addicted to heroin. Most important, the authors suggested that treatments focusing only upon heroin use or those that only supplied methadone would not be able to decrease participants' drug use because of the pervasive nature of substance abuse and the drug-oriented lifestyle of many of their subjects. They proposed that effective treatment would have to change patient lifestyles as well as drug use patterns. In a related study, Wille (1983) evaluated drug use patterns during the period following detoxification in 40 abstinent heroin users in London. Using a retrospective interview technique, he found increases in nonopiate drug use immediately following withdrawal from heroin, with some 90% of the subjects in his sample reporting increases in the use of alcohol, marijuana, amphetamines, and tranquilizers. For all subjects, polydrug use was eliminated by the time the interviews were conducted eight years after detoxification. Wille (1983) concluded that multiple drug use in this group of drug-free addicts was part of the process of becoming abstinent. His findings also confirmed the existence of polydrug use at some point in the careers of most heroin addicts, and emphasized the need for treatment programs to address broad-based substance abuse rather than focusing solely on heroin. Recent findings from the DATOS study (Hubbard, personal communication) confirm the increasing presence of this pattern of multiple drug abuse among opiate users in methadone maintenance treatment. While 49% of patients in methadone maintenance treatment in the DARP study (1969–73) had used nonopioids in combination with daily opioid use, this figure rose to 74% in the DATOS (1991–93) study.

Use of Alcohol and Other Drugs

Alcohol abuse frequently accompanies active opiate use and is a frequent occurrence among treated heroin addicts (see Volume 1, pp. 196–198). In the DARP 12-year follow-up, up to half of the sample drank heavily at some point during their addiction careers, and 11% were found to have had a chronic alcohol problem (Lehman, Barrett, and Simpson, 1990; Lehman and Simpson, 1990b). Alcohol use at treatment entry and throughout the study was related to more frequent use of marijuana and nonopioids, but not necessarily to opioid use. Heavier drinking at Year 12, however, was closely associated with indicators of low social stability (including not being married, high levels of psychological dysfunction, and having unfavorable social comparisons), as well as a past history of alcohol abuse, a finding consistent with that of other investigators (e.g., Bihari, 1974; Green, Jaffe, Carlisi, and Zaks, 1978).

Data reported from the TOPS and DATOS projects have suggested a decline in rates of alcohol use among entrants into treatment at the two points in time, approximately 10 years apart, when the data were collected. Among entrants into treatment in the TOPS (conducted in 1979–1981; N = 4,184) and initial entrants in the DATOS (1991–1993; N = 986) studies, the following rates of weekly or daily alcohol use were present in each treatment modality studied: methadone: TOPS, 47.4%, DATOS: 29.8%; Long-term residential: TOPS: 65%, DATOS: 56.7%; and outpatient methadone: TOPS: 61.7%, DATOS; 47.0%. Thus, in all categories, there was a decline in alcohol use among treatment entrants between 1979–1981 and 1991–1993.

Where, according to Lehman and Simpson (1990b), alcohol had become a substitute for opiates, there was evidence of a history of abusive drinking as well as a history of familial alcoholism and greater vulnerability to peer pressure. Alcohol substitution was also found to be related to continued abusive drinking, elevated levels of use of marijuana and nonopioids, and to be more likely to occur in individuals with higher levels of psychological dysfunction (Lehman and

Simpson, 1990b). The finding of an inverse association between addicts' lifetime use of heroin and alcohol despite their distinct psychopharmacological properties has also been interpreted as a compensation for reduction in one psychoactive substance by increasing consumption of another (Almog, Anglin, and Fisher, 1993).

The "alcohol substitution" interpretation given these findings is not a new one (e.g., Waldorf, 1973; McGlothlin, Anglin, and Wilson, 1977a,b), nor one that has been universally accepted (e.g., Green, Jaffe, Carlisi, and Zaks, 1978; Marcovici, McLellan, O'Brien, and Rosenzweig, 1980). Thus, it is not entirely clear if this finding of a pattern of heavy drinking should be interpreted as reflecting a consequence arising from and substituting for cessation of opiate use or possibly as a return to a problem that may have both preceded and existed concurrently with opiate addiction. This latter interpretation would also seem to be the one suggested by the findings of the Hser, Anglin, and Hsieh (1993) study, in which continued drug use was found to be very common among addicts in their 24-year follow-up study of CAP participants (see Chapter 2). These findings lead to the conclusion that continued drug use involving multiple substances, especially alcohol, was a common pattern among both recovering and continuing addicts.

When use of drugs other than alcohol is examined, major changes are seen to have occurred in the time period between the TOPS (1979-81) and DATOS (1991-93) surveys. These changes are represented in Table 1.4. In general, entrants into treatment showed a decline in heroin use. Entrants into long-term residential and outpatient nonmethadone treatment modalities showed a decline in weekly or daily heroin use, while such use among entrants into methadone maintenance treatment increased. Cocaine was the most frequently abused drug for entrants into the long-term residential and outpatient nonmethadone modalities, and second only in abuse level to heroin for entrants into the methadone maintenance treatment modality. For the 12 months preceding entry into treatment, cocaine was the primary drug of abuse for 67% of those entering the long-term residential and outpatient nonmethadone modalities, and the primary drug of abuse for 10% of those entering methadone maintenance treatment (Robert L. Hubbard, personal communication).

Benzodiazepine abuse is also common among opiate dependent individuals, both in and out of treatment (Kleber and Gold, 1978; Stitzer, Griffiths, McLellan, Grabowski, and Hawthorne, 1981; Woody, O'Brien, and Greenstein, 1975; see also Volume 1, pp. 321-322; and Volume 3, Chapter 3), as is barbiturate use (see Volume 1, pp. 198-200). Stitzer et al. (1981) found that approximately 65-70% of male patients attending two methadone maintenance clinics were found to have abused diazepam during a period of a month. Kleber and Gold (1978) found that many patients used diazepam to "boost" or increase the effects of their methadone dose. Alprazolam has been shown to be a preferred drug of abuse among methadone maintenance patients in Baltimore (Weddington and Carney, 1987). Iguchi, Handelsman, Bickel, and Griffiths (1993), in a study of methadone maintenance patients in the Bronx, Philadelphia, and Baltimore, found lifetime usage of sedative drugs (benzodiazepines and barbiturates) to be 86%, 78%, and 94%, respectively. Past six-month use was 44%, 53%, and 66%, respectively. Among the benzodiazepines; diazepam, lorazepam, and alprazolam were found to be most frequently used for their high-producing effects, as well as for selling to produce income (Iguchi, Handelsman, Bickel, and Griffiths, 1993).

CRIMINAL INVOLVEMENT OF ADDICTS

Criminal involvement is a common characteristic of heroin addicts, and reflects both a means of obtaining funds for purchase of drugs as well as a characteristic of the addict subculture (see Volume 1, pp. 184–185, 202–205). In addition, in a recent survey, large numbers of arrestees, some 60%, according to the Drug Use Forecasting System (DUF), were found to have been using drugs and alcohol at the time of their arrests[1] (Wish and O'Neil, 1991), a figure similar to that for juvenile offenders (Bureau of Justice Statistics, 1988). Criminal involvement is typically used, along with retention in treatment, abstinence from drug use, and employment as a primary indicator of outcome (Institute of Medicine [Gerstein and Harwood], 1990).

Addicts have generally had substantial involvement in criminal activity before becoming addicted (e.g., Anglin and Speckart, 1986; Inciardi, 1987; Johnson, Goldstein, Preble, Schmeidler, Lipton, and Miller, 1985; McGlothlin, Anglin, and Wilson, 1977a). Additionally, evidence exists to the effect that " . . . an increase in criminality commonly occurs in conjunction with increased heroin use in the United States" (Faupel and Klockars, 1987, p. 54). This latter conclusion is further supported by the most recent findings from Simpson and Sells's 12-year follow-up study of DARP patients. In a detailed analysis of these data, Lehman and Simpson (1990a) reported that (a) over half of their subjects had spent a year or longer in jail or prison; (b) a majority admitted to involvement in major crime categories, including crimes against property (73%), crimes of acquisition (72%), and violent crimes (49%); and (c) more than half of males in the study had been involved in criminal acts both before and after active addiction.

Studies conducted in other countries have also found evidence for a drugs-crime relationship. For example, Dobson and Ward (1984) found that nearly 90% of imprisoned drug users in Australia viewed crime as their main source of income, while Parker and Newcombe (1987) found a relationship between a heroin

---

[1]The actual figures in 1990 were that between 1.6 and 26% of arrestees had been using opiates at the time of arrest. Cocaine use ranged from 10.2 to 64.8%, and marijuana use, from 6.7 to 37.9%. Alcohol use was not reported. However, these figures do require some caution in interpretation. A GAO report (1993) noted that these data were not consistently gathered with respect to type of arrest and gender; that some data collection sites included convicted participants; that a lack of privacy at some sites may have resulted in underreporting; and that the figures do not distinguish between prescribed and illicit drugs.

epidemic and a large, and unprecedented, increase in property crimes in Wirral, Merseyside, England. Further analyses in this study indicated that some 50% of burglars were known to be "problem" heroin users; that a relationship existed between heroin use and a history of convictions; and a subgroup of young adults had accelerated their criminal activities since using drugs. Similarly Jarvis and Parker (1989) found, in a study of heroin users in London, that annual rates of convictions for "acquisitive" crime more than doubled following the onset of regular heroin use.

Wish (1988) marshalled several lines of evidence which strongly suggested that addicted offenders are particularly likely to commit both drug- and non-drug-related crimes at high rates: (a) greater crime rates during periods of narcotics use (e.g., Wish and Johnson, 1986); (b) criminals identified as "violent predators" were distinguishable by histories of juvenile drug abuse and adult high-cost heroin habits (e.g., Chaiken and Chaiken, 1982); (c) arrestees in Washington, DC and New York City who, upon arrest, tested positive for drugs had more rearrests than arrestees with negative test results (e.g., Torborg, Bellassai, and Yezer, 1986); (d) treatment-related reductions in the use of narcotics are associated with individual reductions in criminal activity (e.g., McGlothlin, Anglin, and Wilson, 1977b); and (e) a relationship existed between cocaine and street crime (e.g., Collins, Hubbard, and Allison, 1985).

Additionally, Wish (1988) observed that referral to drug abuse treatment while in the criminal justice system, together with urine monitoring, could result in longer tenure in treatment and a reduction in both drug use and crime (e.g., Anglin and McGlothlin, 1984; Collins and Allison, 1983; Stitzer and McCaul, 1987), and that younger offenders presented a promising group for intervention to prevent progression to more extensive drug use (e.g., Dembo, Washburn, Wish, Yeung, Getreu, et al., 1987).

Lehman and Simpson (1990a) also reported that while higher criminality before addiction was associated with deviant friends, alcohol problems, and non-opioid use, postaddiction crime was associated with level of drug and alcohol use as well as preaddiction criminality. While Lehman and Simpson (1990a) found that crime was closely associated with the need to financially support opioid use, much of it also was present outside of the immediate pressure to obtain funds to purchase drugs. On the other hand, Clayton and Tuchfield (1982) have raised questions about the direction of causal relationships between opioid use and criminal behavior. They suggested, for instance, that many addicts do not become involved in criminal behavior until after having established habitual drug use, and then primarily to the extent that they require funds to support their drug habit.

Thus, the studies by Lehman and Simpson (1990a) and Clayton and Tuchfield (1982) represent two differing hypotheses concerning the drugs-crime relationship, each with different policy implications (Faupel, 1987a). The first hypothesis states that heroin addict criminality is a consequence, however indirect, of addiction, and that the addict is increasingly driven into more criminal activity as the need for drugs increases; the other states that it is involvement in, and association with, the criminal subculture by persons who eventually become addicted that accounts for this criminal activity. In the latter case, increases in heroin use are predicted to follow or coincide with periods of criminal involvement.

Utilizing life-history interviews, Faupel (1987a) examined the validity of these two theoretical positions. His findings regarding the drugs-crime relationship were that (a) criminality generally preceded first use of heroin and subsequent addiction; (b) both criminal careers and addiction to heroin proceeded slowly, with a median of 3.5 years intervening between first criminal offense and subsequent criminal activity, and occasional use of heroin and other drugs occurred before moving on to regular use of heroin; and (c) almost all respondents believed that their criminal and addiction careers began separately. Two general factors were found to shape and influence addict careers: (a) *availability* of drugs (rather than tolerance levels) as reflected in quantity available, low cost, resources and opportunities to purchase, as well as the skills necessary to use it (evidenced by the statement "The more you had, the more you did") (p. 57); and (b) *life structure*, or " . . . regularly occurring patterns of daily domestic, occupational, recreational, or criminal activity" (p. 57), whether it be conventional (e.g., work, housekeeping, child-rearing, watching television, etc.), or nonconventional activities (e.g., burglary, prostitution, etc.). A related question addressed by Faupel (1987a,b) was whether heroin addicts were "impulsive and opportunistic criminals" or "sophisticated criminal entrepreneurs." This question was also addressed through career history interviews with a group of "hard core" addicts and it was concluded that both perceptions may be accurate at different points in the addict's career. Four addict roles were identified by Faupel (1987a,b): (a) the *occasional user* role occupied by initiates into heroin use, and characterized by high life structure, low drug availability, and socialization into the drug subculture, with engagement in little or no criminal behavior; (b) the *stabilized addict* role, characterized by a high level of drug availability and high, although modified, life structure, during which there is greater integration into the addict subculture, the acquisition of specialized "hustling" skills, and experimentation with criminal roles, a stage perceived by ethnographic accounts as that of a sophisticated criminal entrepreneur; (c) the *freewheeling addict* role, in which there is a lack of daily structure guiding consumption, sharply escalated drug use, erratic, often out of control behavior; and (d) the *street junkie* role, in which there is low drug availability and minimal life structure, a habit often beyond control with living from fix to fix, perhaps precipitated by personal loss, such as the loss of a loved one or loss of employment. Faupel (1987b) observed that the addict in the street junkie role, often perceived as the "impulsive and opportunistic criminal," was not necessarily an inevitable result of the use of heroin, but emerged in response to external conditions limiting drug availability and disrupting established behavioral patterns. Furthermore, addicts, both male and female, tended to be "specialists" with respect to criminal activities, having a predominant involvement in one type of crime over others (Faupel, 1986), although the area of specialization may change over time, and degree of specialization may vary as a function of intensity of drug use, with daily users more diverse in their criminal activities (Kowalski and Faupel, 1990).

Faupel (1987a) suggested the following research and policy implications of his findings: (a) the drugs-crime connection must be viewed as a complex and dynamic one, with periods during which drug use causes crime, and other periods during which crime facilitates drug use; (b) drug law enforcement may not have as profound an effect upon drug use as previously thought, in that addicts can easily adjust to differing levels of availability during their early phases of use, and even adjust during periods of heavier use, although greater vulnerability to law enforcement activity exists when the addict is in the "street junkie" phase, where removal from the drug subculture can have the effect of disengaging the addict from his or her subculture; (c) to the extent that a long-term reduction in criminality is a central goal of drug treatment, such treatment must address the need for an alternative life structure which contains rewards for conventional behavior, thus reducing demand and fostering re-integration into the community.

Employment and Criminal Activity

A direct relationship between unemployment and criminal activity among addicts is well accepted (e.g., Faupel, 1988; see Volume 1, pp. 184–185). Not surprisingly, addicts appear to rely less on legitimate work as a source of income than on criminal or quasi-criminal activity to maintain their habits (Flaherty, Kotranski, and Fox, 1984; Kozel, DuPont, and Brown, 1972; Nurco, Cisin, and Balter, 1981b). This relationship has also been found among those involved in vocational rehabilitation programs (Brewington, Deren, Arella, and Randell, 1990). Faupel (1988) hypothesized that when a person is employed there is neither the time nor the need to obtain money through illicit sources, and that employment represents the shift of the addict from the drug subculture to mainstream culture.

The complexity of the relationship between crime, employment, and addiction was further explicated in an analysis of the employment-criminality relationship in addicts by Faupel (1988). This author examined addict criminality across employment levels (full-time, part-time, unemployed, or not in labor force), occupational categories (white collar, skilled/semiskilled, or unskilled), and crime types (personal, property, drug sale, or public order offenses) in order to test the hypothesis that occupational status and increased employment levels inhibited criminal involvement. Using data from interviews with 544 daily heroin users in five cities, Faupel (1988) found only partial support for his hypothesis in that the average number of crimes his respondents were involved in was greatest at the two extreme ends of his level of employment scale. Unemployed respondents had the highest levels of criminal activity, followed, in descending order, by full-time workers, part-time workers, and those not in the labor force (i.e., students, home-makers, etc.). When occupational status was examined, however, Faupel (1988) found skilled and semiskilled male workers to have reported the highest levels of criminal involvement among employed respondents, followed by white-collar employees and unskilled workers. Among women, the pattern was different, with the highest level of criminal involvement among unskilled workers followed by white-collar, skilled, and semiskilled workers.

When the type of criminal activity was examined by Faupel (1988), different patterns emerged. Women not in the labor force tended to have committed the most property crimes, and both men and women who were employed full-time tended to have committed the most drug sales offenses (Faupel, 1988). For all crimes except public order offenses (i.e., prostitution, procuring, gambling, and alcohol offenses), full-time workers reported higher averages than part-time workers. Furthermore, with the exception of property crimes committed by women, full-time employees reported more criminal activities than did those not in the labor force.

In a study by Metzger (1987) criminal involvement was found to play only a minor role in explaining the current employment status of methadone patients. Criminal involvement (measured by number of months in jail) was found to be inversely related to the acquisition of employment for African Americans but not to be related to acquisition of employment for whites. Criminality was found to not be related to pattern of employment (i.e., mostly employed, mostly em-ployed, or stably employed) for either African Americans or whites.

ADDICT TYPOLOGIES

Over the past decade, Nurco and his associates[1] have provided an understanding of the heterogeneity to be found among opiate addicts. Among the dimensions on which Nurco and colleagues have found differences are (a) criminality; (b) lifestyle; (c) psychopathology; and (d) attitudes towards narcotic addiction. One important result of this research has been the accumulation of evidence present-ing a view of heroin addicts as being as diverse as any other diagnostic group of medical patients and thus requiring individualized treatment planning. Focusing

---

[1]Nurco, Hanlon, Balter, Kinlock, and Slaught, 1991; Nurco and Shaffer, 1982; Nurco, Shaffer, Hanlon, Kinlock, Duszynski, and Stephenson, 1987; Shaffer, Kinlock, and Nurco, 1982; Shaffer, Nurco, Hanlon, Kinlock, Duszynski, and Stephenson, 1988; Shaffer, Nurco, and Kinlock, 1984; Shaffer, Wegner, Kin-lock, and Nurco, 1983.

on his typologies of addict careers, Nurco (1992) summarized a number of studies which have contributed to the knowledge of the natural history of addiction careers. Avoiding sampling problems inherent in other studies employing "captive" populations, Nurco, Cisin, and Balter (1981a, 1981b, 1981c) utilized police records in Baltimore, Maryland in order to initially obtain and then periodically update information on the active addict population in that city. With this methodology, it was likely that some 90% of narcotic users in Baltimore between 1952 and 1976 were identified. Nurco et al. (1981a, 1981b, 1981c), using the first 10 years of addiction as the period within which to identify typologies, identified five types of addicts, based upon the amounts of time spent in the following status: (a) addicted; (b) in the community and not addicted; or (c) in jail or prison and not addicted. Type I addicts had spent little time either addicted or in jail, with only some 7 1/2 years of the 10 years in the community studied in addiction; Type II addicts spent more time in jail than Type I addicts, with resultant low opportunity for, and low voluntary abstinence from, narcotic drug use; Type III were similar to Type I addicts in having high opportunity to use drugs (relatively low jail time), but they also had more addicted time overall, and less nonaddicted time in the community; Type IV addicts, like Type II addicts, spent over a quarter of their careers in jail, but they had also spent a high proportion of their time in the community nonaddicted; Type V differed from other types in spending more than 75% of their careers addicted, with many being addicted for the entire ten years of the study. With respect to race, African American addicts were found to have spent more of their time addicted as well as having spent more time in jail than whites.

Using the typology they developed to explain antecedent behaviors, Nurco et al. (1981a, 1981b, 1981c) found that (a) early onset of addiction was associated with a high percentage of time spent addicted, particularly for African Americans; (b) Types II and IV addicts (both African American and white), who exhibited more criminality, came from the lowest socioeconomic status backgrounds; (c) Types I and V addicts displayed more job stability, in line with higher levels of generalized social competence; (d) African American addicts overall spent more of their time addicted, as well as having spent more time in jail; (e) Type I addicts, particularly whites, had delinquent and criminal preaddiction careers, yet had been successful in terminating their addiction careers during the study period; and (f) Type V addicts, who appeared to have begun their deviant careers with addiction and greater personal adequacy, had apparent success in avoiding incarceration during their drug using careers.

Interpreting the findings of the Nurco et al. (1981a, 1981b, 1981c) studies within the context of theoretical issues, such as the long-standing debate as to whether addiction or criminality occurs first (Nurco concluded that both views were correct since each was found in an addict type), Nurco (1992) drew the following implications for public policy and treatment programs: (a) treatment strategies should be tailored to the individual case; (b) intervention strategies require an awareness of the patient's background demography; and (c) continued investigation is needed with respect to recruitment into addiction and addiction careers.

In another study of addict typologies, Steer, Platt, Ranieri, and Metzger (1989) identified four types of addicts in a group of 458 methadone maintenance patients: (a) somatic; (b) paranoid; (c) hostile; and (d) anxious-depressed syndrome profiles, as determined by SCL-90 profiles. In an assessment of the relationship of these profiles to psychosocial characteristics, a number of modest relationships were found. For instance, methadone patients with a somatic profile tended to have used marijuana at a younger age, to have sought treatment voluntarily, and to have current medical problems. Patients with paranoid profiles were somewhat more likely to have started marijuana use at an earlier age, and were more likely to be using heroin and marijuana at the time of evaluation. Anxious-depressed patients tended to have used marijuana, recognized the existence of a drug problem, and sought treatment at an earlier age, in addition to being less likely to have physical problems. Hostile addicts were somewhat more likely to have started marijuana use at an earlier age, and to be African American, single, and using amphetamines at the time of evaluation. As Steer, Platt, Ranieri, and Metzger (1989) suggested, these profiles and their associated psychosocial characteristics have implications for treatment. For instance, patients with hostile profiles might be more difficult to engage and assist in a methadone maintenance program, and may benefit from structured skills training on how to deal with authority while the presence of a paranoid profile in an addict recently admitted to treatment should alert staff to the need to work hard to instill trust.

Approaching the development of a typology of addicts from the perspective of patterns of social problem-solving skills, Platt, Husband, Steer, and Iguchi (1994) examined profile patterns of such skills among injecting drug users not in treatment. Five problem-solver types were identified: (a) the *below-average* problem solver; (b) the *causal* problem solver; (c) the *generational* problem solver; (d) the *consequential* problem solver; and (e) the *above average* problem solver. Platt et al. (1994) concluded that the existence of these five types not only suggested the need for prescriptive and somewhat different interventions for each, but also the need for assessment of social problem-solving skills before providing the intervention.

Studies such as those reviewed in this section strongly confirm the view that heroin addicts represent a heterogeneous group with respect to patterns of behavior and skill levels. The implication is that programming for such addicts requires taking into account individual characteristics when planning treatment interventions.

PREDISPOSING VARIABLES FOR DRUG ABUSE

Genetic Predisposition for Drug Abuse

A growing body of evidence exists, primarily based on twin and adoption studies, suggesting the existence of a genetic basis for vulnerability to one form of substance abuse, alcoholism. Schuckit (1992), in a recent review of the clinical literature on this issue, has noted that there is evidence that alcoholism is present intergenerationally in families, and that there is research support for a genetic contribution to this familial pattern of alcoholism (e.g., Cadoret, Cain, and Grove, 1980; Gurling, Oppenheimer, and Murray, 1984; Goodwin, 1985). As a group, children of alcoholic parents tend to show signs associated with alcoholic dependence at an earlier age, to escalate use of alcohol more rapidly, and to experience more severe dependencies than their peers (Goodwin, 1985). Studies of twins and adopted children of alcoholic parents lend support to the inheritability of a predisposition to alcohol abuse (Schuckit, 1985). More recently, findings by Emshoff (in press) have suggested that children of alcoholics may also be at risk for other kinds of drug abuse.

With respect to the influence of familial and/or genetic factors in the development of drug abuse, Maddux and Desmond (1989) provided a review of the literature regarding the family heritability of opioid dependence and alcoholism and presented their own data regarding the family prevalence of the two disorders in opioid users. They noted, for example, that while a genetic vulnerability for opioid dependence had not been directly demonstrated in humans, indirect evidence for a common genetic predisposition for morphine and alcohol was available in both animals (e.g., rats bred for high voluntary morphine consumption after withdrawal from chronic morphine administration also show high voluntary alcohol consumptions [Nichols and Hsiao, 1967]) and humans (e.g., both fathers and mothers of opioid-dependent probands had higher rates of alcoholism than of opioid dependence, while brothers had higher rates of opioid dependence than of alcoholism [Ellinwood, Smith, and Vaillant, 1966; Hill, Cloninger, and Ayre, 1977]). Following the careers of 235 male chronic opioid users (87% of whom had a Latino background) who had been treated at the Public Health Service Hospital in Fort Worth, the results of their study suggested that opioid dependence tended to cluster in the families of opioid-dependent probands, with the lowest rates in mothers, and progressively increasing rates in fathers, sisters and brothers; and that alcoholism did not cluster in the families of opioid-dependent probands. However, an intergenerational reversal in the prevalence of alcoholism and opioid dependence in families of opioid-dependent probands may have been affected by both the availability of opiates and the presence of heroin-using peers. Maddux and Desmond (1989) noted the limitations of their study, including the possibility that such factors as common exposure to a pathogenic environment could have accounted for clustering, and concluded that

[t]he current meager evidence points ambiguously to familial transmission both of a common vulnerability to alcoholism and opioid dependence and of specific vulnerabilities to each (p. 131).

In critiquing the Maddux and Desmond (1989) study, Bucholz and Robins (1991) noted that unlike the Drake and Vaillant study (1988), it did not produce strong evidence for the familial transmission of alcoholism. Bucholz and Robins (1991) suggested some reasons for this discrepancy were that (a) Maddux and Desmond's (1989) definition of alcoholism had included heavy or excessive drinking, which is perhaps less transmissible than alcohol dependence; (b) the use of the family history method, which had perhaps underestimated prevalence of disorders; and (c) the use of an inappropriately matched comparison group for determining lifetime prevalence of opiate dependence. Nonetheless, the Maddux and Desmond (1989) study represented an attempt to explore an area, which while intensively studied in the case of alcoholism, has not yet been adequately investigated with respect to opiate abuse. Croughan (1985), reviewing the results of nine studies on the genetics of alcoholism, found rates of both alcoholism and drug abuse to be somewhat higher among the parents and siblings of addicts than expected rates in the general population, although there were methodological weaknesses present in a number of the studies which were reviewed. Mirin, Weiss, Griffin, and Michael (1991) found higher rates of alcohol use and dependence and drug abuse disorders among male relatives, in contrast to higher rates of affective disorders and anxiety/panic disorders among female relatives of drug users.

In an investigation of the common environmental and genetic factors among those with antisocial personality disorder, alcoholism, and drug abuse, Cadoret, Troughton, O'Gorman, and Heywood (1986) studied 242 male and 201 female adoptees who had been separated from biological parents from birth. They found that (a) drug abuse was highly related to antisocial personality disorder, which in turn was predictable from an antisocial personality biological background; (b) a biological history of alcohol problems was related to increased drug abuse in adoptees who did not have antisocial personalities; and (c) the presence of divorce and psychiatric disturbance in the adoptive family were associated with increased drug abuse. Cadoret et al. (1986) concluded that

(1) antisocial behavior in biologic relatives results in antisocial personality, which in turn is associated with drug abuse, and (2) alcohol problems in biologic relatives appear to be associated with drug abuse (p. 1135),

thus suggesting two genetic pathways to drug abuse—one through antisocial personality, and the second from biologic parents with alcohol problems to offspring who are not antisocial.

Examining psychiatric disorders among 877 first-degree relatives of 201 opiate addicts and a control group of 360 relatives of 82 normal controls, Rounsaville, Kosten, Weissman, Prusoff, Pauls, et al. (1991) found that (a) the relatives of opioid addicts had significantly higher rates of alcoholism and drug abuse, depression, and antisocial disorders than did relatives of the controls; (b) relatives of depressed opiate addict probands had higher rates of major depression and anxiety, but not of other disorders, suggesting that the presence or absence of major depression was a valid variable for subtyping opiate addicts; and (c) relatives of opiate addicts with antisocial personality disorder did not differ from those without antisocial personality disorder with respect to rates of presence for other disorders. Merikangas, Rounsaville, and Prusoff (1992) found a much higher rate of drug use among siblings. Of 477 siblings, 78 (16%) used opioids, 21 (4%) used marijuana only, and 76 (16%) used illicit drugs other than marijuana. Luthar, Anton, Merikangas, and Rounsaville (1992), in a further study of the relationship of the possible increased risk of siblings of addicts in the Rounsaville et al. (1991) study for substance abuse and psychopathology, found that (a) siblings of opiate addicts had substantially higher rates of drug abuse, alcoholism, major depression, antisocial personality, and generalized anxiety, compared with rates in the community; (b) siblings of opiate addicts had higher rates of substance abuse and antisocial personality than did parents of opiate addicts; (c) significant increased risk of substance abuse among siblings was indicated by the presence of a major psychiatric disorder; and (d) with respect to age of onset, psychopathology preceded the development of substance abuse. These findings assume particular importance in that they emerge from the first study of siblings of opiate addicts which has employed structured interviews and specific diagnostic techniques.

Finally, while more in the line of acquired predisposition to drug addiction, it should be noted that a line of research in Sweden has suggested that obstetric practices, including administration of opiates, barbiturates, and nitrous oxide during labor, are associated with the future adult development of drug addiction in offspring (Jacobson, Nyberg, Grönbladh, Eklund, Bygdeman, and Rydberg, 1990; Nyberg, Allebeck, Eklund, and Jacobson, 1992). The Nyberg et al. (1992) study also found that a low socioeconomic level at time of birth was associated with becoming addicted to amphetamines, but not to opiates. Nyberg et al. (1992) interpreted their findings as being in accord with " . . . imprinting in the ethnographic sense . . . " (p. 1676) and as supporting an *obstetric care hypothesis* in explaining the development of drug dependence. A further study (Nyberg, Allebeck, Eklund, and Jacobson, 1993) rejected "contagious transmission" risk factors associated with high-risk residential areas during adolescence as an alternative explanation for this finding.

Early Experience and Later Narcotic Addiction

Etiological studies recently completed by Nurco and his associates have addressed the important issue of why some young males become narcotic addicts; while their peers, having come from the same environments, do not. Such studies address the important question of resistance to the cultural conditions breeding drug addiction. Studying age-11 peers of those subjects who became narcotic addicts, Nurco, Balter, and Kinlock (in press) compared three groups: (a) a community-wide sample of male narcotics addicts; (b) a matched sample of nonaddicted controls who had been age-11 associates of the addicts; and (c) a matched sample of community controls from age 11 who had not been associated with the addicts. Findings included a strong selective association between friendship and deviance among narcotic addicts and their age-11 associates, a much stronger association than was present among members of the other two groups, particularly the community control group. Further, the addicts, at age 11, typically had more association with older deviants than peer or community control subjects. Nurco et al. (in press) noted that these findings, suggesting that conditions facilitating serious deviance were present very early in life, were consistent with previous research showing early age-of-onset for deviant behaviors associated with serious deviance in adulthood (e.g., Loeber and Le Blanc, 1990; Robins, 1978), and deviant activity was associated with involvement with delinquent peers (e.g, Chein, Gerard, Lee, and Rosenfeld, 1964). In a second study, Nurco, Kinlock, and Balter (in press) examined criminal behavior in three groups similar to those in their previous study. Clear differences emerged with respect to the patterns of criminal behavior in the three groups in early adolescence, with the addict groups reporting the most criminal involvement, and community controls the least. Within the addict sample, criminal involvement at different severity levels was consistently inversely related to age-of-onset for narcotic addiction. These findings were interpreted as reflecting a parallel development in addiction and criminal careers as well as a direct and positive association between engaging in the greatest severity of drug addiction and engaging in the most severe types of crime.

CONCLUSIONS

The literature on socioeconomic, gender, ethnic, psychosocial, and other differences among addicts reflects a continuing interest in and recognition of the diversity of the heroin addict population and a continuing investigation of its characteristics. While such research may not provide direct explanations for treatment success or failure, an appreciation of this diversity can be useful in determining the treatment needs, program components, and treatment modalities most likely to affect various heroin addict subgroups. As Rounsaville (1986) noted, the most important addict characteristics may be those that are variable (as opposed to static), and those that are "readily translatable to treatment strategies" (p. 176). In addition, even static characteristics (e.g., gender) can be associated with or contain within them features that permit the elaboration of more specified and more effective treatment approaches. Thus, an understanding of differences among addicts can guide the development of programs and help identify the most efficacious approaches for diverse groups of addicts. Specific conclusions that may be drawn from the body of research presented in this chapter include the following:

• Increasing attention to gender differences among addicts (e.g., Hser et al., 1988; Finnegan et al., 1990) has resulted in the development of a greater understanding of addiction problems among women, and an appropriate increase in the development of interventions to meet gender-specific needs (also see Volume 3, Chapter 2). Similarly, attention to ethnic differences in addict characteristics and addiction patterns (e.g., Desmond and Maddux, 1984; Platt et al., 1989) has identified specific needs and characteristics which are likely to result in better patient-treatment matching, and ultimately, improved treatment outcome.

• As indicated in Chapter 1, patterns of heroin use have changed significantly during the past decade, with use of heroin exclusively declining dramatically in favor of polydrug abuse. Increasing differentiation of patterns of use among drug abusing populations has taken place, however (e.g., Crawford, Washington, and Senay, 1983; Flaherty et al., 1984), allowing for greater specificity in the development of treatment interventions. For example, the development of sex- and culture-specific treatment programming has resulted from studies which have identified specific patterns of need among various subgroups of the addict population.

• There has been a very clear decrease in interest in personality variables as explanatory constructs for both elucidating the etiology of, and understanding the process of recovering from, addiction. This trend may be the result of a failure to understand the theoretical basis, or to appropriately interpret findings relating to personality variables, as suggested by Sutker and Allain (1988). Yet, there are clearly many researchers, and perhaps more clinicians, who believe that such "trait" variables are of value in improving interventions for addicts. Most likely though, with more precise measurement, personality and related constructs will play a part in treatment planning, assignment to treatment, and evaluation of outcome. Where this line of work has been most valuable is at a more integrated level of measurement, such as in Nurco's recent (1992) discussion of the implications of addict typologies for the planning of interventions.

- The interaction of alcohol and heroin use has come to be seen as an increasingly complex one (e.g., Lehman, Joe, and Simpson, 1990; Lehman and Simpson, 1990b). For example, increasing doubt has been cast on the concept of alcohol substitution for heroin among recovering addicts, with such use now having been identified as most likely reflecting a return to pretreatment heroin-use levels (Hser, Anglin, and Hsieh, 1993; Lehman and Simpson, 1990b).

- The abuse of other drugs, particularly cocaine and the benzodiazepines, continues to be common among heroin users, preceding, during, and following treatment for opiate abuse (e.g., Ball and Ross, 1991; Iguchi et al., 1993; Stitzer et al., 1981; also see Volume 1, pp. 321–322). This continued drug use poses a significant challenge both to treatment program personnel and to treatment researchers.

- Interest in competencies, whether labeled as social skills, life skills, or social problem solving (e.g., Platt and Hermalin, 1989; Platt and Husband, 1993) has been on the increase, and parallels the increasing identification of social competence variables (e.g., social and interpersonal affiliations, life events, success at interpersonal tasks, such as maintaining satisfactory relationships with significant others, etc.) which have been identified as being related to recovery from addiction.

- The long-noted relationship between criminal involvement and addiction has increasingly been the subject of theoretical and empirical scrutiny, which has begun to reveal the subtle interactions between these two sets of behaviors (e.g., Lehman and Simpson, 1990a; Wish, 1988). Faupel's (1987, 1988) work in particular has revealed the dynamic and changing nature of the relationship between crime and addiction at various stages of the addiction career(s). Such work has resulted in a clearer basis for evaluating the differential impact of interventions at different points in the careers of addicts.

- The use of typologies to explain the heterogeneity to be found among addicts has now been increasingly done on an empirical basis (Nurco, 1992; Platt et al., 1993; Steer, Platt, Hendriks, and Metzger, 1989). The work of Nurco and his associates (Nurco, 1992; Nurco et al., 1987; Shaffer et al., 1988) in particular, suggests strongly that intervention strategies must be tailored to the individual case.

- Available evidence suggests that vulnerability to one form of addiction, alcoholism, has a genetic basis (e.g., Goodwin, 1985; Schuckit, 1992). Several recent studies have suggested the possibility of such genetic or familial heritability for other forms of substance abuse, including addiction to opiates (e.g., Maddux and Desmond, 1989; Mirin et al., 1991), particularly as such drug abuse is related to antisocial personality disorder (e.g., Cadoret et al., 1986; Merikangas et al., 1993; Rounsaville et al., 1991). Such work does not of course preclude the possibility that early experience may facilitate the development of later deviant behavior, including narcotics addiction (e.g., Nurco et al., in press).

CHAPTER 5

Addict Characteristics and Implications for Treatment: Psychopathology and Personality Disorders

PSYCHOPATHOLOGY AMONG ADDICTS

General Psychopathology

One conclusion of the review of the literature in this area in Volume 1 was that a significant degree of psychopathology exists in the addict population (Volume 1, pp. 137–147). Reviewing the literature since then on psychopathology among opiate addicts, one is struck both by the continued findings of high levels of psychiatric symptomatology present, particularly those related to depression and personality disorder, and the application of these findings to an understanding of factors predictive of treatment outcome (e.g., Kosten, Rounsaville, and Kleber, 1986; McLellan, Woody, Luborsky, O'Brien, and Druley, 1983; McLellan, Luborsky, O'Brien, Barr, and Evans, 1986), as well as a dramatically increased understanding of the implications for structuring treatment interventions.

With respect to recent findings relating to the extent of psychopathology among opiate addicts, Ball and Ross (1991) found the lifetime prevalence of one or more psychiatric symptoms in their sample of 567 male methadone maintenance patients to be 68.4%. The most prevalent clinically significant symptom was anxiety (51.7%), followed by depression (48.3%), difficulty in understanding, concentrating or remembering (28.0%), trouble controlling violent behavior (24.9%), hallucinations (8.6%) suicidal thoughts (15.3%), and suicide attempts (8.5%). The presence of one symptom was reported by 15.7% of their study sample, two by 21.3%, three by 13.1%, four by 8.5%, and five or more symptoms by 9.9%. Similar evidence of psychopathology among substance abusers was obtained by Ross, Glaser, and Germanson (1988). Using the Diagnostic Interview Schedule (DIS) with 501 individuals seeking treatment for both drug and alcohol problems, Ross et al. (1988) found 78% of those seeking admission to display evidence of a lifetime prevalence of another psychiatric disorder; two-thirds had a currently diagnosable psychiatric disorder other than substance abuse. The most frequently occurring lifetime disorders were generalized anxiety (51.6%), antisocial personality disorder (46.9%), phobias (33.7%), psychosexual dysfunctions (32.8%), agoraphobia (25.1%), and major depression (24.3%). Abuse of both alcohol and drugs was found to be most closely associated with the presence of psychiatric impairment, while the presence of a diagnosable psychiatric disorder was more likely to be associated with the presence of more serious drug problems. Other recent studies of addicted populations, both in the United States and in other countries, have suggested similar rates of psychopathology. Swift, Williams, Neill, and Grenyer (1990), for example, reported a current prevalence of psychiatric morbidity of 61% among Australian opioid addicts seeking treatment, a figure very similar to the rate of 59% showing emotional distress obtained by Darke, Wodak, Hall, Heather, and Ward (1992) for Australian opioid addicts in treatment. Taking into account different measurement procedures and instruments, these figures correspond to those obtained in an earlier American study (e.g., Rounsaville, Weissman, Kleber, and Wilber, 1982).

The Dutch have been particularly active in studying psychopathology in heroin addicts. Van Limbeek, Geerlings, Wouters, Beelen, deLeeuw, et al. (1990) reported a study of the prevalence of various types of psychopathology in a random sample of 84 addicts receiving treatment at an outpatient methadone maintenance program in Amsterdam. Utilizing Diagnostic Interview Schedule questions and the Diagnostic and Statistical Manual of Mental Disorders (DSM-III), they found fairly high levels of psychopathology. In terms of lifetime episodes of diagnosable disorders, some 63.3% of the sample had been alcohol dependent, 62.0% were classified as having had antisocial personality disorders, approximately 51.9% had experienced anxiety disorders during their lifetime, and 27.8% had experienced a mood disorder (excluding dysthymia). Though anxiety disorders (36.7%) and alcohol dependence (35.4%) were less prevalent within the year prior to, and at the time of, assessment than for lifetime occurrences, the prevalence of mood disorders and antisocial personality disorders for the year preceding assessment were almost identical to lifetime levels (mood disorders: 25.3% and 27.8% respectively; antisocial personality disorders: 62.0% and 60.8% respectively). Van Limbeek et al. (1990) also found that a classification of antisocial personality was significantly related to alcohol use, while the presence of an anxiety disorder was significantly correlated with a coexisting mood disorder. Similar findings in American addicts, although at higher rates, were reported by Jainchill, De Leon, and Pinkham (1986), who found that nearly all substance abuse patients presenting for inpatient treatment qualified for an additional diagnosis. Similarly, Khantzian and Treece (1985) found a 93% lifetime prevalence rate for one or more psychiatric disorders (other than substance abuse) in a sample of narcotics addicts.

Geerlings, van Limbeek, Wouters, et al. (1990) assessed the level and types of psychopathology found in a nonrandom sample of 118 Dutch addicts obtaining treatment at a methadone maintenance clinic in Rotterdam. Their results were substantially similar in terms of type and frequency of diagnostic classification to those found by van Limbeek et al. (1990). Of the four diagnostic categories most commonly found (antisocial personality disorders, alcohol dependence, mood disorders, and anxiety disorders), only anxiety disorders were significantly less frequent in the Rotterdam sample. A further analysis of these data by Wouters and van Limbeek (1990) suggested a high prevalence of major depressive disorders. In a later report, van Limbeek, Wouters, Kaplan, Geerlings, and van Alem (1992) compared the prevalence and severity of psychopathology among patients in both high- and low-threshhold (i.e., entry dose level) methadone maintenance treatment programs. Over 50% of patients surveyed were found to suffer from a lifetime DSM-III Axis I disorder, with this number rising to 70% when antisocial personality disorder was included. Forty percent were diagnosed with such a disorder in the year preceding their evaluation. Recurrent major depression, phobic disorders, alcohol abuse and dependence, dysthymic disorder, and antisocial disorder were most frequently diagnosed. The prevalence of disorders was higher among patients seeking admission to the high-threshold program. Within treatment programs, three distinct diagnostic subgroups could be distinguished: (a) a DSM-III Axis I lifetime or current psychopathology and/or antisocial personality disorder; (b) antisocial personality disorder only; and (c) neither DSM-III psychopathology or antisocial personality disorder. Van Limbeek et al. (1992) concluded that their data were similar to those obtained by Woody, O'Brien, McLellan, and Luborsky (1986) in that, within each program, " ... three clinically meaningful, mutually exclusive groups could be discerned ... [thus] provid[ing] the opportunity for patient treatment matching on an individual and a group basis" (p. 51).

Hendriks (1990) determined lifetime and six-month prevalence rates of DIS/DSM-III diagnoses in a Dutch detoxification center in The Hague, and found the overall rate of diagnosable psychopathology to be very comparable to those found in American samples (e.g., Khantzian and Treece, 1985; Rounsaville, Kosten, Weissman, and Kleber, 1985), with more than 80% of the sample having at least one recent diagnosable psychiatric disorder in addition to substance abuse. Antisocial personality disorder, depressive disorder, and anxiety-related disorders were most prevalent, and commonly diagnosed in combination. Nearly one-half of those patients with antisocial personality disorder also had a depressive or anxiety-related disorder, and those with this disorder were generally younger, had a lower level of education, and a longer history of heroin and poly-drug use. When Dutch and American methadone maintenance patients were compared on the SCL-90 and Beck Depression Inventory, comparable profiles were obtained on the SCL-90, with the exception that the Dutch sample had somewhat elevated profiles, reflecting more symptom complaints, than did the American sample. Similarly, on the Beck Depression Inventory, the Dutch had higher mean scores, reflecting more severe cognitive and affective symptoms (Hendriks, Steer, Platt, and Metzger, 1990). Thus, one can conclude on the basis of these studies, that similar patterns of psychopathology exist in Dutch and American addicts, although the Dutch had somewhat higher levels. In a study of the similarity of types of self-reported psychopathology in Dutch and American heroin addicts in methadone treatment, Steer, Platt, Hendriks, and Metzger (1989) examined the shape of SCL-90 symptom profiles (syndromes) for the two groups. Comparability was present, with 85% of both groups being classifiable into one of three syndromes, which they labeled as (a) anxious-depressed, accounting for 42% of Dutch and 43% of American addicts; (b) hostile (13% of the Dutch and 10% of the Americans); and (c) paranoid (31% of the Dutch and 34% of the Americans). Steer, Platt, Hendriks, and Metzger (1989) noted the identification of these profile types as having implications for a differential treatment approach. Such cross-cultural findings are important in that knowledge of the characteristics of the respective addict populations facilitates the transfer of treatment technologies developed in one country to the other.

Specifically with respect to personality disorders, Malow, West, Williams, and Sutker (1989) examined their prevalence and symptomatology among opioid- and cocaine-dependent admissions to a Veterans Administration drug dependence treatment unit. Both opioid and cocaine users were found to have higher prevalences of antisocial and borderline symptomatology than other personality disorders. Comparing the two groups, over three-quarters of opioid addicts were classified by at least one personality disorder category in comparison with less than one-third of cocaine users. Additionally, the picture of the typical opioid user was one of borderline and antisocial behavior characterized by inappropriate anger, chronic boredom, affective instability, inconsistent work history, and social nonconformity. Cocaine users, on the other hand, were less maladjusted, and showed much less borderline symptomatology and self-reported affective disturbance. Malow et al. (1989) invoked methodological diversities in the classification of users in explaining the differences in their findings from those of Black, Dolan, Penk, Robinowitz, and Deford (1987), who also used the MMPI, but reported no significant differences between their inpatient cocaine and heroin users. A further study of Veterans Administration opioid- and cocaine-addicted patients by Malow and his associates found that opioid users, in contrast to cocaine users, exhibited more problems with anxiety, depression, and adjustment (Malow, West, Pena, and Lott, 1990). Possibilities proposed by Malow et al. (1990) to account for this finding were that the greater psychopathology seen in opioid users was reflective of an aggregation of symptoms and features, which was chronic and cumulative resulting from (a) opioid addicts having had a longer history of addiction before seeking help; or from (b) cocaine users having reached psychosocial crises earlier than opioid users due to the different nature of drug effects for the two substances.

In turn, many patients presenting with medical problems also have substance abuse problems. Galanter, Castaneda, and Ferman (1988), for example, observed that a "considerable portion" of patients presenting for general psychiatric treatment, sometimes half, were substance abusers. Further, they noted that as many as one-third of general psychiatry admissions can be found to have had their presenting problems strongly influenced, or even precipitated, by substance abuse. This overlap of substance abuse with general medical problems presents considerable difficulty in teasing apart the symptoms of combined addictive and general psychiatric disorders, and compromises the ability of the mental health system to adequately care for either group, particularly as patterns of drug abuse change relatively rapidly.

Depression

In an assessment of the extent to which depression was present among heroin addicts, Steer (1990) compared 71 white heroin addicts beginning methadone maintenance treatment to 99 dysthymic white psychiatric outpatients. The full Beck Depression Inventory (BDI) was administered to each subject during the intake process. Fifteen percent of the dysthymic patients were prescribed psychotropic medication at the point of evaluation; all addicts had initiated methadone treatment and were not experiencing withdrawal symptoms. The results showed moderate levels of depression among dysthymics and mild levels of depression among addicts, though there were no statistically significant differences between groups in terms of these total scores. There were, however, significant differences in the types of response patterns demonstrated by each group. Dysthymic patients scored higher than addicts on the cognitive-affective subscales of the BDI, while the heroin addicts scored higher than dysthymics on the somatic-performance subscales of the BDI. Steer (1990) noted that the sedative effects of methadone were likely to have accounted for the greater somatic-performance scores among addicts, and suggested that the cognitive-affective scale was likely to be the more valid measure of depression in this population. This conclusion confirms the observations of others (e.g., Clark, vonAmmon Cavanaugh, and Gibbons, 1983), and may explain the discrepancy between these and previous findings which have suggested significantly greater levels of depression among addicts (e.g., Rounsaville, Weissman, Crits-Christoph, Wilber, and Kleber, 1982). Also specifically with respect to depression, Joe, Knezek, Watson, and Simpson (1991), using the BDI cutoff scores reported by Beck and Steer (1987) found that 83% of their sample of intravenous drug users in treatment showed evidence of depression (23% severely depressed, 39% moderately depressed, and 21% mildly depressed). Greater levels of depression were noted in women addicts, as well as in those addicts who were younger, white, and less well educated.

Steer's (1990) observation concerning the impact of the sedative effects of heroin upon BDI Somatic-Performance scale scores (see above) might also explain differences between his results and those found in a series of studies conducted in the Netherlands, at least with respect to depressive symptoms.

Interested in determining whether the Cognitive-Affective and Somatic-Performance dimensions of the BDI, which had been found to exist in medical and alcoholic patients, also existed for injection drug users (primarily heroin addicts not in treatment), Steer, Iguchi, and Platt (1992) administered the BDI to 1,290 injection drug users not currently enrolled in a treatment program. Their results indicated that the same factors were also present in injection drug users, thus supporting the appropriateness of existing scoring for this population. Injection drug users not in treatment were found to be mildly to moderately depressed, according to the existing BDI scoring system. Further, scores remained relatively stable in a subsample of 157 injection drug users followed for six months.

Addressing the question of whether the dysphoric mood states seen in heroin addiction were a cause or consequence of heroin addiction, Handelsman, Aronson, Ness, Cochrane, and Kanof (1992) assessed levels of dysphoria and opioid dependence in a sample of male heroin addicts applying for treatment at a Veterans Administration clinic. Both during a period of heroin use prior to application for treatment, and during acute precipitation of withdrawal by means of a pharmacological challenge with 0.4 mg of naloxone, symptom changes with respect to dysphoria were found to be highly correlated with changes in opioid withdrawal symptoms precipitated by naloxone. These findings suggested to the investigators that dysphoric mood changes in addicts may partly be pharmacologic sequelae of chronic drug use and dependence. This study left unanswered, however, the question of whether dysphoria is a cause or consequence of heroin dependence.

Kosten, Rounsaville, and Kleber (1983) investigated the relationship of recent life events to depression in heroin addicts. They found, in their sample of 123 addicts who had been tested before treatment and at a six-month follow-up, that addicts had a significantly greater number of stressful recent life events than a sample of normal individuals or a sample of patients who were diagnosed with depression. Within the addict population studied, the authors also found that stressful recent life events were most strongly related to the continuation of depression, rather than to the onset of depression. Addicts who were depressed at the initial and follow-up evaluation points had higher levels of stressful recent life events during the post-treatment period than did addicts who were asymptomatic or who became depressed during the follow-up period. Further, those subjects who were depressed at both assessment points had experienced more frequent social losses than did subjects who were not depressed at either point. In comparison to addicts who became depressed during the six-month follow-up, those who continued to be depressed had a greater degree of new conflict (i.e., arguments) with members of their social support systems. Social losses seemed to be more strongly related to increased illicit drug use, and arguments more strongly related to continuing depression. The investigators concluded that losses and arguments aggravate rather than cause depression in addicts, and that such events were likely to undermine the addict's ability to recover from depression. They further suggested that skills training and support for coping mechanisms may be required to assist addicts in dealing with the recent life events that aggravate their depression and impede their recovery.

Reporting on a study that utilized multiple measures of functioning at a six-month and a 2.5-year treatment follow-up, Kosten (1986) found that major depression in addicts seemed to lift over time. However, addicts demonstrating major depression at the point of intake into treatment were likely to have had more severe employment, drug use, and psychological problems at the six-month follow-up. Major depression upon intake also tended to predict lower current functioning and psychosocial functioning at the 2.5-year follow-up, while moderate and severe psychological problems upon intake (as assessed by the Addiction Severity Index) tended to predict worse outcomes along a number of measures at follow-up (including psychosocial adjustment, substance use, legal problems, and medical disability). Life events at the time of termination of treatment were prognostic of resumption of drug use by the end of the 2.5-year follow-up. Those addicts experiencing a divorce or a death in the family at the point of treatment exit were significantly more likely to have relapsed to drug abuse than addicts who had not experienced such events. Addicts who were free of such stressful events, who had completed treatment, and who were not depressed at intake, were significantly more likely to be abstinent at the end of the follow-up (75%) than were addicts who had been depressed, unable to complete treatment, and who had experienced stressful life events at the point of treatment exit (24%). Finally,

Kosten (1987) noted that major depression upon intake generally tended to predict higher rates of relapse. He concluded that "the long term prognostic significance of depressive disorders for relapse to drug abuse may be related to a patient's ability to cope with life stresses, particularly losses" (p. 419). Moreover, he suggested that identifying addicts who suffer from psychological distress, and then providing appropriate psychological and pharmacological treatment (as distinct from an exclusive focus on cessation of drug-taking behavior) might prove important in increasing rates of success in treatment and preventing relapse once treatment has ended.

Finally, a study by Nunes, Quitkin, Brady, and Stewart (1991) provided encouraging results with respect to the impact of antidepressant treatment upon drug use. Nunes et al. (1991) employed imipramine in an open pilot trial with 17 consecutive methadone maintenance treatment patients who had received diagnoses of primary depression. Following treatment, nine (53%) improved both with respect to mood and drug abuse, although more with respect to the former than the latter. Despite a number of design limitations noted by the authors, this work clearly warrants further research efforts in the form of controlled trials.

PSYCHOPATHOLOGY AND TREATMENT OUTCOME

A number of studies have examined the relationship of psychopathology to treatment outcome. McLellan, Luborsky, Woody, O'Brien, and Druley (1983), for example, found scores on the Psychiatric Severity scale of the Addiction Severity Index to be the best predictor of treatment outcome across a number of treatment programs, both alcohol and drug. Further, when the study populations were divided on the basis of diagnosis, it was found that (a) low-severity patients showed the most improvement, regardless of the type of treatment they received; (b) mid-severity patients could be matched to the appropriate and cost-effective treatment; while (c) high-severity patients, both alcohol and drug dependent, showed the least improvement and the poorest outcomes regardless of the type of treatment they received. Similarly, McLellan, Luborsky, O'Brien, Barr, and Evans (1986), seeking predictors of treatment outcome from pretreatment information, found that severity of psychiatric, employment, and legal problems were the best of all predictors utilized for both drug- and alcohol-dependent populations.

LaPorte, McLellan, O'Brien, and Marshall (1981) compared admission and six-month follow-up evaluation ASI data on three groups: high-, medium-, and low-severity drug-dependent patients treated in either a therapeutic community or a methadone maintenance program. Their results indicated considerable improvement by all groups on all measures of drug abuse. Improvement also took place in other areas for the low- and medium-severity groups: employment, criminality, and family relations. The least amount of improvement was found for the high-severity group. Overall, Laporte et al. (1981) found that the follow-up status of the three groups with respect to outcome status was in the same order in which they had entered treatment.

When interactions among severity, outcome, and treatment condition were examined for patients in methadone maintenance treatment, there was little difference in outcome for low-severity patients as a function of type of therapy provided (supportive-expressive, cognitive-behavioral, or counseling alone). High-severity patients showed some gains with psychotherapy, but few gains with drug counseling only. The mid-severity group showed more gains with psychotherapy than with only counseling. On the basis of this study, the authors concluded that psychotherapy increased the chances of improvement for high-severity patients over methadone alone (Woody, McLellan, Luborsky, O'Brien, Blaine, et al., 1984). This conclusion has led to the suggestion that high-severity patients, who demand more program resources and make poorer progress than other patients, can be identified early in treatment, provided with additional psychotherapy, and thus have a better chance of improvement, while reducing demands upon counselors (Woody, O'Brien, McLellan, and Luborsky, 1986).

Faced with the dilemma of how to treat the 15 to 20 percent of drug abusers in the high-severity group, McLellan, Childress, Griffith, and Woody (1984) hypothesized that this type of patient was more likely to respond slowly to treatment, and thus required more than the 90 days provided in the therapeutic community program. Examining rates of improvement for 118 patients admitted to the therapeutic community and 154 patients admitted to methadone maintenance treatment during 1980, McLellan, Childress, Griffith, and Woody (1984) generally found a strong and positive relationship between treatment duration and percent improvement. For low-severity patients, a direct relationship was found between time spent in treatment and amount of positive change on all measures. For both methadone maintenance and therapeutic community programs, the most immediate and greatest changes were on the drug use measure, while employment changed more slowly and showed less improvement overall. On the criminality measure, the therapeutic community patients in treatment for under 30 days showed a worsening; with longer stays of up to 90 days, significant positive change took place. Methadone maintenance patients showed the same pattern, but responded sooner, after 70 days. The findings for mid-severity patients was similar and generally comparable to those obtained for low-severity patients. Steeper rates of change for the mid-severity patients, however, suggested a greater effect of treatment duration in this group. Additionally, on both criminality and employment measures for therapeutic community patients, and on criminality and drug use measures for methadone maintenance patients, patients with short durations of stay showed a worsened status at six months than at admission. The high-severity patient group in methadone maintenance treatment showed an improvement similar to that seen in the mid-severity group although with a shallower slope, suggesting an attenuated duration effect. The absolute level of improvement was also lower than for either the low-severity or mid-severity groups. The employment measure did not show a net improvement until after 70 days of treatment, and no change occurred on the criminality measure. The results for the high-severity therapeutic community group were very much different than for any other group or condition. On each measure, there was a negative relationship between time in treatment and percentage improvement, suggesting a worsening of condition over time, especially with respect to drug use and criminality.

McLellan et al. (1984) concluded that treatment, both methadone maintenance and therapeutic community, was associated with significant positive change across most measures, with a clear and direct relationship found between duration of treatment and amount of improvement. A second conclusion reported by McLellan et al. (1984) was that severity of psychiatric status was an important predictor of treatment response generally and of differential treatment response in more impaired drug abuse patients. Another conclusion drawn from the results of this study relates to the counterproductivity of therapeutic community treatment for high-severity patients. One explanation for this finding, put forth by McLellan et al. (1984), was that this type of patient was often younger, used less opiates (but more other drugs), and had fewer personal and social supports than the patient for whom the therapeutic community was originally designed. These patients were thus less prepared to cope with the stresses present in therapeutic community life as a result of community living, group encounter sessions, embarrassing punishments, and the relative absence of psychotropic medications. McLellan et al. (1984) also noted the significance of the fact that the negative relationship between treatment duration and percent improvement was not present in high-severity alcohol patients treated in the alcohol therapeutic community, and that the alcohol therapeutic community did not employ either group encounter sessions or embarrassing punishments, and had a more liberal attitude toward the use of psychotropic medications during treatment.

ANTISOCIAL PERSONALITY DISORDER, PSYCHOPATHOLOGY, AND RESPONSE TO PSYCHOTHERAPY

Conventional wisdom among psychotherapists and drug abuse program personnel holds that many opiate abusers are likely to have antisocial personality disorders and thus are poor candidates for psychotherapeutic interventions (see Volume 1, pp. 122–124 and 145–147). In this regard, Rounsaville, Weissman, and Kleber (1982) found opiate addicts with antisocial personality disorder to have had more legal, employment, and psychosocial problems at follow-up than had opiate addicts without additional psychiatric diagnoses. Yet, Woody, McLellan, Luborsky, and O'Brien (1985) reported that antisocial opiate users who, in addition to their addiction, met DSM-III-R criteria for a lifetime diagnosis of depression had a somewhat better (although only slightly) treatment response than did other antisocial substance abusers in the same program when provided with a six-month course of individual psychotherapy. Among the reasons suggested for this finding were that depression reflected a greater capacity for relating to people and events, and to experience feelings such as guilt and loss. Alternatively, just having a comorbid psychiatric problem that is amenable to treatment may be the salient factor (Woody et al., 1985; 1990).

Noting that little was known about the personality trait dimensions or of Axis II comorbidity among antisocial drug abusers, Brooner, Herbst, Schmidt, Bigelow, and Costa (1993) categorized outpatient opioid drug abusers into four groups: (a) a pure antisocial group; (b) a mixed antisocial group (antisocial plus another Axis II disorder); (c) other Axis II (Axis II diagnosis other than antisocial); and (d) a non-Axis II group. The mixed group was found to be more prone to neuroticism (greater vulnerability to stress and hostility) when compared to the pure group, and also when compared with the non-Axis II group. The mixed group was also found to have lower agreeableness (i.e., higher interpersonal antagonism) than the non-Axis II group, while surprisingly, the pure antisocial group did not differ from the remaining groups.

In a secondary analysis of data from the Woody et al. (1985) study, Gerstley, McLellan, Alterman, Woody, Luborsky, and Prout (1989) hypothesized that those opiate abusers in treatment diagnosed as having antisocial personality disorder who could respond to an interpersonal relationship of the kind formed with a therapist in individual treatment would be more likely to have a positive treatment outcome. While neither the counselors' nor the therapists' assessments of the relationship in general were significantly related to overall treatment outcome, a positive assessment of the therapeutic alliance by either the patient or the psychotherapist was significantly related to improvements in overall functioning, drug use, and employment. Additionally, the magnitude of these changes was not as large as those seen in the other diagnostic subgroups studied by Woody et al. (1985).

In a subsequent report, Gerstley, Alterman, McLellan, and Woody (1990) noted problems inherent in the DSM-III and DSM-III-R criteria for diagnosing antisocial personality disorder in substance abusers in that the criteria failed to require that antisocial behaviors exist independently of the substance abuse. They suggested that the DSM-III and DSM-III-R criteria encompassed two different subgroups of substance abusers which they identified as "true" psychopathic individuals and symptomatic psychopaths with little psychopathy. The latter group was seen as possessing more psychoneurotic symptomatology and favorable treatment responses. One must agree with Gerstley et al. (1990) that the relationship between antisocial personality disorder and substance abuse is not yet fully understood. As with so many other relationships studied in the field of substance abuse, this relationship is complex and its full understanding awaits either the development of more precise measurement or increasingly rigorous experimental design. What is clear, however, is that this entire line of research has opened up an important new avenue in treating what have been thought to be untreatable patients, and also in advancing toward the ultimate goal of matching drug abuse patients to the most appropriate treatment.

THERAPIST EFFECTS IN PSYCHOTHERAPY

The role of the counselor can be crucial in the rehabilitation of the methadone patient. In this regard, several studies have demonstrated significant individual counselor or therapist effects upon patient improvement in methadone maintenance treatment (Luborsky, Crits-Christoph, McLellan, Woody, Piper, et al., 1986; Luborsky, McLellan, Woody, O'Brien, and Auerbach, 1985; McLellan, Woody, Luborsky, and Goehl, 1988; see Chapter 5). Examining the factors which resulted in these outcomes, Woody, McLellan, Luborsky, and O'Brien (1987) checked how closely the therapists and counselors conformed to their treatment manuals in implementing their therapies. Additionally, the patients were asked how much their therapist or counselor was helping them. While the patient's rating of helpfulness was the strongest predictor of outcome, the degree to which the therapist conformed to the specifications of the treatment manual also predicted outcome, although to a lesser extent.

THE DRUG DEPENDENCE SYNDROME

Increasing support has been presented for the existence of a unitary dependence syndrome across all substances of abuse, as proposed in the model articulated by Edwards, Arif, and Hodgson (1981), and as later adopted in DSM-III-R. This model, in the form of a general theory of addiction, proposes that the initiation and maintenance of addiction is a function of both predisposing and immediate variables ranging from the genetic to societal levels. According to Babor, Cooney and Lauerman (1986), this model, labeled the "drug dependence syndrome" (DDS),

. . . maintains that a complete explanation of an individual's substance abuse must include statements concerning the frequency and severity of dependence, the kinds and degrees of disability, and the personal and environmental influences upon substance use (p. 21).

The elements of the drug dependence syndrome, according to Babor, Cooney, and Lauerman (1986), include (a) a narrowing of repertoire around a regular schedule of consumption; (b) the increased salience given to substance-taking over other behaviors, despite its negative consequences; (c) the development of increased tolerance; (d) the appearance of withdrawal symptoms after short periods of abstinence; (e) the use of substances to avoid withdrawal; (f) the development of a compulsion to use the substance, involving craving and impairment of control over intake; and (g) readdiction liability, or an increased likelihood for the syndrome to be rapidly reinstated by use after a period of abstinence. The elements of the syndrome are tied together by a set of "often unstated" assumptions about the learning process underlying the acquisition and maintenance of drug dependence, including classical and operant conditioning, and cognitive mediation. While it is beyond the scope of this volume, the reader is referred to Edwards et al. (1981) for the full explication of the model, as well as to Babor, Cooney, and Lauerman (1986) for a briefer explication and its specific application to the problem of relapse to drug use.

Empirical evidence for the existence of the Drug Dependence Syndrome was presented by Skinner and Goldberg (1986), who found a general dependence factor distinct from social and health problems on a 20-item general drug screening questionnaire, the Drug Abuse Screening Test (DAST; Skinner, 1982). This general dependence factor was characterized by (a) an inability to stop drug use; (b) problems in getting through the week without drugs; and (c) withdrawal symptoms when drug use stopped. In addition, Kosten, Rounsaville, Babor, Spitzer, and Williams (1987) found that opiate, cocaine, and alcohol dependent individuals shared similar factor patterns of dependence; and Hasin, Grant, Harford, and Endicott (1988) found the dependence syndrome, while generalizable across classes of substances, not to be necessarily distinct from the social, health, and other problems that accompany drug abuse. Kosten, Rounsaville, Babor, Spitzer, and Williams (1987), on the other hand, found the DSM-III-R drug-specific dependence criteria to form a single factor for opiate, cocaine, and alcohol, but not for other drugs, with medical and psychological consequences relatively independent of the dependence syndrome, except for alcohol and cocaine, which had some association with other problem areas. Rounsaville, Bryant, Babor, Kranzler, and Kadden (1993) conducted a field test of substance abuse disorders as defined by DSM-III-R, DSM-IV (proposed), and the International Classification of Disease, 10th Edition (ICD-10), and found support for the drug dependence syndrome and for its applicability to a relatively wide range of drugs.

CONCLUSIONS

• Psychopathology is a common and pervasive characteristic of American heroin addicts, with lifetime prevalence of one or more psychiatric disorders of about 65–75% or more (e.g., Ball and Ross, 1991; Malow et al., 1989, 1990; Ross et al., 1988). Antisocial personality disorder and affective disorders predominate among American addicts, and studies conducted in other countries generally show similar patterns for heroin addicts (e.g., Darke, Wodak, Hall, Heather, and Ward, 1992; Ellgring and Vollmer, 1992; Hendriks, 1990; Swift et al., 1990; van Limbeek et al., 1990, 1992).

• Studies of affective disorders in heroin addicts indicate a very high level of prevalence of depression in heroin addicts (e.g., Joe et al., 1991; Steer et al., 1992), although for addicts in methadone treatment, medication effects may depress somatic-performance scores on measures such as the Beck Depression Inventory (Handelsman et al., 1992; Steer, 1990). A recent study by Nunes et al. (1991) suggests that antidepressant treatment of depression may itself reduce illicit drug abuse.

• Pretreatment level of severity of psychopathology has been shown to be related to treatment outcome (McLellan et al., 1986). Low-severity patients tend to do well in treatment (regardless of type of treatment received), while high-severity patients do poorly (Laporte et al., 1981; McLellan, Luborsky, Woody, O'Brien, and Druley, 1983), regardless of the type of treatment which they receive (Woody et al., 1984). Mid-severity patients can be matched to the most appropriate (and cost-effective) treatment (McLellan et al., 1983a). High-severity patients identified early in treatment may do best when provided with additional treatment (this early identification may also reduce demands upon counseling staff) (McLellan et al., 1984; Woody et al., 1986).

• While heroin addicts with antisocial personality disorder tend to have more psychiatric, legal, psychosocial, and employment problems, and typically do not do well in treatment, those with a diagnosis of depression tend to have a somewhat better response to treatment (Woody et al., 1985). Additionally, those addicts with antisocial personality disorder who can form an alliance with their therapist are likely to have better outcomes (Gerstley et al., 1989), as do those who had more psychoneurotic personality structures (Gerstley et al., 1990).

• Evidence is accumulating (e.g., Babor, Cooney, and Lauerman, 1986; Skinner and Goldberg, 1986; Rounsaville, 1993) which supports the concept of a unitary drug dependence syndrome applicable to all drugs of abuse (e.g., Edwards et al., 1981; Babor et al., 1986), although the syndrome may be applicable only to opiates, cocaine, and alcohol and not to other drugs of abuse (Kosten, Rounsaville, Babor, Spitzer, and Williams, 1987).

PART FOUR

Control Approaches to Heroin Addiction

CHAPTER 6

Coercion, Legalization, and Normalization

COMPULSORY TREATMENT

Most drug users are unlikely to enter treatment except when under some form of complusion or coercion. Such coercive forces include pressures from family, friends, or social institutions such as employers or school systems, loss of access to drugs or the means to pay for them, or ultimately, the legal/judicial system, as when the expectation of imminent arrest is present (Platt, Bühringer, Kaplan, Brown, and Taube, 1988).

"Pressures" can be defined as a certain set of operations or activities exercised by others to increase the likelihood that a drug dependent individual will enter and remain in treatment, change his or her behavior in socially appropriate ways, and sustain that change after treatment (p. 508).

Such pressures may be either positive (e.g., the desire to change lifestyle) or negative (e.g., the threat of imprisonment), although it is likely that many addicts may only be responsive to negative pressures at certain points in their addiction careers (Platt et al., 1988).

The place of coercion in substance abuse treatment has increasingly been addressed in recent years, with a number of reviews available on this subject (Rotgers, 1992; Stitzer and McCaul, 1987; Ward, 1979; Webster, 1986; Weissner, 1990). With specific reference to treatment for opiate addiction, this issue was also the focus of a German-American workshop held in 1986 (Brown, Bühringer, Kaplan, and Platt, 1987), and the topic of a special issue of the *Journal of Drug Issues* (Rachin, 1988) as well as a NIDA monograph (Leukefeld and Tims, 1988a). Despite this increasing attention in the literature, most writers are in agreement that only rudimentary knowledge exists on this important issue (e.g., Platt et al., 1990).

Compulsory treatment of drug abusers is not new in the United States. It was first evidenced in the proposal by the Narcotics Unit of the Treasury Department to establish "narcotics farms," which resulted in the establishment of the Public Health Service Hospitals at Lexington, Kentucky in 1935, and at Fort Worth, Texas in 1938. These hospitals were established with the original intention of their serving as separate prison facilities for narcotic addicts, although a high proportion of their admissions eventually were voluntary (see Volume 1, pp. 24–25, 245–247). According to Maddux (1988a,b), treatment provided in the two Public Health Service hospitals consisted of gradual withdrawal from opiates, provision of a drug-free environment within which to recover, psychotherapy, and supervised activities. The last category consisted of work, vocational training, remedial education, and recreational activities. The original treatment course was six months, although this time was later reduced to four months.

Unfortunately, most patients left during or soon after withdrawal (Maddux, 1988a,b). Treatment was thus very often ineffective, with high rates of discharges occurring against medical advice (Rasor and Maddux, 1966), and a very high rate of relapse to narcotics use (Maddux, 1988a,b). With narcotics use having been made a crime in Kentucky in 1946, patients who had left the Lexington hospital were only readmitted if they had pleaded guilty to narcotics use in a Kentucky court. The one-year sentence was then suspended on condition that the addict stayed at Lexington until treatment was completed. This procedure stayed in force until 1956, when it was discontinued, in large part because a criminal conviction was required as a condition of admission to the hospital.

Rotgers (1992) has identified three forms of coercion directed towards inducing the target individual to enter treatment: (a) *informal coercion*, most often experienced in the form of pressure exerted by significant others, including spouses and friends, and carrying no formal sanctions; and (b) *formal noncriminal coercion*, as exerted by noncriminal institutional entities. This latter form included (i) referrals to treatment by employers and employee assistance programs; (ii) sanctions imposed by civil and governmental agencies including probationary monitoring by regulatory and professional licensing boards (e.g., impaired professional programs); (iii) civil commitment procedures involving formal commitment to treatment programs, either within correctional settings or in lieu of such incarceration (e.g., the California Civil Addict Program [see Volume 1, pp. 247-249] and the New York State Narcotic Addiction Control Program [see below]); and (iv) mandated treatment by social service agencies which may direct clients to enter treatment in lieu of having their children removed from the home. The final type of coercion was (c) *formal criminal justice coercion*, including (i) diversion or deferred prosecution, which defers or reduces sanctions contingent upon treatment participation (e.g., probation or parole continuation); (ii) completion of treatment before lifting of sanctions (e.g., completion of treatment before restoration of driving privileges for driving while intoxicated [DWI] offenders); and (iii) treatment completion while incarcerated as a condition of parole to the community.

A number of issues arising in the use of formal coercive measures to induce substance abusers to enter treatment were reviewed by Rotgers (1992). He categorized these issues as follows: (a) *ethical considerations in application* as reflected in the answers to such questions as "Who is the client?" and "What does the coercive (referral) agent need to know about a client's progress?"; (b) *civil rights issues* concerning the extent to which society has, for example, a right to demand constriction in individual rights (i.e., involvement in treatment) in the service of societal aims; (c) the appropriate *diagnostic criteria* upon which to base individual decisions, in that such decisions are often made by nonmental health professionals (e.g., judges and probation officers) so that many offenders for certain offenses (e.g., driving while intoxicated) who may not otherwise come to the attention of the courts are thrust into treatment, thus depleting costly treatment resources; (d) whether coercion, as an extrinsic *motivation for treatment* is likely to be as effective as other, more intrinsically based motivations; (e) the *efficacy of the treatment provided*, in that there is little solid evidence of the efficacy of such widely prescribed treatments such as Alcoholics Anonymous; (f) the *criteria of treatment outcome*, in that court mandated and clinical judgments about what constitute appropriate outcomes may differ significantly; and (g) *systematic issues* that may affect the implementation and effectiveness of coercive measures. Rotgers (1992) notes, for instance:

Given the tendency for coercive agents to refer all clients to one type of treatment (e.g., EAPs tend to refer to private, inpatient treatment facilities [Walsh, Hingson, Merrigan, Levenson, Cupples, et al., 1991]; courts tend to refer opiate addicts to drug-free programs, rather than methadone maintenance programs [Cook and Weinman, et al., 1988]), and for treatment programs to administer their "standard" treatment to all clients (Miller, 1989) regardless of client characteristics or evidence of effectiveness of the particular program's approach with all clients, this question raises the possibility that systematic tendencies may result in some clients being denied access to programs that might be most suitable for them, resulting in an implicit system of socioeconomic class discrimination (pp. 407-408).

Rotgers (1992) went on to review empirical findings on the issue, and concluded that

With few exceptions, the literature to date provides very little useful information about the effects of coercion on substance abuse treatment . . . This state of affairs is due to the paucity of adequately designed research in this area . . . (p. 411).

Rotgers (1992) gave the following reasons for reaching this conclusion: (a) the lack of a clear-cut theoretical framework for the study of coercive motivational techniques, although this deficiency may be remedied by the introduction of models for studying motivation to stop alcohol and drug abuse (e.g., Prochaska and DiClemente, 1986; Cox and Klinger, 1988; and Miller and Rollnick, 1991); (b) lack of a widely accepted definition of coercion that clearly defines the behaviors constituting coercion, as well as their relevant parameters; and (c) the difficulty of conducting well-controlled outcome research. Rotgers (1992) concluded by emphasizing the need for research on the relationship between coercion and treatment outcome, and wider dissemination of research findings to the agents of coercive social control. The reader is referred to this provocative article, as well as to the several other reviews which exist (Rachin, 1988; Ward, 1979; Webster, 1986; Weissner, 1990) for a fuller discussion of these issues and recommendations for their remediation within the context of substance abuse treatment.

With their lengthy aftercare components, civil commitment programs are particularly effective in preventing relapse (Leukefeld and Tims, 1988a). The need for accessible and effective aftercare programs is greatest during the first 90 days following treatment, when exposure to drug-related stimuli, without the support of a structured program, presents the greatest risk of relapse (Tims and Leukefeld, 1986).

In 1985, a United States/Federal Republic of Germany Workshop on the Treatment of Drug Abuse took place at Manresa-on-Severn, Maryland. The purpose of this meeting, a follow-up to an earlier Workshop held in 1983 in Nuremburg, was to determine the different kinds of pressures that influence the behavior of drug addicts, as well as how these pressures could be used to bring addicts into treatment, to change their behavior during the treatment process, and to maintain these changes following treatment. The report of this conference can be found in Brown, Bühringer, Kaplan, and Platt (1987). Platt, Bühringer, Kaplan, Brown, and Taube (1988) presented a synthesis and set of six propositions summarizing the conclusions reached at the 1985 meeting, which reflected the prospects, and limitations of compulsory treatment in drug addiction treatment. The six propositions (in the form of recommendations) were (a) pressure is inherent and pervasive in the social and personal systems of the drug abuser and should be harnessed for use in treatment; (b) some proportion of drug abusers will require pressure to involve themselves in treatment; (c) pressure, appropriately applied, can be a useful element in the treatment experience; (d) the judicial system currently permits and provides the procedures for the application of pressure to induce a drug abuser to enter and remain in treatment; (e) there is a need to assess the pressures that can be applied in order to clarify their application and, if appropriate, to place controls on their use; and (f) the drug-abusing client is within the province of both systems—judicial and health. Therefore, coordination between the two systems is essential and must be enlarged (Platt et al., 1988).

In a study of whether addicts who reported themselves as coerced into treatment by the criminal justice system differed from voluntary admissions, Brecht, Anglin, and Wang (1993) studied 618 methadone maintenance patients admitted to programs in Southern California under high-, moderate-, and low-legal coercion levels. All groups, regardless of coercion level, were similar in showing substantial improvement in levels of narcotics use, criminal activity, and other behaviors during treatment, with some regression following treatment. Brecht et al. (1993) concluded that the similarity of response to treatment regardless of level of coercion, gender, or ethnicity supported the use of coercion as a valid motivation for treatment entry. Chapter 7 discusses the use of coercion to enter treatment in a number of forms, including civil commitment and treatment in lieu of incarceration.

NATIONAL APPROACHES TO HEROIN ADDICTION

This section reviews the approaches taken by four countries (the Netherlands, the United Kingdom, Germany, and the United States) in addressing the heroin problem. To a great extent, the approaches taken by each of these countries may be viewed in terms of the perspective provided by van de Wijngaart (1991). Van de Wijngaart (1991) has provided an analysis of the major differences between the *normalization* and *deterrence* "perspectives" or models for dealing with the problem of drugs at the societal level, each of which he sees as a paradigm within which specific issues, actions, and solutions can be viewed. He identified the points of departure for these two positions as being, in the case of the deterrence perspective, "the best way to prevent the problems arising from the use of drugs is to try and eliminate their use altogether," while in the case of the normalization perspective, it was the proposition that "the problems arising from the use of drugs are not inevitable, and are intensified rather than alleviated by attempts to eliminate their use" (p. 97). The deterrence view is exemplified by the approach associated with the "War on Drugs" declaration made by President Richard Nixon in his message to Congress of June 1971, while the "normalization" view is best exemplified by the societal response to drugs in the Netherlands. Van de Wijngaart (1991) noted, however, that official Dutch drug policy is *not* a purely "normalizing" approach.

Differentiating between the opposing theoretical properties of the normalizing and deterrence viewpoints, van de Wijngaart (1991) pointed out the internal coherence of these two approaches and how each addressed such issues as (a) how drugs are defined; (b) how drugs are supposed to affect their users; (c) the social consequences of drug use; (d) policies recommended at both societal and individual levels; (e) sources of support for each policy; and (f) how the supporters of each position are viewed. Essentially, the deterrence view sought to solve the drug problem by eliminating all use. This view (a) defined drugs legally in terms of their physiological dangerousness; (b) saw addiction as caused by the drugs themselves; (c) saw drugs as threatening society through the breakdown of order and the work ethic; (d) recommended prohibition and a punitive approach as policies; (e) viewed the opposition as escapist, unrealistic, and overpermissive; (f) was supported by the establishment; and (g) employed positivist, determinist, and reductionist models, such as "the medical model." The normalization view, on the other hand, had as its core value the concept that elimination of all use intensifies problems. This view (a) saw no hierarchy of dangerousness possible because of intervening social factors; (b) saw social meaning and pattern of use as mediating drug effects upon users; (c) saw the persecution of users as leading to a criminalized society with an erosion of civil liberties; (d) recommended a policy of decriminalization, and a narrowing of the gap between users and the rest of society; (e) saw the opposition as shortsighted, simplistic, and denying the existence of social problems; (f) had support from groups close to users, sociologists, and the Dutch government; and (g) used arguments of an interpretive, probabilistic, interdisciplinary, and transactional nature. The reader is referred to van de Wijngaart (1991) for his discussion of the implications of these differing approaches.

The Normalization Approach: The Netherlands

Van Vliet (1990) provided a good overview of the normalization approach adopted by the Dutch. He saw the basic elements of this approach, which exists in concert with a strong adherence to international control efforts against narcotics trafficking, as including (a) *decriminalization* of the use and retail trade in products derived from cannabis (e.g., marijuana and hashish), in order to keep persons from experimenting with drugs such as heroin and cocaine; (b) the *separation of markets* concept, which he saw as the foundation of this policy, reflecting an attempt to avoid socially marginalizing youthful users of cannabis, thus driving them towards hard drug use; and (c) *normalization* of drug problems, which while reflecting an admission that drug use, like tobacco and alcohol use, has gained an extensive and firm foothold in society, aims at the normalization or encapsulation of drug abusers within society, with resultant harm minimalization. Such harm minimalization is directed at all levels, the abuser, his environment, and society, and includes AIDS prevention. Van Vliet (1990) observed that Dutch policy has actively sought to avoid two negatively viewed side effects of control of illicit drug trafficking: (a) the possible growth of organized crime to the point where it would eventually control important parts of society, including the media, the police, the judiciary, and even the political systems; and (b) the driving of drug users from society into a true "underground," where they would be beyond the reach of "helping" institutions. Within the Dutch view of drug abuse as " . . . basically and principally a matter of health and social well being . . . " (Altes, 1987, cited by van Vliet), van Vliet (1990) saw this policy as both fitting the needs of the Netherlands and as being consistent with the Dutch tradition of rationally solving social problems in a cost-effective manner. However, the adoption of the normalization approach has inevitably led to an uneasy relationship between both the international drug control system and those countries, including the United States, which have adopted a "War on Drugs" approach to drug abuse control.

The Medical Approach: The United Kingdom

In contrast to the Dutch normalization approach described above, the British approach was initially (in the 1960s, at least) centered on the long-standing, humanely oriented policy of maintenance. As pointed out by Howitt (1990-91), this policy developed out of an international agreement, The Hague Opium Conventions of 1912-13 (see Volume 1, pp. 6-7), rather than being the result of a fully considered appraisal of the domestic situation and its needs. The United Kingdom's Dangerous Drugs Act of 1920 outlawed opium for nonmedical purposes, required registration of persons engaged in the manufacture, sale and distribution of heroin, morphine, cocaine, and other drugs, and set standards, including licensing and record keeping for pharmacists and physicians. However, unlike the situation in the United States, physicians were allowed a wide latitude of discretion with respect to the prescription of narcotic drugs. The Rolleston Committee's Report (Departmental Committee on Morphine and Heroin Addiction, 1926) recommended the prescription of opiate and other controlled drugs under two conditions: (a) when an attempt was made to cure the addiction through gradual withdrawal and (b) when withdrawal would require hospitalization or a normal lifestyle would be disrupted. Weekly visits to a physician were required, and dosages could be prescribed for the period between visits. The approach recommended by the Rolleston Committee, which soon thereafter was translated into law, together with the 1928 Report of the Committee on Homosexual Offenses and Prostitution of 1928 which outlawed behaviors only when they promoted corruption, exploitation, or indecency in public, represented the establishment of a "public health morality" in Britain (Rouse and Johnson, 1991).

However, the appearance of the heroin "epidemic" in the 1960s was accompanied by both a rapid increase in the number of addicts, and a change in demographics (from a middle-aged, middle-class, and largely female user problem to a user population of young, working-class individuals, and was associated with criminality [Howitt, 1990–91]). This change in the user population, according to Howitt, resulted in a increasing perception by the Home Office of a threat to society from both criminality on the part of addicts and overprescription of drugs by physicians.

In 1958, a review of British policy toward addicts had been conducted by the Brain Committee, which essentially reconfirmed the medically oriented approach. A few years later, in 1965, the situation had changed sufficiently for the second Brain Committee to recommend that heroin and opiates only be available to addicts through government clinics, a recommendation which was translated into law through the Dangerous Drug Act of 1967. In addition to establishing government clinics, physicians were required to be specifically licensed to prescribe heroin and cocaine, which could only be used for the alleviation of pain due to injury or disease (although either a maintenance or, more likely, a declining schedule of methadone could still be prescribed for addicts), reporting requirements for drug prescription were established, as was a central registry for drug addicts.

While Britain's approach in the 1980s still focused on heroin, the emphasis was now more concerned with the problems associated with drug use than drug dependence, reflecting a continuation of a policy of control and containment as described by Johnson (1977). In the 1990s, the British approach still appears opposed to the normalization of drug use and users. According to Ghodse and Kaplan (1988), the British have maintained, throughout the 60-year history of opiate prescription, a "medical" rather than a social approach to normalization of addiction, although this approach is seen by Howitt (1990–91) as being similar to that of other countries in that it is an "essentially punitive" one. A full discussion of the British approach up to the early 1980s may be found in Stimson and Oppenheimer (1982), while a more recent view, from a somewhat different perspective, may be found in Howitt (1990–91).

Ghodse and Kaplan (1988) concisely contrasted the differing Dutch and British responses to the problem faced by both countries in the 1970s. Seeing the Dutch response to the drug epidemic as occurring within and reflecting a strongly organized and pragmatic culture, they observed that the Dutch employed a national strategy of channeling drugs through a complex system of social mechanisms into nondestructive paths. Officially adopting a concept of *normalization*, the focus of intervention was on the drug, its associated problems and complications and not on addiction per se. The emphasis on harm reduction, as evidenced by the message "If you use drugs, do so safely," was in contrast to a policy of deterrence. Consistent with the harm-reduction approach was the stabilization of addicts through provision of social support, food, shelter, the ready availability of methadone to reduce suffering, as well as the reduction of the secondary deviance consequences of addiction to heroin. A comprehensive discussion of the evolution of Dutch drug policy, its successes and failures, and its implications for other countries is found in van de Wijngaart (1991).

Addiction as a Psychosocial Disease: Germany

Germany is among the countries in which extensive debate has been taking place regarding the development of addiction treatment policy. This debate has also increasingly involved American policy makers and researchers, and has led, over the last ten years, to several German-American conferences as well as to collaboration, on an individual basis, between German and American researchers (See Bühringer and Platt, 1992, pp. xv–xvi). Drug abuse patterns in Germany differ significantly from those in the United States, reflecting a greater communality with those of other European countries. Recently, however, an increasingly negative attitude toward illicit drug use has been developing in Germany. At the same time, the use of "hard" drugs, including opiates, has generally been on the increase in Germany in recent years (e.g., Reuband, 1992), in part reflecting the increased availability of heroin (Püschel, 1992).

In contrast to the United States, the German government has looked upon the drug problem as a " . . . particular challenge to its societal and health policy," taking the perspective that " . . . drug abuse is understood as a psychological alarm signal, and drug addiction as a psychosocial disease" (Schreiber, 1992, p. 59). Such a view has led to a national plan for drug abuse control which views demand reduction as important as supply reduction, and which emphasizes the importance of maintaining addicts within the social system, rather than treating them as deviant outcasts. Egg (1992) noted the movement in Germany to apply "treatment instead of penalty" to drug users, commenting that

At the least, strong efforts should be made to motivate drug addicts to undergo suitable therapy, and if they agree to it this treatment should be made available. No penalty should stand in the way of treatment (p. 435).

Bühringer (1992) has outlined the following goals of the German treatment system: (a) early intervention for first-time users (e.g., secondary prevention); (b) decreasing time between onset of addiction and first treatment; (c) providing treatment access for a high proportion of addicted persons; and (d) reducing treatment dropout, relapse, periods of addiction, and harm among current users.

With respect to actual service provision, Germany currently has about 600 larger and 300 smaller drug treatment facilities, with a total of about 3,000 beds.

This system provides a high rate of access to treatment for addicts, compared to other countries. Each year about 25,000 drug addicts are treated in outpatient facilities while an additional 7,000–8,000 receive care in residential facilities. These figures amount to an estimate of some 30–40% of addicts being treated annually (Bühringer, 1991). The previously restrictive policy toward methadone maintenance has been relaxed since 1991, and intense discussion is now underway concerning just what the form of the new regulations concerning methadone maintenance treatment should be (Bühringer, 1993, personal communication). For more detailed information concerning the issues underlying the German drug treatment system, its structure, and evaluation, the reader is referred to Bühringer (1992), Ziegler (1992), and Simon, Bühringer, and Strobl (1992) respectively, while Egg (1992) has provided an overview of the interface between criminal law and addiction treatment in Germany.

The Criminalization Approach: The United States

The use of opium, morphine, coca leaf, and cocaine represented a major problem in the United States during the late nineteenth century and early part of this century (Musto, 1973); perhaps as many as two hundred to four hundred thousand people were addicted (Musto, 1973). These drugs were taken as remedies for a wide variety of ailments and also were an ingredient in patent medicines and even soft drinks (Brecher, 1972). Control over this problem was initially implemented (and later, treatment initiated) with the passage of such measures as the Pure Food and Drug Act (1906) and the Harrison Act (1914), followed by the Uniform Narcotics Act (1932), the Comprehensive Drug Abuse Prevention and Control Act (1970), and the Narcotic Addict Treatment Act (1974, 1980) (see Volume 1, Chapter 2). In general, however, the intent of these laws paralleled an increasing view of opiates in this country as a legal, rather than as a medical problem (Bates and Crowther, 1974).

More recently, the Anti-Drug Abuse Act (1988) raised the level of funding for anti-drug programs. At the same time, there has been an increasingly vocal advocacy for legalization in the United States, and while such efforts are unlikely to be successful at present, they likely reflect the beginnings of a shift in public opinion, in large part because of frustration at the failure of a primarily control-oriented policy.

Parallel to the increasing control of narcotic and other drugs on the domestic front, the United States was active in instituting worldwide control through the major international conferences, beginning with the Shanghai Conference of 1909, followed by The Hague Conferences of 1912 and 1913, the Geneva Conference of 1924, the Limitation Convention (1931), the San Francisco Conference (1945), the Opium Limitation Conference (1953), the Single Convention on Narcotic Drugs (1961) and the Amending Protocol to the Single Convention (1972) (see Volume 1, Chapter 1). The United States has been a major sponsor of many of these conferences, the theme of which emphasized increased control over the production, processing, and trade of narcotic drugs. This theme paralleled that taken on the domestic side during this period, except that domestic regulations also addressed the prescription of narcotic drugs by physicians.

The American control strategy has been one of reducing supply of, and to a lesser extent, demand for drugs. As noted by Inciardi (1991), a classic deterrence model served as the basis of American supply- and demand-reduction strategies, involving such elements as (a) implementation of legislation and criminal penalties in order to discourage use; (b) the setting of examples of traffickers in order to discourage dealing; and (c) the implementation of research to improve treatment, education, and prevention. However, when in the early 1970s, this "war on drugs" approach was not being won, and drug abuse was spreading, increased control efforts were instituted, including efforts against organized crime, treaties aimed at extradition of drug traffickers, and the involvement of the U.S. military in interdiction efforts. Finally, in 1988, a policy of "zero tolerance" for drug use was instituted, having at its core the concept of willful use of drugs (rationalizing the options of stopping drug use), the assignment of responsibility for continued use to the user, and the attempted reduction of public tolerance of drug abuse to zero. The goal of prohibition of drug use on the one hand, with criminal penalties for transgression on the other, as evident in American policy, can be conceived of as reflecting a "prohibition-criminalization morality" (Rouse and Johnson, 1991).

At the same time as efforts aimed at control of narcotics continued to increase, there has also been an emphasis in the United States on treatment through publicly supported clinics, many of them providing methadone maintenance, although funding for such programs, once derived primarily from the federal level, has increasingly shifted to state and local government, making access to such treatment by addicts, who are primarily from poor, often minority backgrounds, increasingly more difficult to obtain. Research activity into improved treatment strategies has been primarily supported by the federal government through the leadership of the National Institute on Drug Abuse.

In describing the development of the war on drugs by the United States, Wisotsky (1991) noted that the armamentarium includes not only the Drug Enforcement Agency, the Federal Bureau of Investigation, the Central Intelligence Agency, and the Treasury Department (through efforts at tracing drug money), but also Organized Crime Drug Enforcement Task Forces in 13 cities, the National Narcotics Border Interdiction System, which was designed to coordinate radar surveillance and interdiction efforts along the U.S. border, and the U.S. armed forces. Despite all these efforts, and as well, a dramatic expansion of the

U.S. prison population to house all those arrested and convicted of drug-related crimes (some 40% of those committed), the war has not been going well, for the available supply of drugs does not seem to have been seriously reduced.

HEROIN MAINTENANCE

The Dutch experience with heroin maintenance (see Volume 1, pp. 280–286) appears to have been less than totally positive. Van de Wijngaart (1991) noted that one-third of Dutch heroin addicts he had interviewed in 1982 had no desire to enter a heroin maintenance program, despite the fact that many had the view that heroin maintenance (a) would have a positive effect upon their social functioning, and (b) would lead to a disappearance of the black market for heroin and other opiates. This one-third consisted of those users who had plans to "kick the habit" or were actually doing so, and preferred methadone maintenance for this purpose. Another smaller group desired no control over their use of heroin. According to van de Wijngaart (1991) this picture was not substantially changed 10 years later.

LEGALIZATION OF HEROIN AND OTHER DRUGS

The history of antinarcotics legislation and the criminalization of drug taking in the United States has been described in detail elsewhere (Musto, 1973; see also Volume 1, Chapters 2 and 3). A related issue that arises cyclically is whether heroin and other currently illicit drugs should be legalized as a means of better controlling their use and abuse. Recently, this alternative has again become the source of discussion and debate (perhaps more intensely than previously) due to both a rising frustration with the problem of drug abuse on the part of the public (reflecting the feeling that present policies of control and interdiction are not working) and highly articulate advocates on both sides of the question.

The crux of the argument in favor of legalization is that existing policy is not effective, and that, in fact, it is responsible for increasing crime, among having other adverse effects. As many advocates of legalization have argued, the criminal justice system cannot handle the problem, in part because it is impossible to seal any country's borders. Among other things, opponents of legalization foresee huge increases in drug abuse and addiction rates if drugs are legalized. They also have argued that legalization would signal the loss of "the war on drugs," perhaps before it even started (Massi and Trebach, 1988). Whatever the outcome, it promises to be an uphill battle for those who propose legalization. For the immediate future, such changes in official United States government policy appear unlikely.

A particularly vocal advocate of legalization has been Nadelmann (1989; 1991a,b; 1992), who has written widely on the failure of present United States drug policies, and the need to consider the controlled legalization of illicit drugs. Seeing a losing war on drugs, including the expenditure of significant monies on drug enforcement without much effect on the price, availability, or consumption of illicit drugs, while the use of legal drugs such as alcohol and tobacco has declined, Nadelmann (1991b) has concluded that

Drug laws themselves appear to be responsible for much of the "drug problem." In addition to the criminal production, sale and purchase of drugs, many drug users resort to robbery, burglary, and prostitution to pay for high-priced illegal drugs. Most of the violence associated with drugs is due not to the physiological effects of drugs but rather, to the illegal markets in which they are sold (p. 3).

Nadelmann (1991a) saw the distinction between prohibition and legalization as less one of control of distribution than of emphasis on the use of criminal sanctions to control use *versus* a reliance on public health approaches, nongovernmental approaches, and the private decision of citizens. He has pointed to the need, when analyzing drug legalization, to assess the relative costs, benefits, risks, and advantages of any proffered solution. Some of the costs of present policies include (a) a need on the part of addicts to commit crimes to obtain funds for drugs, (b) the undermining of respect for law and law enforcement, (c) the overburdening of the criminal justice system, (d) increased health costs resulting from present policy, (e) the poor record of current drug policy in dealing with the spread of AIDS and other diseases through intravenous drug use, (f) the prohibition against the use of illicit drugs for medical use for palliative purposes, and (g) the problems associated with the lack of purity and unknown potency of unregulated drugs (Nadelmann, 1989). Not only would legalization eliminate many of these problems, according to Nadelmann, but positive benefits (such as reduced government expenditure for drug law enforcement and tax revenue on legalized drugs) would accrue. Nadelmann's arguments are radical and provocative, yet very appealing in their apparent simplicity, particularly in light of the many failures of the current policy of control. Their greatest value may lie in opening a long-needed, and articulate, debate on the subject.

Inciardi and McBride (1989) summarized the arguments made by supporters of drug legalization as follows: (a) drug laws have created evils—corruption, violence, street crime, and disrespect for the law—far worse than the drugs themselves; (b) demand for drugs has not been reduced by legislation passed for this purpose; (c) the very fact that a large number of people in a society are doing something illegal mitigates against that activity being illegal; and (d) positive benefits would accrue as a result of legalization, including (i) drug prices falling, (ii) the availability of drugs at prices regulated by the government would no longer require users to engage in prostitution and street crime in order to maintain their habits, (iii) a reduction in drug-related crime would result in a freeing up of criminal justice resources, allowing the courts, jails, and prisons to focus on "real criminals," (iv) drug-related activities, and their profits, would be removed from the province of organized crime, (v) drug-related governmental corruption and intimidation would be reduced, and (vi) a general restoration of civil liberties would accrue as a result of the decreased police efforts to enforce drug laws. In addition, Inciardi and McBride (1989) have noted that an assumption is implicit in legalization arguments to the effect that legalization would (a) match current levels of use to demand and that (b) no additional health, safety, behavioral, and other problems would accrue, thus (c) making available billions of dollars currently being spent on enforcement as well as generating revenues from regulated drug sales, monies that could be used for prevention and treatment activities.

Admitting the good intentions on the part of those supporting legalization, Inciardi and McBride (1989) nonetheless saw the arguments given in support of legalization as questionable in their historic, sociocultural, and empirical underpinnings, as well as in their understanding of the negative consequences of a legalized drug market. Noting the absence of a concrete, comprehensive proposal for legalization, they posed the following questions: (a) what drugs should be legalized, according to which criteria, and who should determine the criteria?; (b) for those drugs to be legalized, what potency levels should be legalized?; (c) what age limits, if any, for the use of drugs should be imposed?; (d) who should be allowed to use certain drugs, those already dependent on them, and in what amounts?; (e) where and how should drugs be sold?; (f) where should raw material for drugs originate, and should drugs presently unknown in the United States be allowed?; (g) should the drug market be a free one with issues such as price, purity, potency, and advertising (e.g., endorsements) determined by private industry?; (h) what restrictions should be place on legalized drugs for those workers in critical occupations (e.g., transportation, nuclear power employees)?; (i) what restrictions should be placed on where drugs are sold or consumed (e.g., separate drug use sections in restaurants, creation of "pot breaks")?; and (j) which government bureaucracy should be charged with the enforcement of the legalization statues?

Reviewing a number of issues related to legalization, including the public health and behavioral consequences of drug use, cost/benefit considerations of legalization, drug-related violence, the impact of legalization on poverty groups in our society, and public views towards legalization, Inciardi and McBride (1989) concluded that the perceived

... benefits of legalization are only potential, [while] the costs are readily apparent in existing levels of drug use ... Existing data do not support the utilitarian benefit of legalization (p. 283).

Approaching the legalization argument from an historical perspective, Court-wright (1993), in a reply to prolegalization arguments by Nadelmann (1993), observed that the lessons of history argue against legalization. Some likely outcomes of legalization listed by Courtwright (1993) include (a) an increase in the number of addicted users (perhaps to somewhere between the twelve to fifty-five million suggested by Kleber [cited by Courtwright, 1993, p. 50]), as has happened in countries where narcotics have long been cheap, potent, and readily available, such as Thailand; (b) that a significant increase in drug use would likely occur among occupational groups in our culture, such as physicians, to whom drugs would become even more readily available; (c) rate of use would likely increase among addicts who would use more drugs if the cost was low, with a resultant increase in crime to finance such drug use; (d) rate of drug use among the young would likely increase due to diversion of drugs by adults who sell to them, thus altering and diminishing, but not eliminating, the black market in drugs; (e) this latter problem would likely maintain rates of arrest for violations of law; (f) availability of drugs to persons whose use of them would jeopardize public safety would occur; (g) drugs would be available to pregnant women, the mentally ill, parolees, and other groups at particular risk; (h) the smuggling of drugs to prisoners in correctional settings would likely increase as supplies became more readily available; (i) the windfall in tax revenue as a result of import duties and taxes on sales would result in widespread attempts to evade them, and any reduction in interdiction expenses would likely be balanced to some extent by the increased effort required to neutralize smuggling and illegal manufacturing; (j) the states might not uniformly repeal their antidrug laws, thus exacerbating the problem of interstate smuggling; (k) the possibility that a windfall in increased tax revenues would invite the levying of state taxes, resulting in interstate smuggling to take advantage of variations in such rates, as is the case with cigarettes now; and (l) opportunities for income from illicit sales and smuggling would benefit organized crime, much as organized crime benefited from Prohibition. Courtwright (1993) concluded by noting that while it has appeared that the

... legalization debate [is] an argument about a colossal gamble, whether society should risk an unknown increase in drug abuse and addiction to eliminate the harms of drug prohibition, most of which stem from illegal trafficking ... It would be more accurate to ask whether society should risk an unknown but possibly substantial increase in drug abuse and addiction in order to bring about an unknown *reduction* in illicit trafficking and other costs of drug prohibition (p. 56).

Another view has been provided by Goldstein and Kalant (1990), who observed that a rational drug policy requires striking the appropriate balance between harm reduction resulting from both the use of psychoactive drugs on the one hand, and strict legal prohibitions and their enforcement, on the other. Their position incorporates the following arguments: (a) that psychoactive drugs are dangerous to both users and society, although to varying degrees; (b) availability of drugs has a strong impact upon consumption; (c) other methods in addition to prohibition exist to control availability; (d) demand reduction, rather than supply reduction, is the real solution to the drug problem; and (e) a rational drug policy requires tailoring to the specific dangers presented to both the user and society by each drug. In this well-reasoned and articulate article, Goldstein and Kalant (1990) acknowledged that, given that psychoactive drugs have always been present in society and are unlikely to disappear, the practical aim of drug policy should be harm reduction. They proposed that this be accomplished, for example, by (a) reducing the recruitment of new addicts through making it more difficult and expensive to obtain drugs, as well as through the strengthening of anti-drug education; and by (b) ameliorating the condition of present drug users by considering them " . . . as victims of a life-threatening disease . . . requiring compassionate treatment" (p. 1516).

Jarvik (1990), while more concerned with cocaine than heroin abuse, and taking a somewhat different tack, has also made some innovative suggestions as to how to reduce both demand and abuse, emphasizing the need for empirically derived answers and the application of existing new technologies. His suggestions include (a) reducing drug demand through the implementation and evaluation of preventive techniques, primarily involving "social therapy," such as family planning, job programs, expansion of evaluation of preventive-intervention strategies in the schools, and mass-media campaigns; (b) the investigation of existing treatments, particularly replacement therapies, which while not perfect solutions, are at the least less harmful than illicit drug use; (c) the objective evaluation of funding for supply reduction (interdiction) versus demand reduction (prevention and treatment) in order to determine the best use of resources; (d) the extension of existing chemical and electronic technology, coupled with community pressure, although this option raises potential fourth amendment implications; (e) the introduction of more immediate aversive consequences for illicit drug use, perhaps accomplished through the detection of drug use through telemetering of specific physiological responses to drug use; (f) the development of new pharmacological alternatives, such as mood-altering drugs with slower rates of onset, such as buspirone, or a safe euphoriant or positive reinforcer; and (g) more effective criminal justice responses to drug use, particularly through making the law more enforceable, and more intensive probation, as an intermediate punishment between parole an incarceration.

While Courtwright's (1993) arguments, like those of Nadelmann (1993) and Inciardi and McBride (1989), illucidate the issues in the legalization debate and should be read by all those concerned with this important issue, Goldstein and Kalant's (1990) argument is most persuasive, arguing as it does, for both harm reduction and the matching of control efforts to the actual dangers posed by specific drugs to the user and to society. Jarvik's (1990) emphasis upon technology is unlikely to provide a complete answer to the question of where to go from here with respect to legalization, but it does make the point that there is much to be gained from the application of both empirical methods and existing technology to the seeking of solutions to the problem of drug abuse. After reviewing the pro- and antilegalization literature, one is drawn to Jonas's (1992) point that while properly implemented legalization of drugs would positively affect the *drug-traffic-related crime* problem, it would have little impact upon the *substance abuse* problem.

CONCLUSIONS

*   Coercion may be said to be a common element in entry into addiction treatment. Coercion may be present in many forms, some of which are more formal (e.g., treatment in lieu of incarceration or as a condition of parole) than others (e.g., pressure from friends and family). In a free society, coercion carries with it many implications relating to the rights of the individual, and the ability of the treatment agent to intervene effectively. Recent work has been primarily concerned with defining the nature of coercion (e.g., Rotgers, 1992), the framework within which coercion takes place (e.g., Brown et al., 1988; Platt et al., 1988), as well as the contribution made by coercion to treatment outcome (e.g., Brecht et al., 1993; Stitzer and McCaul, 1987).

*   Addiction has increasingly become an international problem, crossing borders with ease. The development, and patterns of addiction may be very different between countries because of cultural differences. Some countries, fearful of the consequences of suppression, have opted for what is, in practice, a normalization approach to its drug users (e.g., the Netherlands; van de Wijngaart, 1991; van Vliet, 1990), while others (the United States, for instance) have taken a deterrence approach, with an emphasis upon interdiction of drug supplies and criminalization of users. Each of these approaches has both costs and benefits, and few counties have come to terms fully with the implications of the policy which has been adopted. Other countries (e.g., Britain and Germany) appear to be in the process of changing policy, although this may vary with respect to the extent to which it is deliberate (e.g., Germany versus Britain). For many years, Britain followed a medically oriented policy of heroin maintenance, a policy which arose out of The Hague Opium Convention of 1912–13, while its present policy is primarily one of control and containment (e.g., Ghodse and Kaplan, 1988; Howitt, 1990–91). A more societally oriented approach towards heroin addiction has been undertaken by Germany, which has focused upon maintaining and reintegrating the drug user within the social system. As the result of extensive debate over the past several years, the German treatment system has now introduced methadone maintenance treatment, an approach which had been strongly re-

sisted in the past (e.g., Bühringer, 1992; Schrieber, 1992). The United States has continued in effect its deterrence approach to drug use, with its resultant criminalization of drug users.

• One periodically recurring proposal for radical change in drug policy in the United States, that of legalization of drug use, has recently elicited much more controversy than it has in the past. In large part this has been the result of the increased visibility of the drug problem, its association with the AIDS problem, and the increasing frustration on the part of the American public with the drug problem and related issues such as rising crime, as well as the failure to control the importation of drugs, despite massive investments of money. Articulate advocates have also arisen on both sides of the problem, leading to an intensification of debate (e.g., Courtwright, 1993; Goldstein and Kalant, 1990; Inciardi and McBride, 1989; Jarvik, 1990; Nadelmann, 1991b, 1992). Yet, the debate itself serves the purpose of educating the public about drug abuse and its associated problems, and in doing so, may lead to increased concern with the development and/or expansion of appropriate treatment.

CHAPTER 7

Criminal Justice Approaches to Heroin Addiction Treatment

TREATMENT OF THE ADDICT OFFENDER
IN THE CRIMINAL JUSTICE SYSTEM

As Leukefeld (1991) has pointed out, drug abuse treatment has a traditional relationship with the criminal justice system. Milestones in this relationship include the establishment of the Public Health Service "narcotics farms" at Lexington and Fort Worth, which were originally intended for narcotic-addicted federal prisoners; the passage of the Narcotic Addict Rehabilitation Act of 1966 (NARA), which was originally intended to provide court-ordered treatment as an alternative to incarceration, as well as continuing treatment for opiate addicts in the community; and the Treatment Alternatives to Street Crime (TASC) diversion program, which was intended to bridge the gap between criminal justice and drug abuse treatment systems through provision of referral, case management, and monitoring of drug- and alcohol-dependent offenders. Little research evidence exists, however, concerning the effectiveness of correctional programming for drug abuse treatment aside from that available for therapeutic communities (Lipton, Falkin, and Wexler, 1992).

CIVIL COMMITMENT

Civil commitment represents a form of compulsory treatment. Implicit in this treatment approach is the "rational authority" concept proposed by Brill and his associates (Brill and Leiberman, 1969; Brill and Jaffe, 1967; see also Volume 1, p. 227) with respect to the need for compulsory supervision both for the purpose of effecting abstinence and maintaining the addict in treatment. As Inciardi (1988) has noted,

> The theory of civil commitment holds that some heroin and other substance abusers are motivated for treatment, but most are not. As such, there must be some lever for diverting into treatment those who ordinarily would not seek assistance on a voluntary basis (p. 549).

Civil commitment came into existence some 30 years ago, in California, with the establishment of the California Civil Addict Program in 1961. This was likely the first true civil commitment program in the United States. This was followed by the New York Narcotic Addiction Control Commission (NACC), which was noted by Inciardi (1988) to have reportedly been " ... the largest and costliest civil commitment program in history ... " (p. 447). Civil commitment became national policy with the establishment of the Federal Narcotic Addict Rehabilitation Act (NARA) in 1966. (See Maddux, 1988a,b; also Volume 1, pp. 28–29, 245–247 for a description and evaluation of this program.) By 1988, some 25 states had civil commitment statutes (Leukefeld and Tims, 1988a).

Focusing on compulsive drug users who are responsible for committing large numbers of criminal acts, civil commitment procedures essentially increase the likelihood that drug users will enter and remain in treatment, change their behavior so as to conform in socially desirable ways, and maintain that change. Civil commitment, with the intent of controlling and rehabilitating the compulsive drug user, employs drug abuse treatment, monitors drug use, and provides reasonable sanctions for program infractions (Leukefeld and Tims, 1988a).

California Civil Addict Program

This program (see Volume 1, pp. 247–249), in addition to being the first true civil commitment program in the United States, has certainly been the most intensively studied, and perhaps most successful, of three programs which combined treatment in a correctional institution with specialized parole supervision. While the two other civil commitment programs, the Federal Narcotic Addict Rehabilitation Act, and the New York State Civil Commitment Program, were not successful and soon ended (Inciardi, 1988), the California Civil Addict Program (CAP), which began in 1961 and essentially changed its form (and therefore, its original character) in 1969, was quite successful. Intensively studied by McGlothlin and his associates (e.g., McGlothlin, Anglin, and Wilson, 1977a,b) and after McGlothlin's death, by Anglin (e.g., Anglin, 1988c; Anglin, McGlothlin, and Speckart, 1981), this program allowed adjudication of heroin-addicted individuals by means of a civil commitment, in contrast to a criminal sentencing, procedure. Utilizing a seven-year commitment procedure initiated while incarcerated in a medium security prison, typically three-fourths of a seven-year term was spent on parole under community supervision. This supervision was provided by specially trained parole officers with smaller caseloads, limited to 30 parolees. Early release for some of the first admissions due to legal-procedural errors resulted in the possibility of a case-control comparison group, matched for criminal and drug histories and demographics.

The major findings of the evaluation of the CAP program were as follows: (a) During the first year following release from treatment, the CAP group used narcotics at a much lower rate than did the comparison group, receiving only minimal exposure to the program; (b) this difference between groups was maintained over the entire five-year supervision period; (c) following Year 5, increased daily use occurred in both groups; and (d) in addition to a drop in daily drug use, similar positive effects were obtained with respect to criminal involvement, time spent dealing drugs, employment, etc. (Anglin, 1988c).

When the components of civil commitment were examined with respect to their effectiveness, the most efficacious appeared to be close community supervision, accompanied by objective drug testing. The best results were obtained with the use of specially trained parole officers, smaller case loads, and more frequent drug testing. Legal supervision with drug testing followed in effectiveness, while absconded status was associated with the least positive outcomes. Similarly, liberalization of the program with respect to both length of inpatient stay and stringency of outpatient performance requirements resulted in poorer outcomes. Finally, program flexibility (versus rigidity), with greater decision-making power in the hands of the parole officers, resulted in better outcomes (McGlothlin et al., 1977a).

The New York Parole Project

The forerunner of the New York Narcotic Addiction Control Commission, the New York Parole Project (NYPP) was conceptualized as an intensive, authoritatively oriented, community-based program for the supervision of parolees with histories of narcotics use (Diskind, 1960; Diskind and Klonsky, 1964a,b). Elements of this program, *as envisioned,* included specially selected and trained parole officers and small parole officer caseloads; thus permitting intensive supervision.

Reevaluating the original reports by Diskind and Klonsky, Inciardi (1988) found much about the procedures employed in the study that he believed compromised the data and the conclusions drawn from them. These problems included (a) most of the parole officers were not specially, or even well-trained for the task that they were given; (b) biased case selection for the program, with selection limited to those parolees whose records suggested "some chance of success" (p. 550); and (c) the use of rearrest for a new crime as the criterion of parole failure rather than, e.g., drug use. Similarly, failure to report to parole officers did not become a matter of record, and thus was not considered in the follow-up evaluation. In addition, many parolees who had reverted to drug use were undetected, and parole officers would, on occasion and in the interest of building a therapeutic relationship with patients, not report detected drug use. In addition to these problems, Inciardi (1971) also had earlier identified another problem. Due to racial tension, fewer parole supervisory contacts were made in minority areas, thus leading to uninformed parole reports.

New York Narcotic Addiction Control Commission (NACC)

Authorized under the New York State Narcotics Control Act in 1966, the New York Narcotic Addiction Control Commission (NACC) represented a civil commitment program under which individuals could be judicially certified to treatment for periods of three to five years. Inciardi (1988) noted that this program appears to have been " ... founded almost solely because of the misrepresented findings of the New York Parole Project" (p. 553; see above). Inciardi's (1988) estimate of the cost of this program was $200 million during the first three years for the treatment of 4,500 addicts.

Eligibility for commitment under NACC involved having been arrested for drug-related crimes, volunteering for commitment, or having been given a court commitment following a petition by friends, family members, or relatives. Inciardi (1988) listed five mistakes made by NACC: (a) the apparent acceptance of the initial NYPP evaluation findings as the basis for the NACC program; (b) the purchase of state correctional facilities and retention of their guards as "rehabilitation officers," thus maintaining a correctional, in contrast to a therapeutic, atmosphere; (c) inexperienced facility administration, in that the selection of treatment facility directors was made on the basis of political or civil service appointments, rather than demonstrated clinical and administrative skills; (d) the modeling of the aftercare component of the program on the parole system rather than on a therapeutic system, yet at the same time, not giving the "aftercare officers" the arrest powers of parole officers—one result was the high rate of failure to report and abscondance; and (e) the loss of public support through attempts to cover-up program failures.

Inciardi (1988), in his evaluation of the significance of this program, noted that among the elements contributing to failure of the NACC were (a) a too hastily conceived response to the growing epidemics of heroin use and drug-related street crime, thus resulting in staffing patterns tainted by politics and incompetence; (b) large capitalization costs necessary for the creation of new treatment facilities and a comprehensive aftercare network; and (c) the " . . . awesome expenditures of tax dollars . . . [by a political entity] . . . that resulted in cover-up and secrecy" (p. 556). In conclusion, Inciardi (1988) observed that the experience gained from this program, together with that gained from compulsory treatment programs which have had demonstrated success,

> . . . suggest an important lesson for the future direction of mandatory treatment initatives—*that the implementation of any new approaches should avoid, at all costs, the creation of new, large scale treatment bureaucracies* (p. 556).

The Effectiveness of Civil Commitment

Reporting on his clinical experience with opioid addicts at the former Public Health Service Hospitals at Lexington and Fort Worth, Maddux (1988a,b) recalls that the unstable motivation of the addicts in these programs presented a major obstacle to treatment success, with only a minority of patients, about one-third, staying in treatment until discharge to aftercare. One-third of patients admitted to the two PHS hospitals prior to civil commitment were found to have disruptive or dangerous behavior which rendered them unsuitable for treatment, and only a minority stayed beyond detoxification. While Maddux (1988a,b) found that civil commitment provided only a weak coercion into treatment, the results of two follow-up studies (Langenauer and Bowden, 1971; Stephens and Cottrell, 1972) suggested a somewhat better outcome with civil committed, in contrast to voluntary, patients. (For a fuller discussion of outcomes for patients treated at the Lexington and Fort Worth Hospitals, see Volume 1, pp. 245-247.)

Civil commitment procedures, as exemplified by major programs such as the NARA, CAP, and NACC, had focused primarily upon compulsive drug users, especially antisocial addicts heavily involved in criminal activities (Leukefeld and Tims, 1988a). Such programs, however, were only fully operational for the period 1965 to 1975, when they were replaced by the community mental health center system. Leukefeld and Tims (ibid), however, see a renewed need to examine the value of such programs as the result of (a) the need to enroll larger numbers of addicts into treatment; (b) the large number of prisoners with addiction histories; and (c) concerns about the spread of AIDS among injecting drug users and their sexual partners as well as their children.

McGlothlin and Anglin's work on the evaluation of the California Civil Addict Program (CAP) (Anglin, 1987a,c; 1988; Anglin and McGlothlin, 1984; McGlothlin, Anglin, and Wilson, 1977a,b) stands as strong evidence for the effectiveness of coercion as a useful strategy leading to treatment entry on the part of individuals who otherwise would be unlikely to enter treatment by themselves. At the same time, Inciardi's (1988) discussion of the problems involved in the evaluation of the New York Parole Project and the reasons underlying the subsequent failure of the NACC should be mandatory reading for any architects of new civil commitment programs.

Reviewing international issues with respect to civil commitment, Brown (1988) concluded by summarizing six issues which have been described as necessary for the implementation of civil commitment: (a) the presence of an apparent major risk to larger society by a subgroup's inappropriate behavior(s); (b) the capacity to create support for (or diminish opposition to) measures to contain the behavior(s); (c) the ability to identify members of the subgroup with the offending behavior(s); (d) an inability on the part of the offending subgroup to mount competing political pressure on its own behalf; (e) the existence of mechanisms to process, detain, and confine individuals who are seen as inappropriate and threatening; and (f) a belief in the ability of the community to develop incentives that will humanely change the identified behavior(s). Finally, any discussion of civil commitment should note its limitations. Three were identified by Maddux (1988a,b): (a) civil commitment cannot overcome deficits in services, particularly with respect to availability of sufficient adequate treatment; (b) while coercion can bring an individual into treatment, it cannot make him or her actively participate in such treatment; and (c) civil commitment must operate within the constitutional guarantees of individual liberties, which are curtailed when coercion is applied. This last issue is further complicated by the need to balance rights of the individual against those of the community. As noted by Leukefeld (1991), however, the criminal justice system provides an excellent opportunity to identify and refer drug-abusing individuals to appropriate treatment. The Treatment Alternatives to Street Crime (TASC) program provides an excellent case example of a program based upon this concept.

REFERRAL TO TREATMENT

The Treatment Alternatives to Street Crime Program

The Treatment Alternatives to Street Crime (TASC) programs (Cook and Weinman, et al., 1988), which were originally funded by the Drug Abuse Office and Treatment Act of 1972 for implementation in a number of cities and locally administered, were intended to become permanent local- or state-funded programs. Their aim was to identify drug users in the criminal justice system, refer those eligible to treatment, monitor their progress while in treatment, and return violators to the criminal justice system. Thus, the TASC program, in linking the criminal justice and drug abuse treatment systems, provided an alternative to incarceration.

Data provided by the TOPS evaluation (Hubbard, Collins, Rachal, and Cavanaugh, 1988; Hubbard et al., 1989) indicated that about one-half of both TASC and non-TASC clients in outpatient drug-free programs were on probation at the time they were admitted to treatment, as were approximately one-half of the residential clients. The results were consistent with prior research findings (Collins, Hubbard, Rachal, and Cavanaugh, 1988) in that criminal justice clients, particularly those referred by TASC, stayed in treatment substantially longer than did non-criminal justice clients. Compared with noncriminal justice clients, TASC clients stayed 45 days longer in outpatient drug-free treatment, while other criminal justice clients stayed 17 days longer than clients with no criminal justice involvement. Both TASC and non-TASC criminal justice clients stayed 50 days longer in residential treatment than did clients with no criminal justice involvement.

With respect to criminal activity, both TASC and non-TASC criminal justice client status did not predict posttreatment predatory criminal activity, although outpatient drug-free clients were more likely to be arrested posttreatment. Worse outcomes were, however, found for criminal justice referrals with respect to depression and employment. Further, criminal activity of clients with a criminal justice status decreased significantly while in drug abuse treatment. Hubbard et al. (1989) concluded that these findings supported the view that criminal justice clients do as well or better than other clients in drug abuse treatment. Referrals from the criminal justice system, including those for TASC, tend to be younger, to have not been previously treated, and not to be as heavily involved in drug abuse. Thus, referral provides an opportunity for an early interruption of criminal and drug abuse behaviors, as well as increasing retention in treatment, which is in turn associated with better treatment outcomes.

TREATMENT IN CORRECTIONAL INSTITUTIONS

A very high percentage of drug abusers spend time, often in significant amounts, in correctional settings. As Leukefeld and Tims (1992) have noted, " ... the criminal justice system is awash with drug users ... " (p. 279). As noted in Chapter 1, upwards of 40% of offenders admitted to federal prisons during 1988 had a moderate or severe drug problem, while 18% of male and 24% of female state prison inmates reported daily use of cocaine, heroin, PCP, LSD, or illicit methadone during the month before their offense (Bureau of Justice Statistics, 1992).

Inciardi, McBride, Platt, and Baxter (1993), reporting on the injection drug user population of some 26,000 persons sampled by the National AIDS Demonstration Research (NADR) projects, found that some 83% had been incarcerated at least once in their lives. Similarly, Chaiken (1989) found that some 62% of inmates of correctional systems reported having used drugs regularly prior to incarceration. A significant percentage of incarcerated drug users, approximately 20%, were opiate users prior to admission (Bureau of Justice Statistics, 1992).

Correctional settings often provide an unique opportunity to change drug use behaviors (Platt, Labate, and Wicks, 1977b). This is primarily due to enforced abstinence, a severely structured environment, and the opportunity to link highly desirable reinforcements to the achievement of milestones. Additionally, periods of incarceration frequently provide the only time free from addiction for many young addicts (Ball and Corty, 1988). Yet, despite the clear need for drug abuse treatment services in correctional settings, existing programs are neither readily available (e.g., Chaiken [1989] noted that only 11% of those using drugs regularly prior to incarceration were receiving drug abuse treatment while in prison), nor necessarily effective (Wexler, Falkin, and Lipton, 1990), particularly with respect to addressing the unique requirements of incarcerated drug users (Inciardi, Lockwood, and Quinlan, 1993). Thoughtful discussions of the problems and opportunities for drug treatment in prisons may be found in Falkin, Wexler, and Lipton (1990) and Inciardi, Lockwood, and Quinlan (1993). Recently, a promising correctional drug abuse treatment strategy has been developed and implemented on a pilot basis (i.e., Project REFORM; Wexler, Blackmore, and Lipton, 1991).

Joseph (1988) has provided a useful historical overview of the efforts to address opiate addiction within the criminal justice system. He noted that early programs of supervised probation (e.g., the New York Parole Program [Diskind and Klonsky, 1964a,b], the New York Riverside Hospital Program [Brill and Leiberman, 1969] and the Washington Heights Rehabilitation Center [Brill and Leiberman, 1969]) had failed to reduce recidivism, with heroin use following treatment averaging 80%. On the other hand, he noted, therapeutic community programs such as Stay'n Out and methadone maintenance treatment programs have had better outcomes.

Long an advocate of methadone maintenance treatment, Joseph (1988) noted that while not a panacea, this treatment, if correctly administered, can diminish a number of problems associated with addiction, including crime, unemployment, drug and alcohol abuse, high death rates, AIDS, and hepatitis. He concluded that

... addicted probationers who stay in methadone treatment have lower arrest rates and remain in treatment longer than convicted addicts who are supervised in special narcotics units without chemotherapy (p. 122).

Wish (1988) has provided a useful description and evaluation of methods for the identification of drug abusers within the criminal justice system. These include (a) offender self-reports; (b) criminal justice records; (c) urinalysis tests; and (d) radioimmunoassay of hair (RIAH). Wish (1988) noted that several methods are excluded from consideration for use because of specific difficulties: (a) blood tests, because of the problems associated with large-scale blood drawing and fear of AIDS; (b) breathalyzer tests, both because of alcohol not being an illicit drug and because it is not associated with high-rate criminal activity (Wish, Chedekel, Brady, and Cuadrado, 1986); and (c) physical and behavioral signs of drug use and intoxication because of their unreliability.

A recent report by the U.S. General Accounting Office (1993) has strongly recommended the use of hair analysis as a diagnostic measure for the presence of illicit drugs, although a number of threats to accurate measurement and interpretation of findings still exist (e.g., environmental contaminants and their removal, adhesion of the drug to various hair types, the effects of hair treatment on drug removal, and the relationship of drug dose to hair drug level). Mieczkowski (1992) after reviewing the advantages and disadvantages of hair analysis (versus urinalysis), as well as the controversies associated with the procedure, concluded that hair analysis is a useful tool in studying drug epidemiology. Magura and his associates found strong agreement among hair analysis, immunoassay urinalysis, and self-report, which they felt argued for convergent validity of all three drug use indicators (Magura, Freeman, Siddiqi, and Lipton, 1992). Further research is, however, needed focusing on the physiological basis of how substances of abuse are incorporated and retained in hair and large-scale baseline testing of various criminal justice populations.

The Effectiveness of Correctional Drug Abuse Treatment

Despite early pessimism about the effectiveness of correctional treatment (e.g., Lipton, Martinson, and Wilks, 1975; Martinson, 1974), there has been mounting evidence for the effectiveness of correctionally based treatment programs (e.g., Falkin, Wexler, and Lipton, 1990; Gendreau and Ross, 1987; Platt, Labate, and Wicks, 1977b; Ross and Gendreau, 1980). With respect to the content of effective correctional drug abuse treatment programs, Husband and Platt (1993), after reviewing evaluations of such programs, concluded that those which address the cognitive skills of offenders have had better outcomes. They also noted that a number of other writers in the correctional literature have described cognitive, cognitive-behavioral, thinking, skill-building, or problem-solving training as an element in successful prison treatment programs (e.g., Izzo and Ross, 1990; Gendreau and Ross, 1979, 1987; Ross and Fabiano, 1985; Wexler, Lipton, and Johnson, 1988). Husband and Platt (1993) concluded that cognitively based interventions for incarcerated substance abusers hold considerable promise. Two examples of current programs identified by Husband and Platt (1993) as effectively incorporating cognitive elements are "Stay'n Out" (Wexler, Falkin, and Lipton, 1990; see below) and "Time to Think" (Ross and Fabiano, 1985; Fabiano, Porporino, and Robinson, 1991), although the latter has yet to be specifically applied to the treatment of substance abusers.

Falkin, Wexler, and Lipton (1990) provided a list of the elements they saw as necessary for a successful prison drug treatment program: (a) a competent and committed staff; (b) adequate support, both administrative and material, by correctional authorities; (c) separation of the drug treatment population from the general institutional population; (d) incorporation into the program of self-help principles and ex-offender aid; (e) a comprehensive program of intensive therapy directed towards the entire lifestyle of the addict and not just substance abuse; and (f) continuity of care into the parole period, this being seen as an absolutely essential ingredient.

Therapeutic Communities

The IOM report listed three therapeutic community programs which incorporated the above elements and for which there are evaluations available. Two of these, the Stay'n Out and the California Civil Addict Program (CAP), focused on drug abuse outcomes and each employed controlled methodologies and collected data on the entire group of admissions to treatment during specified periods of time. The third program, Cornerstone, used subsequent arrests and reincarceration as outcome variables, but did not examine drug abuse outcomes. The Stay'n Out and Cornerstone programs are described below, while the California Civil Addict Program is described in Volume 1 (pp. 247–249; also see this Chapter, above).

Stay'n Out

This New York program for the treatment of incarcerated drug offenders, which has been identified by the IOM report (1990) as the most influential at the time of the report, is based upon the structure of Phoenix House, a well-known therapeutic community (see Volume 1, pp. 234–238), as applied to the correctional setting. Stay'n Out, which operates a four-unit, 146-bed prison unit for male inmates and a separate 40-bed program for female inmates, works closely with community-based therapeutic communities to extend treatment after discharge from the correctional setting. The evaluation of the Stay'n Out program (Wexler, Falkin, Lipton, 1990; Wexler, Falkin, Lipton, and Rosenbaum, 1992) involved a follow-up study of 682 clients from 1977 through 1984 who were followed for two to nine years after discharge from prison. Comparison groups consisted of clients receiving regular drug abuse counseling ($N = 576$); a quasi-therapeutic community, staff intensive, milieu therapy intervention ($N = 364$); and an untreated waiting list group seeking admission to Stay'n Out ($N = 197$).

The outcome evaluation found that the therapeutic community group was arrested significantly less often than the other groups, some 22% to 35% less often in the case of males, and 25% to 40% less often in the case of females. No substantive findings were obtained between the groups, however, on such variables as rate of reincarceration, rapidity of rearrest, and parole revocation, with one exception—more of the women who had been through Stay'n Out successfully completed their parole term.

Treatment outcomes were found to be a function of time in treatment. For males who stayed less than three months, 49.2% had favorable outcomes while for those who stayed 9 to 12 months, 77.3% had favorable outcomes. For females, favorable outcomes were present in 79% and 92% of cases respectively. Even for those who were rearrested or reincarcerated, more time in treatment was related to better outcomes (i.e., longer times until rearrest or reincarceration). Treatment completers (53% of admissions) also did better than noncompleters (72% not reincarcerated within three years versus 61%).

Cornerstone

This therapeutic community program for alcohol- and drug-dependent offenders, which is located on the grounds of the Oregon State Hospital in Salem, represents the only other correctional drug abuse program for which there is solid, large-scale evaluative evidence indicating effectiveness. In the first of two evaluative studies, program graduates had lower rates of both return to prison and criminal conviction than did each of two control groups (Field, 1985). In the second study, program graduates were compared with nongraduates with varying lengths of stay on outcome measures of recidivism during a three-year follow-up (Field, 1989). The findings were similar to those of the earlier study. Over half of the program graduates were not convicted of a subsequent crime, over three-quarters were not reincarcerated, and about a third were not rearrested. In contrast, the range of those who were not rearrested in the various control groups was from 8% to 21%; for those not convicted it was 11%-28%; and for those not incarcerated it was 15%-37%. In all cases, increased time in treatment was associated with more positive treatment outcomes.

Boot Camps

While not formally directed toward drug abusers, another form of prison-based treatment, also known as "shock incarceration," received a great deal of popular exposure when it was introduced in the 1980s. Originally developed by the State of Georgia as a way of reducing the costs and improving the efficiency of incarceration, it was intended for young offenders. Shock incarceration involves a relatively short period of incarceration (three to six months) spent in a facility organized similarly to either a military boot camp or the Outward Bound program. Emphasizing segregation from the general prison population, physical exercise, and a small-group organizational structure, some (but far from all) such programs incorporate drug treatment components. Findings by Parent (1989) as described in the IOM report (1990) question the effectiveness of shock incarceration in reducing recidivism, and suggest caution in viewing claims of effectiveness until further evaluative data are available. No data are available specifically concerning the impact of this intervention upon drug abuse.

Treatment while in a correctional setting represents an important opportunity for intervening in the drug abuse careers of offenders. Clearly more program development and evaluative research is called for regarding the efficacy of such interventions. The IOM report makes several important points concerning correctional treatment. First, entry into such programs can (and should be) a matter of negotiation or mutual consent, an essential element in the formulation of treatment entry contracts and treatment plans. Second, the primary characteristic a successful treatment program should have is responsiveness to individual client behaviors. Third, adequate material and administrative support from correctional and other authorities is required.

Though addicts are incarcerated numerous times during their addictive careers (Nurco, Ball, Shaffer, and Hanlon, 1985), there continues to be both a surprising lack of theory and research on traditional addiction treatment programs within correctional facilities as well as a lack of correctional drug abuse treatment programs themselves (Peters and May, 1992). Earlier studies of rehabilitation attempts in correctional settings demonstrated moderately positive effects (see Volume 1, pp. 250–255), but one is hard pressed to find reports of follow-up studies or refinements of previous programs in the drug abuse treatment literature.

Clearly, there is now experimental documentation for the effectiveness of correctional treatment, at least in the case of therapeutic communities. Given the low costs of such programs (Lipton, Falkin, and Wexler [1992] estimate the cost at from $200 to $4,000 annually per inmate), and the potentially high return to society in reduced crime and incarceration costs, their implementation seems clearly warranted. Certainly, Project REFORM (Wexler, Blackmore, and Lipton, 1991), which is directed at providing technical assistance to state departments of correction for implementation or enhancement of statewide comprehensive treatment strategies, is having an impact.

Lipton, Falkin, and Wexler (1992) noted that where correctional therapeutic community programs have failed, they have done so for administrative reasons (e.g., staffing, prison administration, overcrowding, budget cuts, and social conflict) rather than for problems inherent in the therapeutic community concept. Accordingly, they made the following suggestions for successful programming:

(a) adequate, well-trained, and well-supported staff; (b) support of the prison administration; (c) the availability of adequate living and therapeutic space apart from the general prison population; (d) adequate financial support, and some insulation from budget cuts, which tend to first target research and planning, followed by treatment programming; and (e) an institutional climate accepting of the therapeutic community concept. Inciardi, Martin, Lockwood, Hooper, and Wald (1992) have made similar suggestions, in addition also noting that (a) a combination of the professional and recovering addict models would be most effective in a correctional setting; (b) before beginning any prison-based therapeutic community, there should be complete agreement of the program staff, correctional officials, and parole authorities on procedures for acceptance, graduation, and movement to work release or parole; (c) new prison-based therapeutic communities should start small and add clientele only after the program is well established, thus allowing time for resolution of problems with correctional officials; (d) planning for postrelease care needs to be done, perhaps through purchasing bedspace in an existing therapeutic community or through funding a separate transitional facility; and (e) the need exists for mechanisms through which individuals could be recruited into drug counseling careers, including entry for ex-offender employment in correctional treatment.

TREATMENT IN LIEU OF OR FOLLOWING INCARCERATION

There has been a renewed interest in treatment in lieu of or following incarceration. This interest is due, in part, to worldwide concern over the role of intravenous drug use in the spread of AIDS (see Volume 3, Chapters 6 and 7), and to the continuing recognition that criminal justice efforts have been unable to effectively prevent the growth of drug addiction in the last two decades (Anglin, 1988a; Brown et al., 1987; Platt, Bühringer, Kaplan, Brown, and Taube, 1988). Because compulsory treatment is a complex issue that raises ethical, legal, and pragmatic concerns, there have been efforts to clarify and address these potential difficulties. One such effort was made by a group of German and American addiction specialists (Brown et al., 1987; Platt et al., 1988). As a result of a series of conferences, six general propositions regarding the existence and use of pressure (i.e., judicial, social, physical, emotional, and treatment/institutional forces) were identified (see Chapter 6). On the basis of these propositions, the group provided some additional recommendations. Among other things, they advised education and training of health and judicial system personnel regarding their complimentary functions, and the "goals, strategies and ethics of cooperative efforts" (Platt et al., 1988, p. 518). They also suggested that nonjudicial pressures should be emphasized, that "the least severe type and . . . quantity of pressure should be applied" (p. 518), and that the implementation of this pressure requires close monitoring to avoid misuse. Finally, the group recommended that research is necessary to understand the effectiveness of strategies with different populations and at different points in an addict's career.

Stitzer and McCaul (1987) provided a comprehensive theoretical analysis of the relationship between the criminal justice system and substance abuse. Using a behavioral framework, they noted that the legal system provides powerful contingencies (usually of an aversive nature) intended to decrease substance abuse, and consistent with a response-suppression model. Criminal intervention strategies include restricting the supply of drugs (i.e., making certain substances illegal), incarceration, community supervision, and compulsory treatment. Stitzer and McCaul (1987) observed that incarceration does not seem to have much impact on substance abuse. They suggested, however, that if participation in treatment or behaviorally designed aftercare plans could use incarceration as a direct and consistent consequence of relapse, its effectiveness as a negative reinforcer could increase participation in treatment by substance abusers, and thus increase the probability of abstinence behavior on the part of addict offenders. Inconsistent, and perhaps nonexistent, consequences for relapse in abusers who are paroled or on probation may be one reason for the ineffectiveness of current practices. The authors concluded that there is a need to utilize and investigate the effectiveness of a behavioral contingency management approach (i.e., the systematic application of rewards and punishments to provide incentives for therapeutically desired behaviors) in the imposition of legal sanctions and the use of compulsory treatment strategies.

Empirical work on the differential impact of legal pressure on individual addicts supports the conclusions and recommendations of participants in the German/American conference. For instance, in an effort to determine factors that discriminated between abstention and continued drug abuse, Goodkin and Wilson (1982) conducted a retrospective study of 52 opiate addicts who were completing parole or probation. Of the 18 variables they assessed, six were found to differentiate subjects who abstained from drug use from those who did not. Using these variables, the investigators developed a discriminant analysis function, correctly classifying 78.8% of their sample as abstinent or drug-involved. Drug-free subjects tended to be less dogmatic, have higher education and personality integration, fewer previous aggressive acts, fewer prior drug arrests, and to be somewhat older. The authors suggested that addict offenders on parole or probation be screened on the basis of the Dogmatism Scale, the Personality Integration subscale of the Tennessee Self-Concept scale, and relevant historical factors, and that those classified as likely to abstain should receive the majority of therapeutic efforts.

Other research indicates that legal pressures might be useful for some addicts, and superfluous for others. Anglin (1988b) summarized findings from a study of the California Civil Addict Program (CAP; see above, also Volume 1, pp. 247–249), a commitment program instituted in the mid-1960s permitting seven years of supervision following an initial short-term inpatient commitment. The overall results give fairly strong support to the utility of compulsory treatment, and suggest that long-term, close outpatient supervision is effective in reducing (though not necessarily eliminating) drug use and criminal involvement and increasing prosocial activities such as employment. In a separate analysis, however, Anglin (1988a) identified subgroups of addicts among which the effects of commitment on drug use and criminal activity differed. Those addicts who were older and less involved in criminal activities (i.e., addicts who were maturing out of addiction) did best, a fairly sizable group who became re-addicted and re-entered treatment did moderately well, and chronic street addicts fared the worst. An earlier study of the parole behavior of methadone maintenance patients (Anglin, McGlothlin, and Speckart, 1981) also found that parole supervision for addicts who were involved in methadone programs did not meaningfully increase success. Taken together, these studies imply that the impact of coercive pressure on drug addiction is not uniform.

In spite of increasingly refined knowledge about the effects of pressure on treatment participation and outcome, there are a number of pragmatic problems in forcing addicts into treatment. For example, treatment services are currently scarce even for addicts who voluntarily seek treatment (Stitzer and McCaul, 1987; Platt, Bühringer, Kaplan, Brown, and Taube, 1988a). Hence, unless more services are made available, urging higher utilization of compulsory treatment services may simply add to waiting lists and put pressure on programs to decrease the number of voluntary slots. In addition, coordination and management of previous compulsory treatment programs have proven to be highly problematic. As Winick (1988) and Inciardi (1988) have observed, the New York civil commitment system suffered from poorly trained judges and treatment staff, as well as from failure to appropriately assign addicts to particular programs according to their needs, to plan referral and follow-up systems, and to provide for regular, formal evaluations of the program. Maddux (1988a,b) also noted that compulsory treatment does not in itself provide assurance that addicts will necessarily participate in treatment, and he pointed out that there is little information available on the long-term impact of forced treatment after compulsory supervision ends. Thus, there are many difficulties that need to be overcome before new attempts to utilize legal pressures to force addicts into treatment are embraced.

RESEARCH AND EVALUATION IN
CORRECTIONAL SETTINGS

While a clearly defined treatment evaluation literature and set of principles for the evaluation of drug abuse treatment effectiveness exists (e.g., Sells, Demaree, Simpson, Joe, and Gorsuch, 1977; Tims, 1982; Wells, Hawkins, and Catalano,

1988a, b), correctional settings may still pose special problems for research concerned with the evaluation of drug abuse program effectiveness (Platt, Labate, and Wicks, 1977b). Fletcher and Tims (1992), using the theoretical schema provided by Campbell and Stanley (1963), addressed several methodological pitfalls which can be encountered in designing and conducting treatment evaluation research with correctional populations. Among the issues addressed are the following: (a) *threats to internal validity*, including history, maturation, testing and instrumentation, statistical regression, selection and selection-maturation interaction, and attrition; and (b) *threats to external validity*, including interaction of pretreatment data collection, interaction of selection biases and treatment, reactive effects of research arrangements and irrelevant responsiveness of measures, multiple treatment interference, and irrelevant treatment replicability. Noting that these same categories of threats to validity occur in community-based as well as criminal justice research, Fletcher and Tims (1992) discuss the "fundamentally unpleasant" nature of correctional settings and the restrictions imposed upon research by them and point out two important challenges for correction-based research: the influence of environmental and situational factors upon treatment implementation and outcome, and the process of transition to the community.

CONCLUSIONS

Leukefeld (1991) has suggested a number of opportunities provided by the criminal justice system for enhancing drug abuse treatment: (a) *early identification* of the large number of drug users, both adult and adolescent, passing through jails and lockups, through use of these natural entry points for early identification, information provision, and treatment referral; (b) *enhancement of behavioral contingencies* through the use of close supervision, together with the control over contingencies provided by the nature of the criminal justice system; (c) *capitalizing on referrals* to drug abuse treatment through establishment of a close working relationship between the criminal justice and drug treatment systems; (d) *use of compulsory treatment*, in the form of civil commitment, to reduce intravenous drug use; (e) *use of court referral* to increase time in drug abuse treatment; and (f) *disrupting the addiction life cycle* through effective case management programs that bridge the gap between the criminal justice and drug abuse treatment systems. Utilization of these points of opportunity would offer significant access to substance abusers, who are more likely to be in frequent contact with the criminal justice system than with any other institution of our society.

    Additionally, there are several specific conclusions that can be drawn on the basis of the research reviewed in this chapter:

- The findings of the California Civil Addict Program (CAP) demonstrated that reported heroin use and total criminality were reduced by approximately one-half in the treatment group versus the comparison group. While this difference between groups narrowed in subsequent years, it was, however, clear that recovery of a significant part of the CAP group was accelerated by the program's residential and community supervision components (McGlothlin et al., 1977b; Anglin and McGlothlin, 1984; Anglin, 1988a,c). The implication of these findings is that the most effective civil commitment approach is to place addicts on long-term parole (5 to 10 years) with close supervision and urine testing following short-term inpatient stabilization, thus allowing for close monitoring of drug use and related behaviors. If relapse to narcotics use or property crime is detected, a brief reincarceration (30–90 days, at most) is required for detoxification and return to supervised parole status.

• The experience gained from the New York Parole Project (NYPP), in contrast to that gained from the CAP program, in effect provided a case study in how *not* to implement a community-based program for paroled narcotics addicts. Poor staff training, biased case selection and assignment, poor outcome criteria (i.e., rearrest for a new crime rather than drug use), and inadequate and inconsistent record keeping all served to ensure failure. The implementation of the New York Narcotic Control Commission (NACC) on the basis of findings from the NYPP made its success unlikely, and this was then compromised further by the correctional orientation of the NACC program. The failure of these large-scale criminal justice programs represent a significant loss of opportunity which, given the present and likely future fiscal constraints of our society, are unlikely to be again attempted. They also suggest that large-scale bureaucratically oriented approaches to treatment are unlikely to be successful (Inciardi, 1988).

• Civil commitment approaches (e.g., NARA, CAP, and NACC) have had mixed success. Their relatively short tenure, however, represents a limited trial of their value that suggests the need to reemploy them on an appropriate scale, and with a full recognition of the strengths and weaknesses which emerged from their prior implementation. In particular, programs which have as their aim, early intervention in criminal and drug use careers would appear to hold the most promise of good outcomes.

• There is no question that, for the reasons noted by Leukefeld (see above), the criminal justice system provides a unique opportunity for intervention. Enforced abstinence, a severely structured environment, and the opportunity for maximal control over reinforcement contingencies all provide an excellent opportunity for ensuring appropriate behavioral change. Yet, correctional drug abuse treatment is neither readily available (e.g., Chaiken, 1989), nor always effective (e.g., Wexler et al., 1990). Programs such as "Stay'n Out" (Wexler et al., 1990) and "Time to Think" (Fabiano et al., 1991), as well as others which incorporate cognitive skill-building elements (e.g., Gendreau and Ross, 1987; Izzo and Ross, 1990) appear to hold promise for successful intervention. Similarly, the therapeutic community approach appears to be likely to be particularly appropriate for treatment in correctional settings (e.g., Inciardi, Martin, Lockwood, Hooper, and Wald, 1992; Lipton et al., 1992). Other recent approaches to correctional programming, such as boot camps, have not received sufficient evaluation to warrant a judgment as to their effectiveness.

- Finally, treatment in lieu of incarceration would appear to be of value with respect to increasing treatment effectiveness, particularly in the light of recent findings which suggest that incarceration by itself does not appear to have much effect upon substance abuse (see, e.g., Stitzer and McCaul, 1987).

PART FIVE

Conclusions
and
Recommendations

CHAPTER 8

Conclusions and Recommendations

In preparing this volume, the author's purpose has been to identify and describe recent developments pertaining to the theoretical and empirical basis underlying the initiation, course, and treatment of heroin use and addiction. Where appropriate, a fuller understanding of a particular issue has been undertaken through elaboration of earlier work, which, in retrospect, has assumed more importance as a result of current findings. What is clear to the author from this review is that current thinking with respect to understanding the basis of, and treatment of, addiction in general, and heroin addiction in particular, is very vigorous, and there is a continuing, even increasing, richness of theorizing and experimentation.

Additionally, policy issues have become a very active focus of discussion in the field, perhaps more so than at any time in the recent past. At one and the same time a repeal of prohibitions against drug use is being urged, while societal, political, and community resistance to treatment interventions (e.g., resistance against methadone maintenance treatment, the establishment of new treatment programs in certain locations, and increased funding for such programs) remains high.

Completing this survey has led the author to a number of conclusions, new opinions, and modifications of existing views. Conclusions relating to the state of the art have been placed at the end of each chapter; conclusions and opinions relating to broader issues follow under three headings: public policy issues; issues relating to treatment effectiveness; and issues related to research.

PUBLIC POLICY ISSUES

The Chronic, Endemic Nature of Heroin Addiction

Heroin addiction remains a chronic, endemic problem, which Americans continue to identify as a major issue facing this country (cited by Harrison, 1992). The high risks associated with becoming a heroin user, including the development of dependence, the risk of contracting life-threatening diseases (i.e., AIDS), and social estrangement, all continue to fail to deter the steady recruitment of initiates into heroin use and addiction. Clearly, heroin addiction is unlikely to disappear from our society without massive intervention, including a broad public health campaign to prevent drug use and the wide availability of treatment for those who become addicted.

Although the initial route by which illicit opiates are administered appears to have shifted somewhat away from injection drug use, there is every reason to expect that new initiates will eventually shift their mode of use to injecting as they pursue new "highs" made increasingly more difficult to obtain through other routes because of the development of tolerance. Additionally, injection drug use is economically more attractive for addicts (i.e., a cheaper means of obtaining a high), and is thus likely to be turned to at some point in an addict's drug use career.

In the United States, heroin addiction remains primarily, but not exclusively, a problem of minorities, and of males. African Americans account for more than one-half of all admissions to treatment programs, with the exception of methadone maintenance where they account for a smaller percentage. The costs of heroin addiction and its complications, both social and medical, are extensive. Injection drug users tend to have high rates of criminal involvement and are arrested frequently. They tend to die at a relatively higher rate compared to the general population, a fact that should not be surprising when the risky practices attendant to injection drug use are examined. The advent of the AIDS epidemic has even further increased the risks of an already risky avocation.

The Will to Address Drug Abuse Problems

Any attempt to deal seriously with the heroin problem in this country must address not only the issues associated with expanding treatment and attracting drug users into such treatment, but also the root causes of addiction. Our culture both promotes "gateway" drug use (i.e., alcohol and tobacco), and tolerates the continued existence of poverty, lack of education, and social alienation (fertile breeding grounds for drug abuse). These conditions, together with the lack of available routes of access to success, almost guarantee the continuation of drug abuse for future decades. Yet societal efforts at (and indeed interest in) ameliorating these conditions, appear to be diminishing.

Closely related to the will to address the drug problem in this country is the ability to identify and implement appropriate national *policy goals*. As noted by Jonas (1992), goals put in place by the White House over the past 10 years have ranged from a 15% reduction in drug use for the near term and a 55% reduction by the year 2000, to an eventual goal of no drug use at all. Such inconsistency in goals, between "drug free" and "drug-use reduction," as well as the failure to include two major drugs of abuse, alcohol and nicotine, on the list of drugs to be addressed, both fail to provide clearly defined national goals, and are inconsistent with human experience.

The Institute of Medicine Report (Gerstein and Harwood, 1990) has called for the universal availability of drug treatment which would be capable of attracting drug users. As the Report notes, such a step can only take place if the federal government commits to a major, near-term expansion of its financial obligation to treatment, as it did in the early 1970s. In so doing, it addresses two major considerations: (a) the effective coordination of drug treatment funds with other elements of the "war on drugs" including related social, health, rehabilitative, and correctional services; and (b) the integration, at both federal and state levels, of the drug treatment system with other health and welfare services.

Interdiction of the Narcotics Supply

Drug supply reduction has represented a mainstay of the national drug abuse control policy for some time. Drug arrests have doubled over the last decade, with a ten-fold increase in numbers of people sentenced for drug offences. Federal expenditures also reflect a punitive approach with 68% of all government expenditures on drug abuse in this country ($10.8 billion in 1991) spent for this purpose compared to only one-third spent on drug treatment and prevention. According to the U.S. Department of Justice, of the $42.78 per capita federal expenditure for drug control in 1991 (Bureau of Justice Statistics, 1992, p. 128) $28.24 was for law enforcement (66.0%), $6.91 for treatment (16.2%), $5.85 for drug abuse prevention (13.7%), and $1.78 for research and development (0.4%). Some 72% of the $1 billion appropriated to the Department of Defense for drug control is allotted to interdiction of illegal drugs. While it is essential that the drug supply should not increase to the point where prices fall sufficiently to encourage more (and younger) persons to begin or increase drug use, allocation of so much of these increasingly scarce funds to control or interdiction efforts, in contrast to treatment efforts, must be questioned. Given a modest average annual cost of $2,048 per individual in methadone maintenance treatment, $1,753 in detoxification, and $1,799 in drug-free treatment (Bureau of Justice Statistics, 1992, p. 133) a simple shift of some percentage of the drug abuse control budget of $10.8 billion would allow substantial expansion of treatment to accommodate more drug abusers. The resultant savings to society in lower criminal justice expenditures, effective prevention, reduction of the number of new cases of AIDS associated with injection drug use, and those benefits calculated in human terms, would represent a substantial financial return on investment.

The Changing Nature of Injection Drug Use

Patterns of drug use have shown an increasing rate of change during the past several decades. Heroin use was the primary drug abuse problem during the 1970s, yielding to polydrug abuse during the 1980s, with cocaine use showing a dramatic increase between 1975 and 1985. The explosive onset of the AIDS epidemic in the early and mid-1980s well illustrates the rapid changes that can take place in drug use patterns and the complications of drug abuse. The very difficulty of predicting, with any certainty, what future trends will be requires flexibility in planning, as well as built-in mechanisms allowing for rapid responses to new situations and conditions. This flexibility should pertain to research priorities and funding mechanisms, as well as to clinical treatment priorities and funding mechanisms.

The Financing of Drug Abuse Treatment at Appropriate Levels

Drug abuse treatment is *not* equally available for all those persons in need, largely because of the present manner of financing such treatment. As pointed out by Gerstein and Harwood, in their report of the findings of the Committee for the Substance Abuse Coverage Study (Institute of Medicine, 1990), there are two highly contrasting tiers of drug treatment—one for the poor under public sponsorship and one for those who can pay with private insurance or out-of-pocket funds (p. 200).

The Institute of Medicine report (Gerstein and Harwood, 1990) estimated that there were some 60 million Americans without specific coverage for drug treatment. Such a state of affairs in the wealthiest nation in the world, in which most of the advances in drug abuse treatment have been developed, is at the least inappropriate. Hopefully, improved and broadened insurance programs currently under discussion will address this problem.

The system available to the drug abuser of little or no means, usually those with serious criminal and other social deficits, is primarily comprised of outpatient care (63%) and residential programs (24%), with private not-for-profit programs receiving just under one-fifth of their revenues from client fees or private reimbursements. The private tier of programs used by the middle or other economic classes, on the other hand, is largely hospital-based and substantially more expensive, costing three times as much as the equivalent outpatient programs, and four times as much as public residential programs. Recent years have seen a shrinkage of public funds, with a resultant decrease in the experience levels of staff, and the extent and breadth of program services provided at the public-tier clinics. At the same time, the private-tier drug treatment system has greatly grown due to the expansion of existing nonmethadone drug and alcohol programs and the creation of new ones, as well as the opening of private methadone clinics to replace closed public-tier clinics (Institute of Medicine [Gerstein and Harwood], 1990). This shift in the configuration of the treatment system has resulted in increased regional differences in treatment capacity, particularly with respect to public-tier methadone and outpatient treatment slots.

The "Denormalization" of Drug Use

To a great extent, much drug use became "normalized" in our culture from the 1960s through the 1980s. This normalization occurred to the extent, notes Kleber (1992), that students who did not use drugs were perceived to be outsiders. LSD and marijuana were used by high school and college students, amphetamines by premedical students, and cocaine by professionals. Now, according to Kleber (1992), there is a "denormalizing" process underway requiring these very same individuals to change their attitudes toward drug use. The national drug strategy requires that the casual drug user, who is seen as the role model for drug-use initiates and as the vector spreading such use, be subject to accountability as stringent as that to which the heavy drug user is held. Efforts at drug abuse prevention require targeting of such locations as schools and the workplace, where children and adults, respectively, spend much of their time.

The Avoidance of Scapegoating

Kleber (1992) has correctly pointed out how easy it is to accept the images created by the media, particularly television and newspapers, and to lose sight of the fact that drug abuse is not just a minority problem in this country. Drug abuse, and particularly heroin use, has become not only an African American or Hispanic problem, but also a problem among almost all ethnic groups in this country (see also *USA Today*, December 20, 1989, p. A1). Acceptance of this false stereotype, combined with the stereotype of criminals as exclusively minority members, allows the majority of Americans to avoid facing the need for treatment and prevention efforts, and emphasizing instead the use of criminal sanctions and imprisonment.

Involvement of the Community in Fighting Drug Abuse

Also essential to dealing with drug abuse is the involvement of the community in grass root and cooperative efforts against drugs. Neighborhood watches, boarding up crack houses and shooting galleries, marches, and other grass root efforts have been used. Further, cooperation with law enforcement agencies in their efforts to reduce drug involvement is essential.

Communities, however, tend to support the punitive efforts against drugs mentioned above. Changes in these attitudes can only occur when members of the community come to accept the widespread nature of drug abuse in "our" neighborhood, and not just in "their's." The community must come to see that treatment of addicts can reduce the harm done to the entire community by drug seeking and using behavior. Furthermore, attention must be paid to the concern that community cooperation with the police can threaten the fabric of a community when family members involved in drugs are arrested.

The Need to View Heroin Addiction as a Medical Problem and Treatment in Community Settings

There should be no question that heroin addiction is a clearly definable illness whose treatment requires the application of a wide array of medical, psychosocial, and behavioral treatments. Despite the large psychosocial component present in heroin addiction, it is primarily a medically defined illness, no different from other medically defined illnesses having a large psychological component to their etiology. If addiction is a medically defined disease, then it should be treated as such. Yet, heroin addiction continues to be treated primarily in community settings, only some of which have a full-time physician present, and almost none of which have the on-site presence of specialists in internal medicine and other appropriate disciplines. We demedicalize the disease further by calling addicted individuals clients, rather than patients, somehow indicating that they are simply consumers of a service, rather than those suffering from a disease. We separate addicts from other patients by providing most community care in unattractive settings and by denying residents and medical students the opportunity to treat them routinely.

ISSUES RELATING TO TREATMENT EFFECTIVENESS

The Establishment of Closer Collaboration Among Elements of the System with Which Addicts Come in Contact

Increasing the number of public-tier treatment slots is needed if the majority of drug users without economic resources are to receive help. However, merely expanding treatment capacity to meet the needs of drug users cannot result in universal treatment entry unless collaboration among the system's elements with which addicts have contact occurs. Programs designed to begin treatment through the criminal justice system (for example, the California Civil Addict Program), facilitate recruitment at earlier stages of involvement with the judicial system (for example, at arraignment), and which include appropriate use of coercion for attendance can facilitate treatment initiation and retention. These methods may be even more effective than incarceration itself in reducing criminal behavior (Institute of Medicine [Gerstein and Harwood], 1990). Moreover, respected community members and organizations, such as schools and churches, can also act as liaisons with treatment facilities.

Addressing Personal Barriers to Treatment

Addicts typically enter treatment with few verbal, social, and vocational skills (although their veneer of verbosity superficially suggests the present of greater cognitive skills levels than is actually the case [Platt and Metzger, 1987a]). Thus, for treatment to be effective in addressing the drug abuse problem, it must also address the underlying client deficits that may have prevented (and will continue to prevent) integration into mainstream society.

Among the first barriers to be addressed, along with the readiness of a patient to enter treatment, is his or her ability to continue in treatment. Motivational strategies, such as those proposed by Miller and Rollnick (1991), may make the difference between retaining the patient in treatment and losing him or her to the street. Once there is some assurance that the patient will return to the treatment site, the building of appropriate skill repertoires should then take place. This skill building should have the following aims:

(a) The development of resistance to relapse to drug use, perhaps through the use of relapse prevention strategies such as those developed by Marlatt and his associates (e.g., Marlatt and Gordon, 1985);

(b) The establishment of the skills necessary to effectively compete with drug use responses, such as social skills (e.g., Platt and Hermalin, 1989) and employment skills (e.g., Hall et al., 1981a,b; Platt et al., 1993); and

(c) For those addicts entering treatment with existing vocational and inter-personal skills, stopping drug use, along with changes in lifestyle may have a dramatic effect on their functioning. For others, a full range of habilitative services is likely to be required (Kleber, 1989).

The resolution of problems in the immediate social environment is a neces-sary early priority in treatment. As pointed out elsewhere (Lamb, Iguchi, Hus-band, and Platt, 1993), significant others in the lives of patients " . . . can provide powerful contingencies and stimuli for either drug use or abstinence. Clearly, when these contingencies and stimuli promote abstinence the patient's likeli-hood of success is greater" (p. 153). In addition, the family of the addict requires attention. Stanton, Todd, and Associates (1982) have provided direction for re-search on this important issue, and findings by Szapocznik, Kurtines, Foote, Perez-Vidal, and Hervis (1986); Schippers, Romijn, and Hermans-van Wordragon (1990); and their associates have demonstrated the value of family therapy both for engaging and retaining the addict in treatment.

Patient-Treatment Matching

Evidence from research findings clearly indicates that the matching of patients to appropriate treatments is likely to result in improved outcomes. Yet, in prac-tice, such patient-treatment matching is rare. Aside from the scarcity of treat-ment slots, treatment programs often have insufficient resources, including too few highly trained staff to provide even basic services to patients, yet alone highly individualized treatment programs. A priority would appear to be the de-velopment of protocols for the rapid assessment of patient treatment needs and assignment to appropriate, truly individualized treatment plans.

Many of the above described differences among heroin users are important to the development of appropriate treatment programs and to a delineation of the impact of treatment on various subgroups within the drug-abusing population. Based upon the population that a particular treatment program aims to serve, different elements of treatment and training will be required. For example, ac-cess to traditional therapeutic community treatment programs may be increased by adding childcare components, or by allowing relatively greater scheduling flexibility to addict mothers. The provision of employment training to minority women addicts is likely to be a necessary factor in increasing the efficacy of treat-ment with this subgroup. The coordination of detoxification with an attempt to make early, high impact interventions as a means of increasing motivational level is also likely to influence the outcome of treatment.

Generally, then, the increasing delineation of distinct types of heroin addicts, as opposed to the maintenance of a generic concept of such individuals, has provided an impetus for the development of more closely targeted, and thus more effective, treatment strategies. It should be noted, however, that the interaction between an addict and a treatment program is a complex, multidetermined phenomenon. As De Leon (1990), Simpson, Joe, and Lehman (1986), and Simpson, Joe, Lehman, and Sells (1986) have observed, there are a number of subtle yet important factors regarding the interactions between patients and treatment modality that have not been adequately investigated. Furthermore, while initial addict characteristics might assist in the determination of appropriate treatment and in the prediction of some treatment outcomes, these characteristics are not very good predictors of long-term success. Therefore, in order to develop a more fine-grained analysis of treatment effects and a deeper understanding of treatment responses of various types of heroin abusers, it will be necessary to continue the search for addict and treatment related factors that influence treatment outcome.

Referrals and Case Management With Appropriate Follow-up

Surprisingly, given the multiple needs presented by injection drug abusers when they enter treatment, case management, a concept applied to other multiple problem, high need, high risk populations (e.g., the homeless, mentally ill, disabled, and those who receive welfare) has not been widely applied to this population. Case management is clearly called for in many cases, in that the creation of linkages with other agencies in order to meet the patient's needs will likely increase the probability of a good treatment outcome. In addition, the use of sanctioned networks to meet client needs can help with the resocialization of the addict into mainstream society. While recent attention has been focused on case management for drug users (Ashery, 1992a), relatively little empirical research exists on the topic.

Retention in Treatment

Research has consistently found that retention in treatment is essential to the successful cessation of drug use. For those who drop out, relapse to drug use occurs fairly quickly. Despite these findings, up to 66% of those in methadone maintenance and up to 96% of those in therapeutic communities drop out before the end of the first year in treatment (Pickens and Fletcher, 1991). Ball and Ross (1991) found that while some of the methadone dropouts were found to have completed detoxification, the overwhelming majority drop out voluntarily (32.4%) or because of clinic disciplinary procedures or noncompliance (20.0%).

Research has begun to determine those factors which lead to dropout, but more is needed and an examination of those variables which could remedy these factors must be conducted.

ISSUES RELATED TO RESEARCH

The Need for Adequate Research Funding, with Continuity of Such Funding

Major advances have been made in the treatment of heroin addiction over the past two decades. The introduction of methadone maintenance treatment has provided a means of both blocking the euphoric effects of heroin and holding individuals in treatment until other treatment elements, usually psychosocial in nature, can be brought to bear and have an impact on the individual. Research on methadone maintenance has continued to refine the treatment process, but it also has demonstrated that methadone by itself, except under extremely limited circumstances, is not sufficient for long-term rehabilitative gains. What we now know about methadone is invaluable and could only have come from carefully controlled (and therefore, expensive) clinical research.

The introduction of new pharmacological agents can only come from (equally expensive) work in the laboratory. Insights will, of course, continue to be the fountain of new innovations, but the careful experimental testing of such insights will require an investment in time and personnel that can only come from grant support. While this support is available, it has been, and appears to continue to be, highly subject to the vagaries of political winds, particularly during times when the American public views prohibition as the only response available to address the drug problem. At such times, research is seen as irrelevant to a control-oriented approach to the drug problem. These changes in funding levels can only result in sporadic research attempts slowing progress toward new interventions.

SPECIFIC RESEARCH ISSUES

An Understanding of the Social Substrates/Context of Drug Abuse

Addiction is a complex, multidetermined behavior arising within a social context. Addicts grow up in a community, they are "trained" by families and peers, they have individual tolerances for stress and pleasure, and they react to the economic and social pressures of the larger society. Prevention of drug use and reintegration of drug users requires a firm understanding of these and other aspects of this social substrate.

The Understanding of Personal "Dynamics" in the Development and Maintenance of Addiction

Psychodynamic views or interpretations of drug-abuse related behaviors often provide insightful and valid explanations of such behavior. From a heuristic viewpoint, however, they have failed to generate very much research, or more important, significant research findings guiding the development of effective interventions for heroin addicts. Behavioral and cognitive-behavioral views have been much more fruitful in contributing to new experiments and ultimately new findings that can be applied in the clinic.

Motivation, for example, represents a major element, if not the major element in the drug abuser's decision to enter treatment. Not only is the addict giving up his or her source of support in coping with the problems, both external (e.g., employment, criminal justice system involvement, etc.) and internal (e.g., boredom, depression, etc.) of everyday life, but also he or she is giving up membership in peer groups in which acceptance, no matter how superficial, is readily available. Kleber (1991), in discussing the role of motivation in entering and remaining in treatment, quite correctly noted that absence from the drug-using life will carry an element of longing for the more fondly remembered positive features of "the life," with a concomitant diminution of memories of the more painful aspects of that life. Motivation, however, is not the sole element explaining treatment success. Additional research designed to gain understanding of other behaviors, such as tolerance for uncertainty, can yield findings as helpful as those on motivation.

The Development of Interventions Appropriate to the Level of Involvement in the Drug Abuse Culture/Habit

The treatment needs of individuals who have recently entered the culture of drug use are very different from those individuals with long histories of addiction. Programs need to differentiate among those persons entering treatment and incorporate such information into their treatment planning. Does the length of time addicted affect the length of time one needs to remain on methadone? Is the family involvement with the "newer" addict stronger than for the more long-term addict? Have coping skills developed differently for someone who enters treatment soon after addiction? Answers to each of these questions would lead to quite different interventions.

Research into Social Habilitation

Reentry into society requires more than merely stopping an addict's use of heroin. Long-standing patterns of behavior, such as committing crime or not maintaining employment, must also be addressed. Prior research has indicated the particularly potent role of employment in the rehabilitation of the addict. The importance of social skills, including those needed for employment, must be further explored as well as the means necessary to develop or refine these skills.

Prevention of Drug Abuse

Gerstein and Harwood (1990), in a summary of the Institute of Medicine report on drug-treatment programs, noted that drug dependence and drug use (both of which are chronic, relapsing disorders involving drug-seeking behavior and its subjective aspect, drug craving) are difficult, but not impossible to extinguish once they have been established. Prevention would appear to be the most effective way to avoid having to face the difficult task of addressing these problems once they have been established.

The Need for a Comprehensive Theory of Addiction

Finally, a theory of addiction should drive research. There has been no shortage of theories of addiction. In fact, a full volume of the NIDA monograph series was devoted to presenting such theories (Lettieri, Sayers, and Pearson, 1980). It is surprising that the existence of so many competing theories has not led to more theory-derived studies in the field, perhaps reflecting the relatively narrow focus of many addiction theories. As commented upon elsewhere (see Volume 1, pp. 105–135 and 348–351), current theories fail to explain all addictive behavior or provide completely effective therapies. Conditioning theory, for example, while making valuable contributions to our understanding of how addiction, once begun, is maintained, and how it may be changed, fails either to satisfactorily explain the root causes of addiction, or to provide procedures effective in fully eliminating targeted behaviors. Likewise, social learning theories, while adequately explaining the cognitive behavior of the addict, particularly relapse, have not yet been fully and successfully applied as the primary basis for a drug abuse intervention. Metabolic deficiency theory still requires more support before it is fully accepted by the addiction community. But each of these theories still drives research, and each has made significant contributions to our understanding and treatment of addiction. There still exists, however, a need for a comprehensive theory of addiction incorporating both physiological and social science findings. The value of such a theory would be in its ability to direct research through the testing of hypotheses drawn directly from the theory, as well as to integrate presently existing findings.

Yet, we are far from having a single theory of addiction adequately explaining the many mechanisms and behaviors which require explanation. In this regard, Orford (1988) listed four aspects of addictive behavior that an adequate science of addiction should take into account:

1. *the need to account for a number of addictive behaviors,* which Orford elsewhere (1985) labeled "excessive appetites" for both substances and non-drug related activities. These would include compulsive disorders of eating and sexual behaviors as well as gambling;
2. *the extremely wide range of different functions that addictive drugs and behaviors can serve.* Although not mentioned by Orford, this point is well illustrated by the finding that heroin addicts, when asked for the reason they used the drug, often cited completely contradictory reasons (see, e.g., Berzins, Ross, English, and Haley, 1974);
3. *disincentives for addictive behaviors,* which may explain why people do not become addicted to some substances or activities while becoming addicted to others, why some individuals stop using a drug while others do not, or why some persons progress to addiction at different rates from others (pressures towards social conformity, both positive and negative, likely play a role here); and
4. *the need to see addictive behavior as a dynamic, rather than static, process* as reflected in the different pressures towards involvement in, or withdrawal from, drug use, and the differential importance of specific drug effects at different stages of a drug-using career.

Orford (1988) warns against reductionism in the study of the psychopharmacology of addiction, and thus the need to consider the principles and findings derived from social science. He noted the difficulty of adequately representing many of the salient variables associated with addiction, which themselves are under the control of other variables (e.g., gender, social status, ethnicity, culture, and historical epoch) under laboratory conditions. This warning is an apt one, for the temptation to try to explain (and then attempt to change) behavior on exclusively pharmacological, behavioral, or sociological levels without consideration of variables at other levels is one to which researchers in the addiction field are particularly susceptible. At different times in recent years there have been decided "tilts" toward either basic science or social science emphases in various aspects of addiction treatment research. Rarely, however, have developments in one or the other field, such as the availability of naltrexone as a long-acting opiate substitute or the use of contingency management in treatment, led to a solution to the problem of addiction.

Despite pessimism from some observers in the field (e.g., Kooyman, 1984), the foregoing review of treatment research literature forms the basis for continuing optimism regarding the ability to be moderately successful in stopping the cycle of addiction. Undoubtedly, heroin addiction treatment and research faces many challenges in the years to come. Foremost among these will be the generation of viable alternatives for addicts who remain beyond the reach of present treatment technologies. In the process of addressing these as well as other challenges, it will be important to understand the complex multidetermined nature of heroin addiction, and the need for multilevel intervention strategies.

Major National Studies of Drug Abuse Treatment Effectiveness

Several major national research evaluations of the effectiveness of drug abuse treatment exist, and have served as the basis for substantial treatment outcome findings. The first of these, the Drug Abuse Reporting Program (DARP) was originally established in 1969 as a national data base which collected treatment records on some 44,000 opiate addicts admitted to drug treatment agencies in the United States and Puerto Rico between 1969 and 1973. Treatment modalities included were methadone maintenance, therapeutic communities, outpatient drug-free programs, detoxification, and "intake-only" clients who had completed intake but who never returned for treatment. Spanning over 20 years, DARP provided an assessment of the early impact of the establishment of community-based drug abuse treatment. A number of studies were carried out on client characteristics and background, treatment delivery and characteristics, and in-treatment assessments of retention and effectiveness. Several overviews of the development of DARP exist (Simpson, 1990, 1993; Simpson and Sells, 1990). Prospective, multisite, and multimodality in scope, DARP continued until 1973 when the Client Oriented Data Acquisition Process (CODAP), which reported information on clients admitted to all federally funded drug abuse treatment agencies was implemented.

In 1985, the Treatment Outcome Prospective Study (TOPS), which was similar in many ways to DARP, was begun as a research adjunct to the CODAP system. The TOPS program accomplished a research purpose similar to DARP—a national evaluation of community-based treatment—by intensively studying a number of representative treatment programs (Allison, Hubbard, and Rachal, 1985). In contrast to the group targeted by the DARP study, those entering treatment in the late 1960s and early 1970s, TOPS studied a cohort which had entered treatment in 41 agencies from 1979 through 1981 (Hubbard, Marsden, Rachal, Harwood, Cavanaugh, and Ginzburg, 1989). In all, the TOPS program studied 11,750 admissions to 370 methadone, residential, outpatient drug-free programs in 10 cities for a follow-up period of up to five years. Many of the TOPS findings served to confirm the original DARP findings.

During the 1980s, however, a number of rapid changes in the nature of the drug abusing population, the close association between injection drug use and AIDS, the recognition of drug abuse treatment as an intervention for slowing the rate of spread of AIDS, changes in the funding of drug abuse treatment (i.e., more state, third-party, and self-pay), and increased diversity in drug abuse treatment providers (i.e., the existence of more private treatment programs) had all necessitated a new, broadly based national study of drug abuse treatment. To meet this need, the Drug Abuse Treatment Outcome Study (DATOS) was implemented, in 1991, following the DARP model as a major national longitudinal evaluation study of drug abuse treatment. Comparable to the past longitudinal studies, and collecting treatment program data very similar to those collected by TOPS, DATOS was expanded to include as measures of other factors in treatment effectiveness such variables as client psychiatric co-morbidity and the process and structure of treatment services. Designed as a longitudinal study based on a cohort of 20,000 adult clients in 50 drug treatment programs, approximately 4,500 patients were to be followed at 12 months posttreatment. The DATOS study assumed particular importance as the first large-scale evaluation of treatment outcome since block-grant funding had been implemented. DATOS-A, a drug abuse treatment outcome study for adolescents, was established in 1992, and is expected to have studied some 6,000 adolescents admitted to drug abuse treatment by 1994.

Finally, two national reviews of drug abuse treatment in the United States have recently been conducted. The first was conducted by the Institute of Medicine of the National Academy of Sciences (Gerstein and Harwood, 1990) with the aim of examining the status of drug abuse treatment in the United States and making recommendations for policy actions, while the second, an assessment of drug abuse treatment effectiveness, was carried out by the Office of Technology Assessment of the Congress of the United States (U.S. Congress, Office of Technology Assessment, September 1990).

Bibliography

Alemi, F., Stephens, R. C., and Butts, J. (1992). Case management: A telecommunication practice model. In R. S. Ashery (Ed.). *Progress and issues in case management* (NIDA Research Monograph No. 127). Rockville, MD: NIDA, pp. 261–273.

Allison, M., Hubbard, R. L., and Rachal, J. V. (1985). *Treatment process in methadone, residential, and outpatient drug free programs* (NIDA Treatment Research Monograph). Rockville, MD.

Almog, Y. J., Anglin, M. D., and Fisher, D. G. (1993). Alcohol and heroin use patterns of narcotic addicts: Gender and ethnic differences. *American Journal of Drug and Alcohol Abuse, 19(2)*, 219–238.

Altes, F. K. (1987). Address by His Excellency Mr. F. Korthals Altes, Minister of the Justice of Kingdom of the Netherlands, International Conference on Drug Abuse and Illicit Trafficking, Vienna, June 17–26 1987. Cited by van Vliet, 1990.

American Medical Association (1993). *Factors contributing to mental health care cost problem.* Chicago: American Medical Association.

Anglin, M. D. (1987). Review of *Alcohol, drug abuse and aggression. Journal of Studies on Alcohol, 48(3)*, 281–282.

Anglin, M. D. (1988a). Civil commitment as a model for reducing drug demand. *Perspectives in Drug Abuse.*

Anglin, M. D. (1988b). Etiological and epidemiological aspects of drug abuse. AIDS outreach pilot demonstration project for neighborhood outreach workers training seminar.

Anglin, M. D. (1988c). The efficacy of civil commitment in treating narcotic addiction. In C. G. Leukefeld and F. M. Tims (Eds.). *Compulsory treatment of drug abuse: Research and clinical practice* (NIDA Research Monograph No. 86). Rockville, MD: NIDA, pp. 8–34.

Anglin, M. D., and Hser, Y. I. (1990). Treatment of drug abuse. In M. Tonry and J. Q. Wilson, (Eds.). *Crime and justice: An annual review of research, Vol. 13.* Chicago: University of Chicago Press, pp. 393–460.

Anglin, M. D., and McGlothlin, W. H. (1984). Outcome of narcotic addict treatment in California. F. M. Tims and J. P. Ludford (Eds.). *Drug abuse treatment evaluation:*

Strategies, progress, and prospects (NIDA Research Monograph No. 51). Rockville, MD: NIDA, pp. 106–128.

Anglin, M. D., and Powers, K. I. (1991). Individual and joint effects of methadone maintenance and legal supervision on the behavior of narcotics addicts. *Journal of Applied Behavioral Science, 27*(4), 515–531.

Anglin, M. D., and Speckart, G. R. (1986). Narcotics use, property crime, and dealing: Structural dynamics across the addiction career. *Journal of Quantitative Criminology, 2*(4), 355–375.

Anglin, M. D., Brecht, M.- L., Woodward J. A., and Bonett, D. G. (1986). An empirical study of maturing out: Conditional factors. *International Journal of the Addictions, 21*(2), 233–246.

Anglin, M. D., Hser, Y. I., and McGlothin, W. A. (1987). Sex differences in addict careers. 2. Becoming addicted. *American Journal of Drug and Alcohol Abuse, 13*(1&2), 59–71.

Anglin, M. D., McGlothlin, W. H., and Speckart, G. (1981). The effect of parole on methadone patient behavior. *American Journal of Drug and Alcohol Abuse, 8*(2), 153–170.

Apsler, R., (1991). Evaluating the cost-effectiveness of drug abuse treatment services. In W. S. Cartwright, and J. M. Kaple, (Eds.). *Economic costs, cost-effectiveness, financing, and community-based drug treatment* (NIDA Research Monograph No. 113). Rockville, MD: NIDA, pp. 57–66.

Apsler, R., and Harding, W. M. (1991). Cost-effectiveness analysis of drug abuse treatment: Current status and recommendations for future research. In *Drug abuse services research series, No. 1: Background papers on drug abuse financing and services approach.* NIDA, DHHS Pub. No. (ADM) 91-17777. Washington, DC: Govt. Printing Office.

Arella, L., Deren, S., and Randell, J. (1988). *Issues affecting the utilization of vocational/educational services in drug treatment.* Unpublished manuscript.

Arella, L., Deren, S., Randell, J., and Brewington, V. (1986, August). *Vocational rehabilitation: Obstacles for treatment programs.* Paper presented at the 94th Annual Convention of the American Psychological Association, Washington, DC.

Ashery, R. S. (1979). Self-help groups serving drug abusers. In: B. S. Brown, (Ed.). *Addicts and aftercare: Community integration of the former drug user.* Beverly Hills: Sage, pp. 135–154.

Ashery, R. S. (Ed.) (1992). *Progress and issues in case management* (NIDA Research Monograph No. 127). Rockville, MD: NIDA.

Aston-Jones, G., Rajkowski, J., Kubiak, P., and Akaoka, H. (1992). Acute morphine induces oscillatory discharge of noradrenergic locus coeruleus neurons in the waking monkey. *Neuroscience Letter, 140,* 219–224.

Azrin, N. H., and Besalel, V. B. (1982). *Finding a job.* Berkeley, CA: Ten Speed Press.

Azrin, N. H., Flores, T., and Kaplan, S. J. (1975). Job-finding club: A group assisted program for obtaining employment. *Behaviour Research and Therapy, 13,* 17–27.

Babor, T. F., Cooney, N. L., and Lauerman, R. J. (1986). The drug dependence syndrome concept as an organizing principle in the explanation and prediction of relapse. In F. M. Tims and C. G. Leukefeld (Eds.). *Relapse and Recovery in Drug Abuse* (NIDA Research Monograph No. 72). Washington, DC: NIDA, pp. 20–35.

Ball, J. C., and Corty, E. (1988). Basic issues pertaining to the effectiveness of methadone maintenance treatment. In C. G. Leukefeld and F. M. Tims (Eds.). *Compulsory treatment of drug abuse: Research and clinical practice* (NIDA Research Monograph No. 86). Rockville, MD: NIDA, pp. 178–191.

Ball, J. C., and Ross, A. R. (1991). *The effectiveness of methadone maintenance treatment: Patients, programs, services, and outcome.* New York: Springer-Verlag.

Ball, J. C., Lange, W. R., Myers, C. P., and Friedman, S. R. (1988). Reducing the risk of AIDS through methadone maintenance treatment. *Journal of Health and Social Behavior, 29,* 214–226.

Ball, J. C., Rosen, L., Flueck, J. A., and Nurco, D. N. (1981). The criminality of heroin addicts: When addicted and when off opiates. In J. A. Inciardi (Ed.). *The Drugs-Crime Connection.* Beverly Hills, CA: Sage Publications, pp. 39–65.

Bass, U. F., and Woodward, J. A. (1978). Skill training and employment for ex-addicts in Washington, DC: A report on TREAT. National Institute on Drug Abuse Services Research Report. (DHHS Publication Number [ADM] 78-694). Washington, D.C.: Superintendent of Documents, U.S. Government Printing Office.

Bates, W., and Crowther, B. (1974). *Towards a typology of opiate users.* Cambridge, MA: Schenkman.

Bejerot, N. (1980). Addiction to pleasure: A biological and social-psychological theory of addiction. In D. J. Lettieri, M. Sayers, and H. W. Pearson (Eds.). *Theories on drug abuse: Selected contemporary perspectives* (NIDA Research Monograph No. 30) Washington, DC: NIDA, pp. 246–55.

Berzins, J. I., Ross, W. F., English, G. E., and Haley, J. V. (1974). Subgroups among opiate addicts-Typological investigation. *Journal of Abnormal Psychology, 83,* 65–73.

Biernacki, P. (1986). *Pathways from heroin addiction: Recovery without treatment.* Philadelphia, PA: Temple University Press.

Bihari, B. (1974). Alcoholism and methadone maintenance. *American Journal of Drug and Alcohol Abuse, 1(1),* 79–87.

Black, J. L., Dolan, M. P., Penk, W. E., Rabinowitz, R., and DeFord, H. A. (1987). The effect of increased cocaine use on drug treatment. *Addictive Behaviors, 12(3),* 289–292.

Bokos, P. J., Mejta, C. L., Mickenberg, J. H., and Monks, R. L. (1992). Case management: An alternative approach to working with intravenous drug users. In R. S. Ashery (Ed.). *Progress and issues in case management* (NIDA Research Monograph No. 127). Rockville, MD: NIDA, pp. 92–111.

Bonham, G. S., Hague, D. E., Abel, M. E., Cummings, P., and Deutsch, R. S. (1990). Louisville's Project Connect for the homeless alcohol and drug abuser. In M. Argeriou and D. McCarty (Eds.). *Treating alcoholism and drug abuse among the homeless: Nine community demonstration grants.* Binghamton, NY: Haworth Press, pp. 57–78.

Boyer, W. F., and Feighner, J. P. (1989). An overview of fluoxetine, a new serotonin-specific antidepressant. *Mount Sinai Journal of Medicine, 56(2),* 136–140.

Bozarth, M. A., and Wise, R. A. (1981). Heroin reward is dependent on a dopaminergic substrate. *Life Sciences, 29(18),* 1881–1886.

Brecher, E. M. (1972). *Licit and illicit drugs.* Boston: Little, Brown.

Brecht, M-L., Anglin, M. D., and Wang, J. C. (1993). Treatment effectiveness for legally co-erced versus voluntary methadone maintenance clients. *American Journal of Drug and Alcohol Abuse, 19*(1), 89–106.

Brewington, V., Arella, L., Deren, S., and Randell, J. (1987). Obstacles to the utilization of vocational services: An analysis of the literature. *International Journal of the Addictions, 22*(11), 1091–1118.

Brewington, V., Deren, S., Arella, L., and Randell, J. (1990). Obstacles to vocational rehabilitation: The clients' perspectives. *Journal of Applied Rehabilitation Counseling, 21*(2), 27–37.

Brill, L., and Jaffe, J. H. (1967). The relevancy of some newer American treatment approaches for England. *British Journal of Addiction, 62*, 375–386.

Brill, L., and Lieberman, L. (1969). *Authority and addiction.* Boston: Little, Brown.

Brooner, R. K., Bigelow, G. E., Strain, E., and Schmidt, C. W. (1990). Intravenous drug abusers with antisocial personality disorder: Increased HIV risk behavior. *Drug and Alcohol Dependence, 26*, 39–44.

Brooner, R. K., Greenfield, L., Schmidt, C. W., and Bigelow, G. E. (1993). Antisocial personality disorder and HIV infection among intravenous drug abusers. *American Journal of Psychiatry, 150(1)*, 53–58.

Brooner, R. K., Herbst, J. H., Schmidt, C. W., Bigelow, G. E., and Costa, P. T. (1993). Antisocial personality disorder among drug abusers: Relations to other personality diagnosis and the five-factor model of personality. *Journal of Nervous and Mental Disease, 181(5)*, 313–319.

Brown, B., Hickey, J., Chung, A., Craig, R., and Jaffe, J. (1988). Waiting for treatment: Behaviors of cocaine users on a waiting list. In L. S. Harris, (Ed.). *Problems of Drug Dependence, 1987.* (NIDA Research Monograph No. 90). Rockville, MD: NIDA, p. 351.

Brown, B. S. (1985). Federal drug abuse policy and minority group issues—Reflections of a participant-observer. *International Journal of the Addictions, 20*(1), 203–215.

Brown, B. S. (1988). Civil commitment-international issues. In C. G. Leukefeld and F. M. Tims (Eds.). *Compulsory treatment of drug abuse: Research and clinical practice* (NIDA Research Monograph No. 86). Rockville, MD: NIDA, pp. 192–208.

Brown, B. S. (1992). A report on the National AIDS Demonstration Research Program. In G. Bühringer and J. J. Platt (Eds.). *Drug addiction treatment research: German and American perspectives.* Malabar, FL: Krieger, pp. 519–528.

Brown, B. S., Bühringer, G., Kaplan, C. D., and Platt, J. J. (1987). German/American report on the effective use of pressure in the treatment of drug addiction. *Psychology of Addictive Behaviors, 1(1)*, 38–54.

Brown, S., and Yalom, I. D. (1977). International group therapy with alcoholics. *Journal of Studies on Alcohol, 38(3)*, 426–456.

Brunswick, A. F. (1985–86). Dealing with drugs: Heroin abuse as a social problem. *International Journal of the Addictions, 20*(11&12), 1773–1791.

Brunswick, A. F., and Messeri, P. A. (1986). Pathways to heroin abstinence: A longitudinal study of urban black youth. *Advances in Alcohol and Substance Abuse, 5*, 111–135.

Bucholz, K. K., and Robins, L. N. (1991). Recent epidemiologic alcohol research. In P. E. Nathan, J. W. Langebucher, W. Frankenstein, and B. S. McCrady (Eds.). *Annual Review of Addictions Research and Treatment*, 1, pp. 3–14.

Bühringer, G. (1992). The treatment of drug addicts: Fluctuations of health policy or a well-organized, adaptive learning system? In G. Bühringer and J. J. Platt (Eds.). *Drug addiction treatment research: German and American perspectives*. Malabar, FL: Krieger, pp. 67–90.

Bühringer, G., and Platt, J. J. (Eds.) (1992). *Drug addiction treatment research: German and American perspectives*. Malabar, FL: Krieger.

Bureau of Justice Statistics (1988). Survey of youth in custody, 1987. Washington, D.C.: U.S. Department of Justice.

Bureau of Justice Statistics (1992). *Drugs, crime, and the justice system*. Washington, DC: U.S. Department of Justice.

Bureau of Justice Statistics (1993). *National corrections reporting program, 1990*. Washington, DC: U.S. Department of Justice.

Bux, D. A., Iguchi, M. Y., Lidz, V., Baxter, R. C., and Platt, J. J. (1993). Participation in an outreach-based coupon distribution program for free methadone detoxification. *Hospital and Community Psychiatry, 44*(11), 1066–1072.

Cadoret, R. J., Cain, C. A., and Grove, W. M. (1980). Development of alcoholism in adoptees raised apart from alcoholic biologic relatives. *Archives of General Psychiatry, 37*, 561–563.

Cadoret, R. J., Troughton, E., O'Gorman, T. W., and Heywood, E. (1986). An adoption study of genetic and environmental factors in drug absue. *Archives of General Psychiatry, 43*, 1131–1136.

Campbell, D. T., and Stanley, J. C. (1963). *Experimental and quasi-experimental designs for research. Chicago: Rand McNally.*

Caplovitz, D. (1976). *The working addict*. New York: City University of New York.

Cartwright, W. S. and Kaple, J. M. (1991). Recommendations. In W. S. Cartwright, and J. M. Kaple (Eds.). *Economic costs, cost-effectiveness, financing, and community-based drug treatment* (NIDA Research Monograph No. 113). Rockville, MD: NIDA, pp. 205–211.

Casriel, C., Des Jarlais, D. C., Rodriguez, R., Friedman, S. R., Stepherson, B., and Khuri, E. (1990). Working with heroin sniffers: Clinical issues in preventing drug injection. *Journal of Substance Abuse Treatment, 7*, 1–10.

Casriel, C., Rockwell, R., and Stepherson, B. (1988). Heroin sniffers: Between two worlds. *Journal of Psychoactive Drugs, 20*(4), 437–440.

Catalano, R. F., and Hawkins, J. D. (1985). Project Skills: Preliminary results from a theoretically based aftercare experiment. In R. S. Ashery (Ed.). *Progress in the development of cost-effective treatment for drug abusers* (NIDA Research Monograph No. 58). Rockville, MD: NIDA, pp. 157–81.

Catalano, R. F., Howard, M. O., Hawkins, J. D., and Wells, E. A. (1988). Relapse in the addictions: Rates, determinants, and promising relapse prevention strategies. Surgeon General's Report, *The Health Consequences of Smoking: Nicotine Addiction*. Washington, DC.

Chaiken, J., and Chaiken, M. (1982). *Varieties of criminal behavior.* Santa Monica, CA: Rand Corporation.

Chaiken, M. R. (1986). Crime rates and substance abuse among types of offenders. In: B. D. Johnson and E. D. Wish (Eds.). *Crime rates among drug-abusing offenders: Final report to the National Institute of Justice.* New York: Narcotic and Drug Research, Inc.,

Chaiken, M. R. (1989). Prison programs for drug-involved offenders. Washington, D.C.: National Institute of Justice.

Chamberlain, R. and Rapp, C. A. (1991). A decade of case management: A methodological review of outcome research. *Community Mental Health Journal, 27*(3), 171-188.

Chaney, E. F., and Roszell, D. K. (1985). Coping in opiate addicts maintained on methadone. In S. Shiffman and T. A. Wells (Eds.). *Coping and substance use.* New York: Academic Press.

Chaney, E. F., Roszell, D. K., and Cummings, C. (1982). Relapse in opiate addicts: A behavioral analysis. *Addictive Behaviors, 7*, 291-297.

Charlesworth, E. A., and Dempsey, G. (1982). Trait anxiety reductions in a substance abuse population trained in stress management. *Journal of Clinical Psychology, 38(4)*, 764-768.

Chein, I., Gerard, D. L., Lee, R. S., and Rosenfeld, E. (1964). *The road to H*: Narcotics, delinquency and social policy. New York: Basic Books.

Childress, A. R., McLellan, A. T., and O'Brien, C. P. (1984). Measurement and extinction of conditioned withdrawal-like responses in opiate-dependent patients. In L. S. Harris (Ed.). *Problem of Drug Dependence, 1983* (NIDA Research Monograph No. 49). Rockville, MD: NIDA, pp. 212-219.

Childress, A. R., McLellan, A. T., and O'Brien, C. P. (1985). Assessment and extinction of conditioned withdrawal-like responses in an integrated treatment for opiate dependence. In L. S. Harris (Ed.). *Problems of Drug Dependence, 1984* (NIDA Research Monograph No. 55). Rockville, MD: NIDA, pp. 202-210.

Childress, A. R., McLellan, A. T., and O'Brien, C. P. (1986a). Conditioned responses in a methadone populations: A comparison of laboratory, clinic and natural settings. *Journal of Substance Abuse Treatment, 3*, 173-179.

Childress, A. R., McLellan, A. T., and O'Brien, C. P. (1986b). Nature and incidence of conditioned responses in a methadone population: A comparison of laboratory, clinic, and naturalistic settings. In L. S. Harris (Ed.). *Problems of drug dependence* (NIDA Research Monograph No. 67). Rockville, Maryland: NIDA, pp. 366-372.

Childress, A. R., McLellan, A. T., Ehrman, R., and O'Brien, C. P. (1988). Classically conditioned responses in opioid and cocaine dependence: A role in relapse? In B. A. Ray (Ed.). *Learning factors in substance abuse* (NIDA Research Monograph No. 84). Washington, DC: NIDA, pp. 25-43.

Childress, A. R., McLellan, A. T., Ehrman, R. N., and O'Brien, C. P. (1987). Extinction of conditioned responses in abstinent cocaine or opioid users. In L. S. Harris, (Ed.). *Problems of Drug Dependence, 1986* (NIDA Research Monograph No. 76). Rockville, MD: NIDA, pp. 189-195.

Childress, A. R., McLellan, A. T., Natale, M., and O'Brien, C. P. (1987). Mood states can elicit conditioned withdrawal and craving in opiate abuse patients. In L. S. Harris, (Ed.). *Problems of Drug Dependence 1986* (NIDA Research Monograph No. 76). Rockville, MD: NIDA, pp. 137–144.

Clark, D. C., vonAmmon Cavanaugh, S., and Gibbons, R. D. (1983). The core symptoms of depression in medical and psychiatric patients. *Journal of Nervous and Mental Disease, 171*(12), 705–713.

Clayton, R. R. and Tuchfield, B. S. (1982). The drug-crime debate: Obstacles understanding the relationship. *Journal of Drug Issues, 12*, 153–166.

CODAAP (Coordinating Office on Drug and Alcohol Abuse Programs). (1985). *Uniform data collection system annual.* City of Philadelphia: Department of Health.

Coggans, N., and Davies, J. B. (1988). Explanations for heroin use. *Journal of Drug Issues, 18(3),* 457–465.

Coleman, J. S. (1958). Relational analysis: The study of social organizations with survey methods. *Human Organization, 17*, 28–36.

Collins, J. J., and Allison, M. (1983). Legal coercion and retention in drug abuse treatment. *Hospital and Community Psychiatry, 34*, 1145–49.

Collins, J. J., Hubbard, R. L., and Allison, M. (1985). Expensive drug use and illegal income: A test of explanatory hypotheses. *Criminology, 23*, 743–764.

Collins, J. J., Hubbard, R. L., Rachel, J. V., and Cavanaugh, E. (1988). Effects of legal coercion on drug abuse treatment. In M. D. Anglin (Ed.). *Compulsory treatment of opiate dependence.* New York: Haworth.

Comfort, M., Shipley, T. E., White, J., Griffith, M. E., and Shandler, I. W. (1990). Family treatment for homeless alcohol/drug-addicted women and their preschool children. In M. Argeriou and D. McCarty (Eds.). *Treating alcoholism and drug abuse among the homeless: Nine community demonstration grants.* Binghamton, NY: Haworth Press, pp. 129–147.

Condelli, W. S., and De Leon, G. (1993). Fixed and dynamic predictors of client retention in therapeutic communities. *Journal of Substance Abuse Treatment, 10*, 11–16.

Condelli, W. S., and Dunteman, G. H. (1993). Exposure to methadone programs and heroin use. *American Journal of Drug and Alcohol Abuse, 19*(1), 65–78.

Cook, L. F., and Weinman, B. A., et al. (1988). Treatment alternatives to street crime. In C. G. Leukefeld and F. M. Tims (Eds.). *Compulsory treatment of drug abuse: Research and clinical practice* (Research Monograph No. 86). Rockville, MD: NIDA, pp. 99–105.

Courtwright, D. T. (1993). Should we legalize drugs? History answers. No. *American Heritage,* (Feb-Mar.), 41, 43, 50–56.

Cox, W. M., and Klinger, E. (1988). A motivational model of alcohol use. *Journal of Abnormal Psychology, 97*(2), 168–180.

Craig, R. J. (1982). Personality characteristics of heroin addicts: Review of empirical research 1976-1979. *International Journal of the Addictions, 17*(2), 227–248.

Craig, R. J. (1985a). Reducing the treatment drop out rate in drug abuse programs. *Journal of Substance Abuse Treatment, 2*, 209–219.

Craig, R. J. (1985b). Multimodal treatment package for substance abuse treatment programs. *Professional Psychology: Research and Practice, 16*(2), 271–285.

Crawford, G. A., Washington, M. C., and Senay, E. C. (1983). Careers with heroin. *International Journal of the Addictions, 18(5)*, 701–715.

Croughan, J. L. (1985). The contributions of family studies to understanding drug abuse. In L. N. Robins (Ed.). *Studying drug abuse.* New Brunswick, NJ: Rutgers University Press, pp.

Csikszentmihalyi, M., and Larson, R. (1987). Validity and reliability of Experience-Sampling Method. *Journal of Nervous and Mental Diseases, 175(9)*, 526–536.

D'Aunno, T., and Vaughn, T. E. (1992). Variation in methadone treatment practices: Results from a national study. *Journal of the American Medical Association, 267*(2), 253–258.

Dafters, R. and Anderson, G. (1982). Conditioned tolerance to the tachycardia effect of ethanol in humans. Psychopharmacology, 78(4), 365–367.

Darke, S., Wodak, A., Hall, W., Heather, N., and Ward, J. (1992). Prevalence and predictors of psychopathology among opioid users. *British Journal of Addiction, 87(5)*, 771–776.

De Leon, G. (1986). Therapeutic community research: Overview and implications. In G. De Leon and J. T. Ziegenfuss (Eds.). *Therapeutic Communities for Addictions.* Springfield, Il: Charles C. Thomas, pp. 85–95.

De Leon, G. (1990). Effectiveness of therapeutic communities. In J. J. Platt, C. D. Kaplan, and P. J. McKim (Eds.). *The effectiveness of drug abuse treatment: Dutch and American perspectives.* Malabar, FL: Krieger, pp. 113–126.

De Leon, G. (1991). Retention in drug-free therapeutic communities. In R. W. Pickens, C. G. Leukefeld, and C. R. Schuster (Eds.). *Improving drug abuse treatment* (NIDA Research Monograph No. 106). Rockville, MD: NIDA, pp. 218–244.

De Leon, G., and Jainchill, N. (1986). Circumstances, motivation, readiness, and suitability as correlates of treatment tenure. *Journal of Psychoactive Drugs, 18(3)*, 203–208.

Dembo, R., Washburn, M., Wish, E. D., Yeung, H., Getreu, A., Berry, E., and Blount, W. R. (1987). Heavy marijuana use and crime among youths entering a juvenile detention center. *Journal of Psychoactive Drugs, 19*(1), 47–56.

Denis, A., Küfner, H. Roch, I., and Böhmer, M. (1992). Factors influencing dropout from drug abuse treatment programs. In G. Bühringer and J. J. Platt (Eds.). *Drug addiction treatment research: German and American perspectives.* Malabar, FL: Krieger, pp. 241–251.

Dennis, D. L., Buckner, J. C., Lipton, F. R., and Levine, I. S. (1991). A decade of research and services for homeless mentally ill persons: Where do we stand? *American Psychologist, 46(11)*, 1129–1138.

Dennis, M. L., Karuntzos, G. T., and Rachal, J. V. (1992). Accessing additional community resources through case management to meet the needs of methadone clients. In R. S. Ashery (Ed.). *Progress and issues in case management* (NIDA Research Monograph No. 127). Rockville, MD: NIDA, pp. 54–78.

Department of Health and Human Services (1991). *Drug abuse and drug abuse treatment.* Rockville, MD: Department of Health and Human Services.

Departmental Committee on Morphine and Heroin Addiction (1926). *Report.* London: HMSO.

Deren, S., and Randell, J. (1988). *The results of the Venus Project: Increasing programs utilization of vocational services* (Treatment issues report #68). New York: New York State Division of Substance Abuse Services.

Desmond, D. P., and Maddux, J. F. (1984). Mexican-American heroin addicts. *American Journal of Drug and Alcohol Abuse, 10(3),* 317–346.

deVries, M. (Ed.) (1992). *The experience of psychopathology: Investigating mental disorders in their natural settings.* Cambridge: Cambridge University Press.

deVries, M. W., Kaplan. C., Dijkman-Caes. C., and Blanche, P. (1990). The experience of drug craving in daily life. In J. J. Platt, C. D. Kaplan, and P. J. McKim (Eds.). *The effectiveness of drug abuse treatment: Dutch and American Perspectives.* Malabar, FL: Krieger, pp. 127–143.

Dickinson, K., and Maynard, E. S. (1981). The impact of supported work on ex-addicts. *Financial report on the supported work evaluation,* Vol. 4, New York: Manpower Demonstration Research Corporation.

Dinwiddie, S. H., Reich, T., and Cloninger, C. R. (1992a). Patterns of lifetime drug use among intravenous drug users. *Journal of Substance Abuse, 4,* 1–11.

Dinwiddie, S. H., Reich, T., and Cloninger, C. R. (1992b). Lifetime complications of drug use in intravenous drug users. *Journal of Substance Abuse, 4,* 13–18.

Dinwiddie, S. H., Reich, T., and Cloninger, C. R. (1992c). Prediction of intravenous drug use. *Comprehensive Psychiatry, 33(3),* 173–179.

Diskind, M. H. (1960). New horizons in the treatment of narcotic addiction. *Federal Probation, 24,* 56–63.

Diskind, M. H., and Klonsky, G. (1964a). A second look at the New York State parole drug experiment. *Federal Probation, 28,* 34–41.

Diskind, M. H., and Klonsky, G. (1964b). *Recent developments in the treatment of paroled offenders addicted to narcotic drugs—Parts I and II.* New York: State Division of Parole.

Dobson, I., and Ward, P. (1984). *Drugs and crime:* Sydney. Bureau of Crime Statistics and Research.

Dolan, M. P., Black, J. L., DeFord, H. A., Skinner, J. R., and Robinowitz, R. (1987). Characteristics of drug abusers that discriminate needle-sharers. *Public Health Reports, 102,* 395–398.

Dole, V. P., and Nyswander, M. E. (1967). Rehabilitation of the street addict. *Archives of Environmental Health, 14*(3), 477–480.

Double, W. G., and Koeningsberg, L. (1977). Private employment and the ex-drug abuser: A practical approach. *Journal of Psychedelic Drugs, 9*(1), 51–58.

Drake, R. E., and Vaillant, G. E. (1988). Predicting alcoholism and personality disorder in a 33-year longitudinal study of children of alcoholics. *British Journal of Addiction, 83,* 799–807.

Drake, R. E., Osher, F. C., and Wallach, M. A. (1991). Homelessness and dual diagnosis. *American Psychologist, 46(11)*, 1149–1158.

Edwards, G., Arif, A., and Hodgson, R. (1981). Nomenclature and classification of drugs- and alcohol-related problems: A WHO Memorandum. *Bulletin of the World Health Organization, 59*(2), 225–242.

Egg, R. (1992). Criminal law and the treatment of drug addicts. In G. Bühringer and J. J. Platt (Eds.). *Drug addiction treatment research: German and American perspectives.* Malaber, FL: Krieger, pp. 433–448.

Eisenhandler, J., and Drucker, E. (1993). Opiate dependency among the subscribers of a New York area private insurance plan. *Journal of the American Medical Association, 269(22)*, 2890–2891.

Ellgring, H., and Vollmer, H. C. (1992). Changes of personality and depression during treatment of drug addicts. In G. Bühringer and J. J. Platt (Eds.). *Drug addiction treatment research: German and American perspectives.* Malabar, FL: Krieger, pp. 197–209.

Ellinwood, E. H., Smith, W. G., and Vaillant, G. E. (1966). Narcotic addiction in males and females: A comparison. *International Journal of the Addictions, 1(2)*, 33–45.

Emrick, C. D. (1987). Alcoholics Anonymous: Affiliation processes and effectiveness as treatment. *Alcoholism, 11(5)*, 416–423.

Emshoff, J. G. (in press). A preventive intervention with children of alcoholics. In R. P. Lorion (Ed.). *Protecting the children: Strategies for optimizing emotional and behavioral development.* New York: Haworth Press.

Evans, M. E., and Dollard, N. (1992). Intensive case management for youth with serious emotional disturbance and chemical abuse. In R. S. Ashery (Ed.). *Progress and issues in case management* (NIDA Research Monograph No. 127). Rockville, MD: NIDA, pp. 289–315.

Fabiano, E. A., Porporino, F. J., and Robinson, D. (1991). Canada's cognitive skills program corrects offenders' faulty thinking. *Corrections Today, 53*, 102–108.

Falck, R. S., Siegal, H. A., and Carlson, R. G. (1992). Case management to enhance AIDS risk reduction for injection drug users and crack cocaine users: Practical and philosophical considerations. In R. S. Ashery (Ed.). *Progress and issues in case management* (NIDA Research Monograph No. 127). Rockville, MD: NIDA, pp. 167–180.

Falkin, G. P., Wexler, H. K., and Lipton, D. S. (1990). Drug treatment in state prisons. In D. R. Gerstein and H. J. Harwood (Eds.). *Treating drug problems* (Vol. 2), Washington, DC: National Academy Press, pp. 89–131.

Faupel, C. E. (1986). Heroin use, street crime, and the "main hustle": Implications for the validity of official crime data. *Deviant Behavior, 7*, 31–45.

Faupel, C. E. (1987). Heroin use and criminal careers. *Qualitative Sociology, 10(2)*, 115–131.

Faupel, C. E. (1988). Heroin use, crime and employment status. *Journal of Drug Issues, 18(3)*, 467–479.

Faupel, C. E., and Klockars, C. B. (1987). Drugs-crime connections: Elaborations from the life histories of hard-core heroin addicts. *Social Problems, 34*(1), 54–68.

Ferguson, J. M. (1986). Fluoxetine-induced weight loss in overweight, nondepressed subjects. *American Journal of Psychiatry, 143*, 1496.

Field, G. (1985). The Cornerstone program: A client outcome study. *Federal Probation, 49*, 50–55.

Field, G. (1989). The effects of intensive treatment on reducing the criminal recidivism of addicted offenders. *Federal Probation, 63*, 51–56.

Finnegan, L. P., Kaltenbach, K., Ehrlich, S., and Regan, D. O. (1990). Beyond adolescent drug use and pregnancy: Life history data on addicted mothers in treatment. In J. J. Platt, C. D. Kaplan, and P. J. McKim (Eds.). *The effectiveness of drug abuse treatment: Dutch and American perspectives.* Malabar, FL: Krieger, pp. 177–197.

Finney, J. W., and Moos, R. H. (1986). Matching patients with treatments: Conceptual and methodological issues. *Journal of Studies on Alcohol, 47*(2), 122–134.

Fischer, P. J. (1989). Estimating the prevalence of alcohol, drug, and mental health problems in the contemporary homeless population: a review of the literature. *Contemporary Drug Problems, 16*, 333–390.

Fischer, P. J., and Breakey, W. R. (1991). The epidemiology of alcohol, drug, and mental disorders among homeless persons. *American Psychologist, 46*(11), 1115–1128.

Flaherty, E. W., Kotranski, L., and Fox, E. (1984). Frequency of heroin use and drug users' lifestyle. *American Journal of Drug and Alcohol Abuse, 10*(2), 285–314.

Fletcher, B. W., and Tims, F. M. (1992). Methodological issues: Drug abuse treatment research in prisons and jails. In C. G. Leukefeld and F. M. Tims (Eds.). *Drug Abuse Treatment in Prisons and Jails* (NIDA Research Monograph No. 118). Rockville, MD: NIDA, pp. 246–260.

Frederick, C. J. (1980). Drug abuse as learned behavior. In D. J. Lettieri, M. Sayers, and H. W. Pearson (Eds.). *Theories on drug abuse: Selected contemporary perspectives* (NIDA Research Monograph No. 30). Rockville, MD: NIDA, pp. 191–194.

Friedman, L. N. (1978). *The Wildcat experiment: An early test of supported work in drug abuse rehabilitation* (NIDA Services Research Monograph). Rockville, MD: NIDA.

Galanter, M., Castaneda, R., and Ferman, J. (1988). Substance abuse among general psychiatric patients: Place of presentation, diagnosis, and treatment. *American Journal of Drug and Alcohol Abuse, 14*(2), 211–235.

GAO [General Accounting Office] (1993). *Drug Use Measurement: Strengths, limitations, and recommendations for improvement.* Washington, D.C.: U.S. General Accounting Office.

Geerlings, P., van Limbeek, J., Wouters, L., de Leeuw, M., van Iperen, H. J., Bouman Stichting, H. K., d'Hont, F. A., Edelbroek, W., Rooyen, T.v., and Goris, A. (1990). Psychopathology and drug abuse. In J. J. Platt, C. D. Kaplan, and P. J. McKim (Eds.). *The effectiveness of drug abuse treatment: Dutch and American Perspectives.* Malabar, FL: Krieger, pp. 147–159.

Gendreau, P., and Ross, R. R. (1979). Effective correctional treatment: Bibliography for cynics. *Crime and Delinquency, 25*(4), 463–489.

Gendreau, P., and Ross, R. R. (1987). Revivification of rehabilitation: Evidence from the 1980's. *Justice Quarterly, 4*, 349–408.

General Accounting Office. (1990a). *Methadone maintenance: Some treatment programs are not effective; greater federal oversight needed* (GAO/HRD-90-104). Washington, DC: U.S. General Accounting Office.

Gerstein, D. R., and Harwood, H. J. (Eds.) (Institute of Medicine) (1990). *Treating drug problems Vol. 1. A study of the evaluation, effectiveness, and financing of public and private drug treatment systems.* Washington, DC: National Academy Press.

Gerstein, D. R., and Lewin, L. S. (1990). Treating drug problems. *New England Journal of Medicine, 323*(12), 844–848.

Gerstley, L., McLellan, A. T., Alterman, A. I., Woody, G. E., Luborsky, L., and Prout, M. (1989). Ability to form an alliance with the therapist: A possible marker of prognosis for patients with antisocial personality disorder. *American Journal of Psychiatry, 146*(4), 508–512.

Gerstley, L. J., Alterman, A. I., McLellan, A. T., and Woody, G. E. (1990). Antisocial personality disorder in patients with substance abuse disorders: A problematic diagnosis? *American Journal of Psychiatry, 147*(2), 173–178.

Ghodse, A. H., and Kaplan, C. (1988). Anglo-Dutch responses to drug problems (editorial). *Journal of the Royal Society of Medicine, 81(9)*, 497–498.

Glynn, T. J., Boyd, G. M., and Gruman, J. C. (1990). Essential elements of self-help/minimal intervention strategies for smoking cessation. *Health Education Quarterly, 17*(3), 329–345.

Gold, M. S., Dackis, C. A., and Washton, A. M. (1984). The sequential use of clondine and naltrexone in the treatment of opiate addicts. *Advances in Alcohol and Substance Abuse, 3*(3), 19–39.

Goldstein, A., and Kalant, H. (1990). Drug policy: Striking the right balance. *Science, 249*, 1513–1521.

Goodkin, K., and Wilson, K. E. (1982). Amenability to counseling of opiate addicts on probation or parole. *International Journal of the Addictions, 17(6)*, 1047–1053.

Goodman, L. A. (1961). Snowball sampling. *Annals of Mathematical Statistics, 32*, 148–170.

Goodwin, D. W. (1980). The bad-habit theory of drug abuse. In D. J. Lettieri, M. Sayers, and H. W. Pearson (Eds.). *Theories on drug abuse: Selected contemporary perspectives* (NIDA Research Monograph No. 30). Washington, DC: NIDA, pp. 12–17.

Goodwin, D. W. (1985). Alcoholism and genetics: The sins of the fathers. *Archives of General Psychiatry, 42*, 171–174.

Gorman, D. M., and Brown, G. W. (1992). Recent developments in life-event research and their relevance for the study of addictions. *British Journal of Addiction, 87(6)*, 837–849.

Gossop, M. (1988). Clonidine and the treatment of the opiate withdrawal syndrome. *Drug and Alcohol Abuse, 21(3)*, 253–259.

Gossop, M., Green, L., Phillips, G., and Bradley, B. (1987). What happens to opiate addicts immediately after treatment: A prospective follow up study. *British Medical Journal, 294*, 1377–1380.

Gossop, M., Griffiths, P., Powis, B., and Strang, J. (1992). Severity of dependence and route of administration of heroin, cocaine and amphetamines. *British Journal of Addiction, 87(11)*, 1527-1536.

Graeven, D. B., and Graeven, K. A. (1983). Treated and untreated addicts: Factors associated with participation in treatment and cessation of heroin use. *Journal of Drug Issues, 2*, 287-218.

Greaves, G. B. (1980). An existential theory of drug dependence. In D. J. Lettieri, M. Sayers, and H. W. Pearson (Eds.). *Theories on drug abuse: Selected contemporary perspectives* (NIDA Research Monograph No. 30). Washington, DC: NIDA, pp. 24-28.

Green, J., Jaffe, J. H., Carlisi, J. A., and Zaks, A. (1978). Alcohol use in the opiate use cycle of the heroin addict. *International Journal of the Addictions, 13*(7), 1021-1033.

Greenfield, S. F., Weiss, R. D., and Griffin, M. L. (1992). Patients who use drugs during inpatient substance abuse treatment. *American Journal of Psychiatry, 149(2)*, 235-239.

Grey, C., Osborn, E., and Reznikoff, M. (1986). Psychosocial factors in outcome in two opiate addiction treatments. *Journal of Clinical Psychology, 42*(1), 185-189.

Gurling, H. M., Oppenheimer, B. E., and Murray, R. M. (1984). Depression, criminality and psychopathology associated with alcoholism: Evidence from a twin study. *Acta Geneticae Medicae Gemellologiae, 33*(2), 333-339.

Hall, S. M., Loeb, P., Norton, J., and Yang, R. (1977). Improving vocational placement in drug treatment clients: A pilot study. *Addictive Behaviors, 2*, 227-234.

Hall, S. M., Loeb, P., Coyne, K., and Cooper, J. (1981). Increasing employment in ex-heroin addicts. I: Criminal justice sample. *Behavior Therapy, 12*, 443-452.

Hall, S. M., Loeb, P., LeVois, M., and Cooper, J. (1981). Increasing employment in ex-heroin addicts. II: Methadone maintenance sample. *Behavior Therapy, 12*, 453-460.

Hall, S. M. (1984b). Clinical trials in drug treatment: Methodology. In: F. M. Tims and J. P. Ludford (Eds.). *Drug abuse treatment evaluation: Strategies, progress, and prospects* (NIDA Research Monograph No. 51). Rockville, MD: NIDA, pp. 88-105.

Hall, S. M. (1984a). The abstinence phobias: Links between substance abuse and anxiety. *International Journal of the Addictions, 19*(6), 613-631.

Hall, S. M., Loeb, P. C., and LeVois, M. (1985). *Job seekers' workshop: Leaders' manual for a vocational rehabilitation strategy.* Washington, DC: NIDA.

Hall, S. M., and Havassy, B. E. (1986). Commitment to abstinence and relapse to tobacco, alcohol, and opiates. In F. M. Tims and C. G. Leukefeld (Eds.). *Relapse and Recovery in Drug Abuse* (NIDA Research Monograph No. 72). Washington, DC: NIDA, pp. 118-135.

Hall, S. M., Havassy, B. E., and Wasserman, D. A. (1990). Commitment to abstinence and acute stress in relapse to alcohol, opiates, and nicotine. *Journal of Consulting and Clinical Psychology, 58(2)*, 175-181.

Handelsman, L., Aronson, M. J., Ness, R., Cochrane, K. J., and Kanof, P. D. (1992). The dysphoria of heroin addicton. *American Journal of Drug and Alcohol Abuse, 18(3)*, 275-287.

Harlow, L. L., and Anglin, M. D. (1984). Time series design to evaluate effectiveness of methadone maintenance intervention. *Journal of Drug Education, 14*(1), 53-72.

Harrison, L. D. (1992). Trends in illicit drug use in the United States: Conflicting results from national surveys. *International Journal of the Addictions, 27(7)*, 817–847.

Hasin, D. S., Grant, B. F., Harford, T. C., and Endicott, J. (1988). The drug dependence syndrome and related disabilities. *British Journal of Addiction, 83*, 45–55.

Hawkins, J. D., and Catalano, R. F. (1985). Aftercare in drug abuse treatment. *International Journal of the Addictions, 20*(6–7), 917–945.

Hawkins, J. D., Catalano, R. F., and Wells, E. A. (1986). Measuring effects of a skills training intervention for drug abusers. *Journal of Consulting and Clinical Psychology, 54(5)*, 661–664.

Hawkins, J. D., Catalano, R. F., Gillmore, M. R., and Wells, E. R. (1989). Skills training for drug users: Generalization, maintenance, and effects on drug use. *Journal of Consulting and Clinical Psychology, 57*, 559–563.

Hendriks, V. M. (1990). Psychiatric disorders in a Dutch addict population: Rates and correlates of DSM-III diagnosis. *Journal of Consulting and Clinical Psychology, 58(2)*, 158–165.

Hendriks, V. M., Steer, R. A., Platt, J. J., and Metzger, D. S. (1990). Psychopathology in Dutch and American heroin addicts. *International Journal of the Addictions, 25(9)*, 1051–1063.

Herbst, K. (1992). Prediction of dropout and relapse. In G. Bühringer, and J. J. Platt, (Eds.). *Drug addiction treatment research: German and American perspectives*. Malabar, FL: Krieger, pp. 291–299.

Hermalin, J. A., Steer, R. A., Platt, J. J., and Metzger, D. S. (1990). Risk characteristics associated with chronic unemployment in methadone clients. *Drug and Alcohol Dependence, 26*, 117–125.

Hill, S. Y., Cloninger, C. R., and Ayre, F. R. (1977). Independent familial transmission of alcoholism and opiate abuse. *Alcoholism: Clinical and Experimental Research, 1*(4), 335–342.

Howitt, D. (1990–91). Britain's "substance abuse policy": Realities and regulation in the United Kingdom. *International Journal of the Addictions, 25*(3A), 353–376.

Hser, Y-I., Anglin, M. D., and Chou, C. (1988). Evaluation of drug abuse treatment: A repeated measures design assessing methadone maintenance. *Evaluation Review, 12*(5), 547–570.

Hser, Y-I., Anglin, M. D., and Hsieh, S-C. (1993). Heroin cessation and other substance abuse. In L. S. Harris (Ed.) *Problems of Drug Dependence, 1993*. (NIDA Research Monograph) Washington, D.C.: U.S. Government Printing Office.

Hser, Y-I., Anglin, M. D., and McGlothin, W. (1987). Sex differences in addict careers. 1. Initiation of use. *American Journal of Drug and Alcohol Abuse, 13*(1 and 2), 33–57.

Hser, Y-I., Anglin, M. D., and Powers, K. (1993). A 24-year follow-up of California narcotics addicts. *Archives of General Psychiatry, 50*, 577–584.

Hubbard, R. (1981). *Employment related services in drug treatment programs* (NIDA Research Monograph). Washington, DC: NIDA.

Hubbard, R. L., and Marsden, M. E. (1986). Relapse to use of heroin, cocaine, and other drugs in the first year after treatment. In F. M. Tims and C. G. Leukefeld (Eds.). *Relapse and recovery in drug abuse* (NIDA Research Monograph No. 72). Washington, DC: NIDA, pp. 157–166.

Hubbard, R. L., Allison, M., Bray, R. M., Craddock, S. G., Rachal, J. V., and Ginzburg, H. M. (1983). An overview of client characteristics, treatment services, and during-treatment outcomes for outpatient methadone clinics in the Treatment Outcome Prospective Study (TOPS). In J. R. Cooper, F. Altman, B. S. Brown, and D. Czechowicz (Eds.). *Research on the treatment of narcotic addiction: State of the art.* (DHHS Publication No. ADM83-1281). Washington, DC National Institute on Drug Abuse, pp. 714–751.

Hubbard, R. L., Collins, J. J., Rachal, J. V., and Cavanaugh, E. R. (1988). The criminal justice client in drug abuse treatment. In C. G. Leukefeld and F. M. Tims (Eds.). *Compulsory treatment of drug abuse: Research and clinical practice* (Research Monograph No. 86). Rockville, MD: NIDA, pp. 57–80.

Hubbard, R. L., Marsden, M. E., Cavanaugh, E., Rachal, J. V., and Ginzburg, H. M. (1988). Role of drug-abuse treatment in limiting the spread of AIDS. *Review of Infectious Diseases, 10*(2), 377–384.

Hubbard, R. L., Marsden, M. E., Rachal, J. V., Harwood, H. J., Cavanaugh, E. R., and Ginzburg, H. M. (1989). *Drug abuse treatment: A national study of effectiveness.* Chapel Hill, N. C.: The University of North Carolina Press.

Hubbard, R. L., Rachal, J. V., Craddock, S. G., and Cavanaugh, E. R. (1984). Treatment outcome prospective study (TOPS): Client characteristics and behaviors before, during, and after treatment. In F. M. Tims and J. P. Ludford (Eds.). *Drug abuse treatment evaluation: Strategies, progress, and prospects* (NIDA Research Monograph No. 51). Rockville, MD: NIDA, pp. 42–68.

Hunt, D. E., Lipton, D. S., and Spunt, B. (1984). Patterns of criminal activity among methadone clients and current narcotic users not in treatment. *Journal of Drug Issues, 14*, 687–702.

Hunt, W. A., and Bespalec, D. A. (1974). Relapse rates after treatment for heroin addiction. *Journal of Community Psychology, 2*, 85–87.

Hunt, W. A., Barnett, L. W., and Branch, L. G. (1971). Relapse rates in addiction programs. *Journal of Clinical Psychology, 27*(4), 455–456.

Husband, S. D., and Platt, J. J. (1993). The cognitive skills component in substance abuse treatment in correctional settings: A brief review. *Journal of Drug Issues, 23*(1), 031–042.

Iguchi, M. Y., Handelsman, L., Bickel, W. K., and Griffiths, R. R. (1993). Benzodiazepine and sedative use/abuse by methadone maintenance clients. *Drug and Alcohol Dependence, 32*, 257–266.

Iguchi, M. Y., Platt, J. J., French, J., Baxter, R. C., Kushner, H., Lidz, V. M., Bux, D. A., Rosen, M., and Musikoff, H. (1992). Correlates of HIV seropositivity among injection drug users not in treatment. *Journal of Drug Issues, 22(4)*, 849–866.

Iguchi, M. Y., Stitzer, M. L., Bigelow, G. E., and Liebson, I. A. (1988). Contingency management in methadone maintenance: Effects of reinforcing and aversive consequences on illicit polydrug use. *Drug and Alcohol Dependence, 22*, 1–7.

Inciardi, J. A. (1971). The use of parole prediction with institutionalized narcotic addicts. *Journal of Research in Crime and Delinquency, 8*, 65–73.

Inciardi, J. A. (1981). *The drugs-crime connection*. Beverly Hills: Sage.

Inciardi, J. A. (1987). *Criminal justice*. San Diego: Harcourt Brace Jovanovich.

Inciardi, J. A. (1988). Compulsory treatment in New York: A brief narrative history of misjudgment, mismanagement, and misrepresentation. *Journal of Drug Issues, 18*(4), 547–560.

Inciardi, J. A. (1991). American drug policy and the legalization debate. In J. A. Inciardi (Ed.). *The drug legalization debate*. Newbury Park, CA: Sage Publications, pp. 7–15.

Inciardi, J. A., and McBride, D. (1989). Legalization: A high-risk alternative in the war on drugs. *American Behavioral Scientist, 32*(3), 259–289.

Inciardi, J. A., Isenberg, H., Lockwood, D., Martin, S. S., and Scarpitti, F. R. (1992). Assertive community treatment with a parolee population: An extension of case management. In R. S. Ashery (Ed.). *Progress and issues in case management* (NIDA Research Monograph No. 127). Rockville, MD: NIDA, pp. 350–367.

Inciardi, J. A., Lockwood, D., and Quinlan, J. A. (1993). Drug use in prison: Patterns, processes, and implications for treatment. *Journal of Drug Issues, 23(1)*, 119–129.

Inciardi, J. A., Martin, S. S., Lockwood, D., Hooper, R. M., and Wald, B. M. (1992). Obstacles to the implementation and evaluation of drug treatment programs in correctional settings: Reviewing the Delaware KEY experience. In C. G. Leukefeld and F. M. Tims (Eds.). *Drug abuse treatment in prisons and jails* (NIDA Research Monograph No. 118), Rockville, MD: NIDA, pp. 176–191.

Inciardi, J. A., McBride, D. C., Platt, J. J., and Baxter, S. (1993). Injecting drug users, incarceration and HIV: Some legal and social service delivery issues. In B. S. Brown & G. M. Beschner, with the National AIDS Research Consortium (Eds.). *Handbook on risk of AIDS: Injection drug users and sexual partners*. Westport, CT: Greenwood Press, pp. 337–351.

Inciardi, J. A., Tressell, P. A., Pottieger, A. E., and Rosales, T. A. (1992). A heroin revival in Miami: Notes from a street survey. *Journal of Psychoactive Drugs, 24*(1), 57–62.

Institute of Medicine (1989). *Prevention and treatment of alcohol problems: Research opportunities*. Washington, DC: National Academy Press.

Irwin, S., Blachly, P. H., Marks, J., Carlson, E., Loewen, J., and Reade, N. (1976). The behavioral, cognitive, and physiologic effects of long-term methadone and methadyl treatment. In J. D. Blaine and P. F. Renault (Eds.). *Rx: 3x/week LAAM: Alternative to methadone* (NIDA Research Monograph No. 8) Rockville, MD: NIDA, pp. 66–67.

Izzo, R. L. and Ross, R. R. (1990). Meta-analysis of rehabilitation programs for juvenile delinquents: A brief report. *Criminal Justice and Behavior, 17*, 143–142.

Jackson, J. F., Rotkiewicz, L. G., Quinones, M. A., and Passannante, M. R. (1989). A coupon program—drug treatment and AIDS education. *International Journal of the Addictions, 24*(11), 1035–1051.

Jacobson, B., Nyberg, K., Grönbladh, L., Eklund, G., Bygdeman, M., and Rydberg, U. (1990). Opiate addiction in adult offspring through possible imprinting after obstetric treatment. *British Medical Journal, 301*, 1067–1070.

Jainchill, N., De Leon, G., and Pinkham, L. (1986). Psychiatric diagnosis among substance abusers in therapeutic community treatment. *Journal of Psychoactive Drugs, 18*(3), 209–213.

Jarvik, M. E. (1990). The drug dilemma: Manipulating the demand. *Science, 250,* 387–392.

Jarvis, G., and Parker, H. (1989). Young heroin users and crime: How do the "new users" finance their habits? *British Journal of Criminology, 29(2),* 175–185.

Joe, G. W., and Simpson, D. D. (1990). Death rates and risk factors. In D. D. Simpson and S. B. Sells (Eds.). *Opioid addiction and treatment: A 12-year follow-up.* Malabar, FL: Krieger, pp. 193–202.

Joe, G. W., Chastain, R. L., and Simpson, D. D. (1990a). Length of careers. In D. D. Simpson and S. B. Sells, (Eds.). *Opioid addiction and treatment: A 12-year follow-up.* Malabar FL: Krieger, pp. 103–119.

Joe, G. W., Chastain, R. L., and Simpson, D. D. (1990b). Reasons for addiction stages. In D. D. Simpson and S. B. Sells (Eds.). *Opioid addiction and treatment: A 12-year follow-up.* Malabar, FL: Krieger, pp. 73–102.

Joe, G. W., Chastain, R. L., Marsh, K. L., and Simpson, D. D. (1990). Relapse. In D. D. Simpson and S. B. Sells (Eds.). *Opioid addiction and treatment: A 12-year follow-up.* Malabar, FL: Krieger, pp. 121–136.

Joe, G. W., Knezek, L., Watson, D., and Simpson, D. D. (1991). Depression and decision making among intravenous drug users. *Psychological Reports, 68,* 339–347.

Johnson, B. D. (1977). How much heroin maintenance (containment) in Britain? *International Journal of the Addictions, 12*(2–3), 361–398.

Johnson, B. D. (1980). Toward a theory of drug subcultures. In D. J. Lettieri, M. Sayers, and H. W. Pearson (Eds.). *Theories on drug abuse: Selected contemporary perspectives* (NIDA Research Monograph No. 30). Washington, DC: NIDA, pp. 110–119.

Johnson, B. D., Goldstein, P. G., Preble, E., Schmeidler, J., Lipton, D. S., Spunt, B., and Miller, T. (1985). *Taking care of business: The economics of crime by heroin abusers.* Lexington, MA: Lexington Books.

Johnson, P. and Rubin, A. (1983). Case management in mental health: A social work domain? *Social Work, 1,* 49–55.

Jonas, S. (1992). Public health approach to the prevention of substance abuse. In J. H. Lowinson, P. Ruiz, R. B. Millman, and J. G. Langrod (Eds.). *Substance abuse: A comprehensive textbook.* Baltimore, MD: Williams and Wilkins, pp. 928–943.

Jones, E. E. (1988). Black-white comparisons: Invidious or inevitable? *Contemporary Psychology, 33,* 251.

Jones, J. M., Levine, I. S., and Rosenberg, A. A. (1991). Homelessness research, services, and social policy. *American Psychologist, 46(11),* 1109–1111.

Jorquez, J. S. (1983). The retirement phase of heroin using careers. *Journal of Drug Issues, 13(3),* 343–365.

Jorquez, J. S. (1984). Heroin use in the barrio: Solving the problem of relapse or keeping the tecato gusano asleep. *American Journal of Drug and Alcohol Abuse, 10*(1), 63–75.

Joseph, H. (1988). The criminal justice system and opiate addiction: A historical perspective. In C. G. Leukefeld and F. M. Tims (Eds.). *Compulsory treatment of drug abuse: Research and clinical practice* (NIDA Research Monograph No. 86). Rockville, MD: NIDA, pp. 106–125.

Kadden, R. M., Cooney, N. L., Getter, H., and Litt, M. D. (1989). Matching alcoholics to coping skills or interactional therapies: Posttreatment results. *Journal of Consulting and Clinical Psychology, 57*(6), 698–704.

Kail, B. L., and Lukoff, I. F. (1984a). Differentials in the treatment of black female heroin addicts. *Drug and Alcohol Dependence, 13*(1), 55–63.

Kail, B. L., and Lukoff, I. F. (1984b). The black female addict's career options: A typology and theory. *American Journal of Drug and Alcohol Abuse, 10*(1), 39–52.

Kampe, H., and Kunz, D. (1981). Sprachliches Interaktionsverhalten Drogenabhängiger als Parameter des theapeutischen Prozesses. In W. Keup (Ed.). *Behandlung der Sucht und des Missbrauches chemischer Stoffe.* Stuttgart: Thieme, pp. 152–164.

Kampe, H., and Kunz, D. (1984). Integration und Fehlanpassung Drogenabhängiger nach der Behandlung in einer Therapeutischen Gemeinschaft. *Praxis der Kinderpsychologie und Kinderpsychiatrie,* 33(2), 49–55.

Kampe, H., and Kunz, D. (1992). Factors influencing relapse and treatment dropout. In G. Bühringer and J. J. Platt (Eds.). *Drug addiction treatment research: German and American perspectives.* Malabar, FL: Krieger, pp. 301–319.

Kampe, H., Kunz, D., and Kremp, M. (1986). Sondersprachgebrauch drogenabhhangiger in ihren Lebensläufen. *Suchtgefahren, 32,* 103–111.

Kaplan, C. D. (1992). Drug craving and drug use in the daily life of heroin addicts. In M. W. deVries (Ed.). *The experience of psychopathology: Investigating mental disorders in their natural settings.* Cambridge, MA.: Cambridge University Press, pp. 193–218.

Kaplan, C. D., Dorf, D., and Sterk, C. (1987). Temporal and social contexts of heroin-using populations: An illustration of the snowball sampling technique. *The Journal of Nervous and Mental Disease, 175*(9), 566–574.

Keefe, F. J., Gil, K. M., and Rose, S. C. (1986). Behavioral approaches in the multidisciplinary management of chronic pain. *Clinical Psychology Review, 6,* 87–113.

Khantzian, E. J., and Treece, C. (1985). DSM-III psychiatric diagnosis of narcotic addicts: Recent findings. *Archives of General Psychiatry, 42,* 1067–1071.

Kleber, H. D. (1989). Treatment of drug dependence: What works. *International Review of Psychiatry, 1,* 81–99.

Kleber, H. D. (1991). Tracking the cocaine epidemic: The Drug Abuse Warning Network. *Journal of the American Medical Association, 266*(16), 2272–2273.

Kleber, H. D. (1992). Federal role in substance abuse policy. In J. H. Lowinson, P. Ruiz, R. B. Millman, and J. G. Langrod (Eds.). *Substance abuse: A comprehensive textbook.* Baltimore, MD: Williams & Wilkins, pp. 32–38.

Kleber, H. D., and Gold, M. S. (1978). Use of psychotropic drugs in treatment of methadone maintained narcotic addicts. In B. Kissin, J. H. Lowinson, and R. B. Millman (Eds.). *Recent developments in chemotherapy of narcotic addiction. Annals of the New York Academy of Science, 311,* 81–98.

Klingemann, H.K-H. (1991). The motivation for change from problem alcohol and heroin use. *British Journal of Addiction, 86*, 727–744.

Kooyman, M. (1984). The drug problem in The Netherlands. *Journal of Substance Abuse Treatment, 1*, 125–130.

Kosten, T. R. (1986). Diagnosing depression with the DST and TRH in cocaine and opioid abusers. *Journal of Substance Abuse Treatment, 3(1)*, 47–49.

Kosten, T. R., Rounsaville, B. J., and Kleber, H. D. (1983). Concurrent validity of the Addiction Severity Index. *Journal of Nervous and Mental Disease, 171*(10), 606–610.

Kosten, T. R., Rounsaville, B. J., and Kleber, H. D. (1986). A 2.5 year follow-up of depression, life crises, and treatment effects on abstinence among opioid addicts. *Archives of General Psychiatry, 43*(8), 733–738.

Kosten, T. R., Rounsaville, B. J., and Kleber, H. D. (1987a). A 2.5 year follow-up of cocaine abuse among treated opioid addicts: Have our treatments helped? *Archives of General Psychiatry, 44*, 281–285.

Kosten, T. R., Rounsaville, B. J., and Kleber, H. D. (1987b). Multidimensionality and prediction of treatment outcome in opioid addicts: 2.5-year follow-up. *Comprehensive Psychiatry, 28*(1), 3–13.

Kosten, T. R., Rounsaville, B. J., Babor, T. F., Spitzer, R. L., and Williams, J. B. (1987). Substance-use disorders in DSM-III-R: Evidence for the dependence syndrome across different psychoactive substances. *British Journal of Psychiatry, 151*, 834–843.

Kowalski, G. S., and Faupel, C. E. (1990). Heroin use, crime, and the "main hustle." *Deviant Behavior, 11*, 1–16.

Kozel, N.J., DuPont, R. L., and Brown, B. S. (1972). Narcotics and crime: A study of narcotic involvement in an offender population. *International Journal of the Addictions, 7*(3), 443–450.

Kozlowski, L. T., and Wilkinson, D. A. (1987). Use and misuse of the concept of craving by alcohol, tobacco, and drug researchers. *British Journal of Addiction, 82*, 31–36.

Kranzler, H. R., and Orrok, B. (1989). The pharmacotherapy of alcoholism. In A. Tasman, R. E. Hales, and A. J. Frances (Eds.). *Review of Psychiatry, Vol. 8*, Washington, DC: American Psychiatric Press, pp. 359–379.

Kreutzer, A., Römer-Klees, R., and Schneider, H. (1992). Drugs and delinquency: Some results of a current self-report of university students and of recent in-depth interviews with drug addicts. In G. Bühringer and J. J. Platt (Eds.). *Drug addiction treatment research: German and American perspectives*. Malabar, FL: Krieger, pp. 409–431.

Krueger, D. W. (1981). Stressful life events and the return to heroin use. *Journal of Human Stress, 7*(2), 3–8.

Küfner, H., Denis, A., Roch, I., and Bhmer, M. (1992). The dropout rate among drug addicts during the first ninety days of residential treatment. In G. Bühringer and J. J. Platt (Eds.). *Drug addiction treatment research: German and American perspectives*. Malabar, FL: Krieger, pp. 227–240.

Kunz, D. (1988). *Analyse des Therapieabbruches in einer stationären Behandlungseinrichtung für Drogenabhängige. Untersuchung zur Entwicklung eines Bedingungsmodelles mittels multivariater Korrelationsstudien*. Bonn: Universitätsdruckerei Bonn.

Kunz, D. (1992). Therapeutic accessibility of drug addicts during treatment in therapeutic communities. In G. Bühringer and J. J. Platt (Eds.). *Drug addiction treatment research: German and American perspectives.* Malabar, FL: Krieger, pp. 271–289.

Kunz, D., and Kampe, H. (1985). Zum problem des therapieabbruches von heroinabhangigen. *Suchtgefahren, 31*, 146–154.

Lamb, R. J., Iguchi, M. Y., Husband, S. D., and Platt, J. J. (1993). A behavioral model for the treatment of cocaine addiction. In J. A. Inciardi, F. M. Tims, and B. W. Fletcher (Eds.). *Innovative approaches in the treatment of drug abuse: Program models and strategies.* Westport, CT: Greenwood Press, pp. 149–160.

Lampinen, T. M. (1991). Cost-effectiveness of drug abuse treatment for primary prevention of Acquired Immunodeficiency Syndrome: Epidemiologic considerations. In W. S. Cartwright and J. M. Kaple (Eds.). *Economic costs, cost-effectiveness, financing, and community-based drug treatment* (NIDA Research Monograph No. 113). Rockville, MD: NIDA, pp. 114–128.

Langenauer, B. J. and Bowden, C. L. A. (1971). A follow-up study of narcotic addicts in the NARA program. *American Journal of Psychiatry, 128*, 41–46.

LaPorte, D. J., McLellan, A. T., O'Brien, C. P., and Marshall, J. R. (1981). Treatment response in psychiatrically impaired drug abusers. *Comprehensive Psychiatry, 22(4)*, 411–419.

Legarda, J. J., Bradley, B. P., and Sartory, G. (1990). Effects of drug-related cues in current and former opiate users. *Journal of Psychophysiology, 4*, 25–31.

Lehman, W. E. K., and Simpson, D. D. (1990a). Appendix: Development of outcome composite measures. In D. D. Simpson, and S. B. Sells (Eds.). *Opioid addiction and treatment: A 12-year follow-up.* Malabar, FL: Krieger, pp. 253–263.

Lehman, W. E. K., and Simpson, D. W. (1990b). Predictions of 12-year outcomes. In D. D. Simpson and S. B. Sells (Eds.). *Opioid addiction and treatment: A 12-year follow-up.* Malabar, FL: Krieger, pp. 203–220.

Lehman, W. E. K., and Joe, G. W. (1987). Longitudinal behavior as a predictor of follow-up outcomes for opioid addicts. *Psychology of Addictive Behaviors, 1*, 173–184.

Lehman, W. E. K., Barrett, M. E., and Simpson, D. D. (1990). Alcohol use by heroin addicts 12 years after drug abuse treatment. *Journal of Studies on Alcohol, 51(3)*, 233–244.

Lehman, W. E. K., Joe, G. W., and Simpson, D. D. (1990). An integrative model. In D. D. Simpson and S. B. Sells, (Eds.). *Opioid addiction and treatment: A 12-year follow-up.* Malabar, FL: Krieger, pp. 221–237.

Leiby, J. (1978). *A history of social welfare and social work in the United States.* New York: Columbia University Press.

Lettieri, D. J., Sayers, M., and Pearson, H. W. (Eds.). (1980). *Theories on drug abuse: Selected contemporary perspectives* (NIDA Research Monograph No. 30). Rockville, MD: NIDA.

Leukefeld, C. G. (1991). Opportunities for enhancing drug abuse treatment with criminal justice authority. In R. W. Pickens, C. G. Leukefeld, and C. R. Schuster, (Eds.). *Improving drug abuse treatment* (NIDA Research Monograph No. 106), Rockville, MD: NIDA, pp. 328–337.

Leukefeld, C. G., and Tims, F. M. (1986). Relapse and recovery: Some directions for research and practice. In F. M. Tims and C. G. Leukefeld (Eds.). *Relapse and recovery in drug abuse* (NIDA Research Monograph Series, No. 72). Washington, DC: NIDA, pp. 185–190.

Leukefeld, C. G., and Tims, F. M. (1988). Compulsory treatment: A review of findings. In C. G. Leukefeld and F. M. Tims (Eds.). *Compulsory treatment of drug abuse: Research and clinical practice* (NIDA Research Monograph No. 86). Rockville, MD: NIDA, pp. 236–251.

Leukefeld, C. G., and Tims, F. M. (1992). Directions for practice and research. In C. G. Leukefeld and F. M. Tims (Eds.). *Drug abuse treatment services in prisons and jails* (NIDA Research Monograph No. 118). Rockville, MD: NIDA, pp. 279–293.

Levy, J. A., Gallmeier, C. P., Weddington, W. W., and Wiebel, W. W. (1992). Delivering case management using a community-based service model of drug intervention. In R. S. Ashery (Ed.). *Progress and issues in case management* (NIDA Research Monograph No. 127). Rockville, MD: NIDA, pp. 145–166.

Lidz, V., Bux, D. A., Platt, J. J., and Iguchi, M. Y. (1992). Transitional case management: A service model for AIDS outreach projects. In R. S. Ashery (Ed.). *Progress and issues in case management* (NIDA Research Monograph No. 127). Rockville, MD; NIDA, pp. 112–144.

Lipton, D. S., Falkin, G. P., and Wexler, H. K. (1992). Correctional drug abuse treatment in the United States: An overview. In C. G. Leukefeld and F. M. Tims (Eds.). *Drug abuse treatment in prisons and jails* (NIDA Research Monograph No. 118). Rockville, MD: NIDA, pp. 8–30.

Lipton, D. S., Martinson, R., and Wilks, J. (1975). *The effectiveness of correctional treatment.* New York: Praeger.

Loeber, R., and LeBlanc, M. (1990). Toward a developmental criminology. *Crime and Justice, 12*, 375.

Luborsky, L., Crits-Christoph, P., McLellan, A. T., Woody, G. E., Piper, W., Liberman, B., Imber, S., and Pilkonis, P. (1986). Do therapists vary much in their effectiveness?: Findings from four outcome studies. *American Journal of Orthopsychiatry, 56*(4), 501–512.

Luborsky, L., McLellan, A. T., Woody, G. E., O'Brien, C. P., and Auerbach, A. (1985). Therapist success and its determinants. *Archives of General Psychiatry, 42*, 602–611.

Lubran, B. G. (1990). Alcohol and drugs among the homeless population: A national response. In M. Argeriou and D. McCarthy (Eds.). *Treating alcoholism and drug abuse among the homeless: Nine community demonstration grants.* Binghamton, NY: Haworth Press, pp. 11–23.

Ludwig, A. M., Wikler, A., and Stark, L. H. (1974). The first drink: Psychobiological aspects of craving. *Archives of General Psychiatry, 30*(4), 539–547.

Luthar, S. S., Anton, S. F., Merikangas, K. R., and Rounsaville, B. J. (1992). Vulnerability to substance abuse and psychopathology among siblings of opioid abusers. *Journal of Nervous and Mental Disease, 180(3)*, 153–161.

Maddux, J. F. (1988a). Clinical experience with civil commitment. *Journal of Drug Issues, 18*(4), 575–594.

Maddux, J. F. (1988b). Clinical experience with civil commitment. In C. G. Leukefeld and F. M. Tims (Eds.). *Compulsory treatment for drug abuse: Clinical practice and research* (NIDA Research Monograph No. 86), Rockville, MD: NIDA, pp. 35–56.

Maddux, J. F., and Desmond, D. P. (1986). Relapse and recovery in substance abuse careers. In F. M. Tims and C. G. Leukefeld (Eds.). *Relapse and recovery in drug abuse* (NIDA Research Monograph No. 72). Rockville, MD: NIDA, pp. 49–71.

Maddux, J. F., and Desmond, D. P. (1989). Family and environment in the choice of opioid dependence or alcoholism. *American Journal of Drug and Alcohol Abuse, 15(2)*, 117–134.

Maguire, P., Davies, M. F., Villar, H., and Leow, G. (1992). Pharmacological evidence for more than two benzodiazepine receptor sites. In L. Harris (Ed.). *Problems of Drug Dependence, 1991* (NIDA Research Monograph No. 119). Rockville, MD: NIDA, p. 387.

Magura, S., Freeman, R. C., Siddiqi, Q., and Lipton, D. S. (1992). The validity of hair analysis for detecting cocaine and heroin use among addicts. *International Journal of the Addictions, 27(1)*, 51–69.

Malow, R. M., West, J. A., Pena, J. M., and Lott, W. C. (1990). Affective and adjustment problems in cocaine and opioid addicts. *Psychology of Addictive Behavior, 4(1)*, 6–11.

Malow, R. M., West, J. A., Williams, J. L., and Sutker, P. B. (1989). Personality disorders classification and symptoms in cocaine and opioid addicts. *Journal of Consulting and Clinical Psychology, 57(6)*, 765–767.

Mann, N. R., Charuvastra, V. C., and Murthy, V. K. (1984). A diagnostic tool with important implications for treatment of addiction: Identification of factors underlying relapse and remission time distributions. *International Journal of the Addictions, 19*(1), 25–44.

Manpower Demonstration Research Corporation (1980). *Summary and findings of the National Supported Work Demonstration.* Cambridge, MA: Ballinger.

Marcovici, M., McLellan, A. T., O'Brien, C. P., and Rosenzweig, J. (1980). Risk for alcoholism and methadone treatment: A longitudinal study. *Journal of Nervous and Mental Disease, 168(9)*, 556–558.

Marlatt, G. A., and Gordon, J. R. (1980). Determinants of relapse: Implications for the maintenance of behavior change. In P. O. Davidson and S. M. Davidson (Eds.). *Behavioral medicine: Changing health lifestyles.* New York: Brunner/Mazel, pp. 410–472.

Marlatt, G. A., and Gordon, J. R. (Eds.). (1985). *Relapse prevention: Maintenance strategies in the treatment of addictive behaviors.* New York: Guilford Press.

Marsh, K. L., Joe, G. W., Simpson, D. D., and Lehman, W. E. K. (1990). Treatment history. In D. D. Simpson and S. B. Sells (Eds.). *Opioid addiction and treatment: A 12-year follow-up.* Malabar, FL: Krieger, pp. 137–156.

Martin, S. S., and Scarpitti, F. R. (1993). An intensive case management approach for paroled IV drug users. *Journal of Drug Issues, 23(1)*, 43–59.

Martinson, R. (1974). What works? Questions and answers about prison reform. *Public Interest, 35*, 22–45.

McAuliffe, W. E. (1990). A randomized controlled trial of recovery training and self-help for opioid addicts in New England and Hong Kong. *Journal of Psychoactive Drugs,* *22*(2), 197–209.

McAuliffe, W. E., and Ch'ien, J. M. N. (1986). Recovery training and self-help: A relapse-prevention program for treated opiate addicts. *Journal of Substance Abuse Treatment,* *3*, 9–20.

McAuliffe, W. E., Ch'ien, J. M. N., Launer, E., Friedman, R., and Feldman, B. (1985). The Harvard Group Aftercare Program: Preliminary evaluation results and implementation issues. In R. S. Ashery (Ed.). *Progress in the development of cost effective treatment of drug abusers.* (NIDA Research Monograph No. 58). Rockville, MD: NIDA, pp. 147–156.

McAuliffe, W. E., Feldman, B., Friedman, R., Launer, E., Magnuson, E., Mahoney, C. Santangelo, S., Ward, W., and Weiss, R. (1986). Explaining relapse to opiate addiction following successful completion of treatment. In F. M. Tims and C. G. Leukefeld (Eds.). *Relapse and recovery in drug abuse* (NIDA Research Monograph No. 72). Washington, DC: NIDA, pp. 136–156.

McBride, D. C., Inciardi, J. A., Chitwood, D. D., McCoy, C. B., and the National AIDS Research Consortium (1992). Crack use and correlates of use in a national population of street heroin users. *Journal of Psychoactive Drugs, 24(4),* 411–416.

McCarthy, E. P., Feldman, Z. T., and Lewis, B. F. (1992). Development and implementation of an interoganizational case management model for substance abuse. In R. S. Ashery (Ed.). *Progress and issues in case management* (NIDA Research Monograph No. 127). Rockville, MD: NIDA, pp. 331–349.

McCarthy, J. J., and Borders, O. T. (1985). Limit setting on drug abuse in methadone maintenance patients. *American Journal of Psychiatry, 142(12),* 1419–1423.

McCarty, D., Argeriou, M., Huebner, R. B., and Lubran, B. (1991). Alcoholism, drug abuse, and the homeless. *American Psychologist, 46(11),* 1139–1148.

McCarty, D., Argeriou, M., Krakow, M., and Mulvey, K. (1990). Stabilization services for homeless alcoholics and drug abusers. In M. Argeriou and D. McCarty (Eds.). *Treating alcoholism and drug abuse among homeless: Nine community demonstration grants.* Binghamton, NY: Haworth Press, pp. 31–46.

McCoy, H. V., Dodds, S., Rivers, J. E., and McCoy, C. B. (1992). Case management services for HIV-seropositive IDUs. In R. S. Ashery (Ed.). *Progress and issues in case management* (NIDA Research Monograph No. 127). Rockville, MD: NIDA, pp. 181–207.

McGlothlin, W. H., and Anglin, M. D. (1981). Shutting off methadone: Costs and benefits. *Archives of General Psychiatry, 38,* 885–892.

McGlothlin, W. H., Anglin, M. D., and Wilson, B. D. (1977a). *An evaluation of the California Civil Addict Program* (NIDA Services Research Monograph Series). DHEW Pub. No. (ADM) 78-558. Rockville, MD: NIDA, p. 102.

McGlothlin, W. H., Anglin,, M. D., and Wilson, B. D. (1977b). A follow-up of admissions to the California Civil Addict Program. *American Journal of Drug and Alcohol Abuse,* *4*(2), 179–199.

McLellan, A. T., and Alterman, A. I. (1991). Patient-treatment matching: A conceptual and methodological review with suggestions for future research. In R. W. Pickens, C. G.

Leukefeld, and C. Schuster (Eds.). *Improving drug abuse treatment* (NIDA Research Monograph No. 106). Rockville, MD: NIDA, pp. 114–135.

McLellan, A. T., Childress, A. R., Griffith, J., and Woody, G. E. (1984). The psychiatrically severe drug abuse patient: Methadone maintenance or therapeutic community? *American Journal of Drug and Alcohol Abuse, 10(1),* 77–95.

McLellan, A. T., Luborsky, L., O'Brien, C. P., Barr, H. L., and Evans, F. (1986). Alcohol and drug abuse treatment in three different populations: Is there improvement and is it predictable? *American Journal of Drug and Alcohol Abuse, 12*(1&2), 101–120.

McLellan, A. T., Luborsky, L., O'Brien, C. P., Woody, G. E., and Druley, K. A. (1982). Is treatment for substance abuse effective? *Journal of the American Medical Association, 247(10),* 1423–1428.

McLellan, A. T., Luborsky, L., Woody, G. E., O'Brien C. P., and Druley, K. A. (1983). Predicting response to alcohol and drug abuse treatments: Role of psychiatric severity. *Archives of General Psychiatry, 40,* 620–625.

McLellan, A. T., Woody, G. E., Luborsky, L., and Goehl, L. (1988). Is the counselor an "active ingredient" in substance abuse treatment? *Journal of Nervous and Mental Disease, 176(7),* 423–430.

McLellan, A. T., Woody, G. E., Luborsky, L., O'Brien, C. P., and Druley, K. A. (1983). Increased effectiveness of substance abuse treatment: A prospective study of patient-treatment "matching." *Journal of Nervous and Mental Disease, 171(10),* 597–605.

McMillan, D., and Cheney, R. (1992). Aftercare for formerly homeless, recovering women: Issues for case management. In R. S. Ashery (Ed.). *Progress and issues in case management* (NIDA Research Monograph No. 127). Rockville, MD: NIDA, pp. 274–288.

Merikangas, K. R., Rounsaville, B. J., and Prusoff, B. A. (1992). Familial factors in vulnerability to substance abuse. In M. Glantz and R. Pickens (Eds.). *Vulnerability to drug abuse.* Washington, DC: APA Press, pp. 75–97.

Metzger, D. S. (1987). *Predicting the employment status of methadone patients.* Doctoral Dissertation, Rutgers University, New Brunswick, New Jersey.

Metzger, D. S., Platt, J. J., and Morton-Bey, I. (1986). *Psychological symptomatology and employment among heroin addicts.* Paper presented at the American Psychological Association Annual Meeting, Washington, DC. (Abstract #303).

Meyer, R. E. (1988). Conditioning phenomena and the problem of relapse in opioid addicts and alcoholics. In B. A. Ray (Ed.). *Learning factors in substance abuse* (NIDA Research Monograph No. 84). Rockville, MD: NIDA, pp. 161–179.

Mieczkowski, T. (1992). New approaches in drug testing: A review of hair analysis. *Annals of the American Academy of Political and Social Science,* 132–150.

Milkman, H., and Frosch, W. (1980). Theory of drug use. In D. J. Lettieri, M. Sayers, and H. W. Pearson (Eds.). *Theories on drug abuse: Selected contemporary perspectives* (NIDA Research Monograph No. 30). Washington, DC: NIDA, pp. 38–45.

Miller, W. R. (1989). Matching individuals with interventions. In R. K. Hester and W. R. Miller (Eds.). *Handbook of alcoholism treatment approaches: Effective alternatives.* Elmsford, NY: Pergamon, pp. 261–271.

Miller, W. R., and Hester, R. R. (1986). Matching problem drinkers with optimal treatments. In W. R. Miller and N. Heather (Eds.). *Treating addictive behaviors: Processes of change.* New York: Plenum, pp. 175–203.

Miller, W. R., and Rollnick, S. (Eds.) (1991). *Motivational interviewing: Preparing people to change addictive behaviors.* New York: Guilford.

Mirin, S. M., Weiss, R. D., Griffin, M. L., and Michael, J. L. (1991). Psychopathology in drug abusers and their families. *Comprehensive Psychiatry, 32*(1), 36–51.

Moise, R., Reed, B. G., and Ryan, V. (1982). Issues in the treatment of heroin-addicted women: A comparison of men and women entering two types of drug abuse programs. *International Journal of the Addictions, 17*(1), 109–139.

Moring, J., and Strang, J. (1989). Cue exposure as an assessment technique in the management of a heroin addict: Case report. *Drug and Alcohol Dependence, 24,* 161–167.

Murphy, P. N., and Bentall, R. P. (1992). Motivation to withdraw from heroin: A factor-analytic study. *British Journal of Addiction, 87*(2), 245–250.

Murphy, P. N., Bentall, R. P., and Owens, R. G. (1989). The experience of opioid abstinence: The relevance of motivation and history. *British Journal of Addiction, 84*(6), 673–679.

Musto, D. F. (1973). *The American disease: Origins of narcotic control.* New Haven: Yale University Press.

Nadelmann, E. A. (1989). Drug prohibition in the United States: Costs, consequences, and alternatives. *Science, 245,* 939–947.

Nadelmann, E. A. (1991a). Beyond drug prohibition: Evaluating the alternatives. In M. B. Krauss and E. P. Lazear (Eds.). *Searching for alternatives: Drug-control policy in the United States.* Palo Alto, CA: Hoover Institution Press, pp. 241–250.

Nadelmann, E. A. (1991b). A rational approach to drug legalization. *American Journal of Ethics and Medicine,* (Spring), 3–7.

Nadelmann, E. A. (1992). Thinking seriously about alternatives to drug prohibition. *Daedalus, 121*(3), 85–132.

Nadelmann, E. A. (1993). Should we legalize drugs? History answers. Yes. *American Heritage,* (Feb-Mar.), pp. 41–42, 44–48.

Nathan, P. E. (1988). The addictive personality is the behavior of the addict. *Journal of Consulting and Clinical Psychology, 56*(2), 183–188.

Newman, R. G. (1983). Sounding board: The need to redefine "addiction." *New England Journal of Medicine, 308*(18), 1096–1098.

Nichols, J. R., and Hsiao, S. (1967). Addiction liability of albino rats: Breeding for quantitative differences in morphine drinking. *Science, 157,* 561–563.

NIDA (National Institute on Drug Abuse) (1981). *Effectiveness of drug abuse treatment programs* (NIDA Treatment Research Monograph). Washington, DC: NIDA.

NIDA (1982). *Data from the client oriented data acquisition process (CODAP): Trend report. January 1978–September 1981. (NIDA Statistical Series, No. 24).* Washington, DC: U.S. Government Printing Office. DHHS Publication No. ADM 82-1214.

NIDA. (1992a). *National household survey on drug abuse: Population estimates 1991.* Washington, D.C.: Dept. of Health and Human Services, DHHS Pub. No. (ADM) 92-1887.

NIDA. (1992b). *Annual Emergency Room Data 1991, Data from the Drug Abuse Warning*

Network (DAWN): Series 1, No. 11-A. Washington, D.C.: Dept. of Health and Human Services, DHHS Pub. No. (ADM) 92-1955.

NIDA. (1992c). *Annual Medical Examiner Data 1991: Data from the Drug Abuse Warning Network (DAWN):* Series 1, No. 11-B. Washington, D.C.: Dept. of Health and Human Services, DHHS Pub. No. (ADM) 92-1955.

Novaco, R. W. (1977). Stress inoculation: A cognitive therapy for anger and its application to a case of depression. *Journal of Counsulting and Clinical Psychology, 45*(4), 600–608.

Nunes, E. V., Quitkin, F. M., Brady, R., and Stewart, J. W. (1991). Imipramine treatment of methadone maintenance patients with affective disorder and illicit drug use. *American Journal of Psychiatry, 148*(5), 667–669.

Nurco, D. N. (1992). Variations in behavior among narcotic addicts. In G. Bühringer and J. J. Platt (Eds.). *Drug addiction treatment research: German and American perspectives.* Malabar, FL: Krieger, pp. 211–224.

Nurco, D. N., and Shaffer, J. W. (1982). Types and characteristics of addicts in the community. *Drug and Alcohol Dependence, 9*(1), 43–78.

Nurco, D. N., Ball, J. C., Shaffer, J. W., and Hanlon, T. E. (1985). The criminality of narcotic addicts. *Journal of Nervous and Mental Disease, 173*(2), 94–102.

Nurco, D. N., Balter, M. B., and Kinlock, T. (in press). Vulnerability to narcotic addiction: Preliminary findings. *Journal of Drug Issues.*

Nurco, D. N., Cisin, I. H., and Balter, M. B. (1981a). Addict careers I: A new typology. *International Journal of the Addictions, 16*(8), 1305–1325.

Nurco, D. N., Cisin, I. H., and Balter, M. B. (1981b). Addict careers II: The first ten years. *International Journal of the Addictions, 16*(8), 1327–1356.

Nurco, D. N., Cisin, I. H., and Balter, M. B. (1981c). Addict careers III: Trends across time. *International Journal of the Addictions, 16*(8), 1357–1372.

Nurco, D. N., Hanlon, T. E., Balter, M. B., Kinlock, T. W., and Slaught, E. (1991). A classification of narcotic addicts based on type, amount and severity of crime. *Journal of Drug Issues, 21*(2), 429–448.

Nurco, D. N., Shaffer, J. W., Hanlon, T. E., Kinlock, T. W., Duszynski, K. R., and Stephenson, P. (1987). Attitudes toward narcotic addiction. *Journal of Nervous and Mental Disease, 175*(11), 653–660.

Nurco, D. N., Wegner, N., Stephenson, P., Makofsky, A., and Shaffer, J. W. (1983). *Ex-addicts' self-help groups: Potentials and pitfalls.* New York: Praeger.

Nyberg, K., Allebeck, P., Eklund, G., and Jacobson, B. (1992). Socio-economic versus obstetric risk factors for drug addiction in offspring. *British Journal of Addiction, 87*, 1669–1676.

Nyberg, K., Allebeck, P., Eklund, G., and Jacobson, B. (1993). Obstetric medication versus residential area as perinatal risk factors for subsequent adult drug addiction in offspring. *Pediatrics and Perinatal Epidemiology, 7*, 23–32.

O'Brien, C. P., Childress, A. R., and McLellan, A. T. (1991). Conditioning factors may help to understand and prevent relapse in patients who are recovering from drug dependence. In R. W. Pickens, C. G. Leukefeld, and C. R. Schuster (Eds.). *Improving drug abuse treatment* (NIDA Research Monograph No. 106). Rockville, MD: NIDA, pp. 293–312.

O'Brien, C. P., Childress, A., McLellan, A., Ehrman, R., and Ternes, J. (1988a). Progress in understanding the conditioning aspects of drug dependence. In L. S. Harris (Ed.). *Problems of Drug Dependence, 1987* (Research Monograph Series No. 81). Washington, DC: NIDA, pp. 395–404.

O'Brien, C. P., Childress, A. R., McLellan, A. T., Ehrman, R., and Ternes, J. W. (1988b). Types of conditioning found in drug-dependent humans. In B. A. Ray (Ed.). *Learning factors in substance abuse* (NIDA Research Monograph No. 84). Rockville, MD: NIDA, pp. 44–61.

O'Brien, C. P., Childress, A. R., McLellan, A. T., Ternes, J., and Ehrman, R. N. (1984). Use of naltrexone to extinguish opioid-conditioned responses. *Journal of Clinical Psychiatry, 45*(9, Sec 2), 53–56.

Office of Applied Studies, Substance Abuse and Mental Health Sciences Administration (1993). *National Drug and Alcohol Treatment Unit Survey.* Rockville, MD: (author).

Oppenheimer, E., Sheehan, M., and Taylor, C. (1988). Letting the client speak: Drug misusers and the process of help seeking. *British Journal of Addiction, 83,* 635–647.

Orford, J. (1985). *Excessive appetites: A psychological view of addictions.* New York: Wiley.

Orford, J. (1988). Psychopharmacology and social psychology: Complementary or contradictory? In M. Lader (Ed.). *The psychopharmacology of addiction.* Oxford: Oxford University Press, pp. 168–179.

Parent, D. G. (1989). *Shock incarceration: An overview of existing programs.* National Institute of Justice. Washington, DC: U.S. Department of Justice.

Parker, H., and Newcombe, R. (1987). Heroin use and acquisitive crime in an English community. *British Journal of Sociology, 38(3),* 331–350.

Parker, H., Newcome, R., and Bakx, K. (1987). The new heroin users: Prevalence and characteristics in Wirral, Merseyside. *British Journal of Addiction, 82*(2), 147–157.

Peele, S. (1989). *Diseasing of America—Addiction treatment out of control.* Lexington, MA: Lexington Books.

Perl, H. I., and Jacobs, M. L. (1992). Case management models for homeless persons with alcohol and other drug problems: An overview of the NIAAA research demonstration program. In R. S. Ashery (Ed.). *Progress and issues in case management* (NIDA Research Monograph No. 127). Rockville, MD: NIDA, pp. 208–222.

Peters, R. H., and May, R. (1992). Drug treatment services in jails. In C. G. Leukefeld and F. M. Tims (Eds.). *Drug abuse treatment in prisons and jails* (NIDA Research Monograph No. 108). Rockville, MD: NIDA, pp. 38–50.

Pickens, R. W., and Fletcher, B. W. (1991). Overview of treatment issues: Improving drug abuse treatment. In R. W. Pickens, C. G. Leukefeld, and C. R. Schuster (Eds.). (NIDA Research Monograph No. 106). Rockville, MD: NIDA, pp. 1–19.

Pickens, R. W., and Johanson, C-E. (1992). Craving: Consensus of status and agenda for future research. *Drug and Alcohol Dependence, 30,* 127–131.

Platt, J. J. (1986). *Heroin addiction: Theory, research, and treatment.* (Second Edition) Melbourne, Florida: Krieger (second printing, 1988).

Platt, J. J. (1994). Vocational rehabilitation of drug addicts. *Psychological Bulletin,* in press.

Platt, J. J., Bühringer, G., Kaplan, C. D., Brown, B. S., and Taube, D. O. (1988). The prospects and limitations of compulsory treatment for drug addiction. *Journal of Drug Issues, 18*(4), 505–525.

Platt, J. J., and Hermalin, J. (1989). Social skill interventions for substance abusers. *Psychology of Addictive Behaviors, 3(3),* 114–133.

Platt, J. J., and Husband, S. D. (1993). An overview of problem-solving and social skills approaches in substance abuse treatment. *Psychotherapy, 30(2),* 276–283.

Platt, J. J., Husband, S. D., Hermalin, J., Cater, J., and Metzger, D. (1993). A cognitive problem-solving employment readiness intervention for methadone clients. *Journal of Cognitive Psychotherapy: An International Quarterly, 7*(1), 21–33.

Platt, J. J., Husband, S. D., Steer, R. A., and Iguchi, M. Y. (1994). Cognitive problem-solving types among high-risk injection drug users not in treatment. *Journal of Substance Abuse Treatment,* in press.

Platt, J. J., and Labate, C. (1977). Wharton Tract Narcotics Treatment Program: Parole outcome and related studies. In J. J. Platt, C. Labate and R. J. Wicks (Eds.) *Evaluative research in correctional drug abuse treatment: A guide for professionals in criminal justice and the behavioral sciences.* Lexington, MA: Lexington Books/D.C. Health, pp. 185–196.

Platt, J. J., Labate, C., and Wicks, R. J. (1977a). Evaluation of the Wharton Tract Narcotics Treatment Program. In J. J. Platt, C. Labate, and R. J. Wicks (Eds.) *Evaluative research in correctional drug abuse treatment: A guide for professionals in criminal justice and the behavioral sciences.* Lexington, MA: Lexington Books/D.C. Health, pp. 149–170.

Platt, J. J., Labate, C., and Wicks, R. J. (Eds.) (1977b). *Evaluative research in correctional drug abuse treatment: A guide for professionals in criminal justice and the behavioral sciences.* Lexington, MA: Lexington Books/D.C. Health.

Platt, J. J., and Metzger, D. S. (1987a). Cognitive interpersonal problem-solving skills and the maintenance of treatment success in heroin addicts. *Psychology of Addictive Behaviors, 1*(1), 5–13.

Platt, J. J., and Metzger, D. S. (1987b). *Role of work in the rehabilitation of methadone clients.* (Final Report, Vol. 1, NIDA Grant #DAO3445). Camden, NJ: University of Medicine and Dentistry of New Jersey.

Platt, J. J., Prout, M. F., and Metzger, D. S. (1986). Interpersonal Cognitive Problem-Solving Therapy (ICPS). In W. Dryden and W. Golden (Eds.). *Cognitive-behavioral approaches to psychotherapy.* London: Harper and Row, pp. 261–289.

Platt, J. J., and Spivack, G. (1977). *Measures of interpersonal cognitive problem-solving for adults and adolescents.* Philadelphia: Hahnemann Medical College.

Platt, J. J., Steer, R. A., Ranieri, W. F., and Metzger, D. S. (1989). Differences in the Symptom Check List-90 profiles of black and white methadone patients. *Journal of Clinical Psychology, 45(2),* 342–345.

Platt, J. J., Taube, D. O., Metzger, D. S., and Duome, M. J. (1988b). Training in interpersonal problem solving (TIPS). *Journal of Cognitive Psychotherapy: An International Quarterly, 2*(1), 5–34.

Powell, J., Bradley, B., and Gray, J. (1992). Classical conditioning and cognitive determinants of subjective craving for opiates: An investigation of their relative contirbutions. *British Journal of Addiction, 87*, 1133–1144.

Prochaska, J. O., and Costa, A. (1989). *A cross-sectional comparison of stages of change for pre-therapy and within-therapy clients.* Unpublished manuscript, Universtiy of Rhode Island, Kingston.

Prochaska, J. O., and DiClemente, C. C. (1982). Transtheoretical therapy: Toward a more integrative model of change. *Psychotherapy: Theory, Research and Practice, 20*, 161–173.

Prochaska, J. O., and DiClemente, C. C. (1986). Toward a comprehensive model of change. In W. R. Miller and N. Heather (Eds.). *Treating addictive behaviors: Processes of change.* New York: Plenum Press, pp. 3–27.

Prochaska, J. O., and DiClemente, C. C. (1992). Stages of change in the modification of problem behaviors. In M. Hersen, R. M. Eisler, and P. M. Miller (Eds.). *Progress in behavior modification.* Sycamore, IL: Sycamore Press, pp. 184–214.

Prochaska, J. O., DiClemente, C. C., and Norcross, J. C. (1992). In search of how people change: Applications to addictive behaviors. *American Psychologist, 47*(9), 1102–1114.

Prochaska, J. O., Norcross, J. C., Fowler, J. L., Follick, M. J., and Abrams, D. B. (1992). Attendance and outcome in a work-site weight control program: Processes and stages of changes as process and predictor variables. *Addictive Behaviors, 17*, 35–45.

Public Health Service (1988). Report of the second Public Health Service AIDS prevention and control conference. *Public Health Reports, 193* (suppl 1), 66–77.

Püschel, K. (1992). Drug-related death. In G. Bühringer and J. J. Platt (Eds.). *Drug addiction treatment research: German and American perspectives.* Malabar, FL: Krieger, pp. 17–33.

Rachin, R. L. (1988). A social policy analysis of compulsory treatment for opiate dependence. *Journal of Drug Issues, 18*(4), 503–697.

Rahdert, E. R. (1992). Case management systems represented in the NIDA-supported "Perinatal-20" treatment research demonstration projects. In R. S. Ashery (Ed.). *Progress and issues in case management* (NIDA Research Monograph No. 127). Rockville, MD: NIDA, pp. 251–260.

Raines, G. (1988, Dec. 11). New York's bold AIDS project. *San Francisco Examiner,* A-1, A-16.

Rapp, R. C., Siegal, H. A., and Fisher, J. H. (1992). A strengths-based model of case management/advocacy: Adapting a mental health model to practice work with persons who have substance abuse problems. In R. S. Ashery (Ed.). *Progress and issues in case management* (NIDA Research Monograph No. 127). Rockville, MD: NIDA, pp. 79–91.

Rasor, R. W., and Maddux, J. F. (1966). Institutional treatment of narcotic addiction by the U.S. Public Health Service. *Health Education Welfare Indicators*, March:11–24.

Raymond, J. S., and Hurwitz, S. (1981). Client preference-treatment congruence as a facilitator of length of stay: Supporting an old truism. *International Journal of the Addictions, 16(3)*, 431–441.

Reuband, K-H. (1992). The epidemiology of drug use in Germany: Basic data and trends. In G. Bühringer and J. J. Platt (Eds.). *Drug addiction treatment research: German and American perspectives*. Malabar, FL: Krieger, pp. 3–16.

Rhoads, D. L. (1983). A longitudinal study of life stress and social support among drug abusers. *International Journal of the Addictions, 18*(2), 195–222.

Rice, D. P., Kelman, S., and Miller, L. S. (1991). Economic cost of drug abuse. In W. S. Cartwright and J. M. Kaple (Eds.). *Economic costs, cost-effectiveness, financing, and community-based drug treatment* (NIDA Research Monograph No. 113). Rockville, MD: NIDA, pp. 10–32.

Ridgely, M. S., and Willenbring, M. L. (1992). Application of case management to drug abuse treatment: Overview of models and research issues. In R. S. Ashery (Ed.). *Progress and issues in case management* (NIDA Research Monograph No. 127). Rockville, MD: NIDA, pp. 12–33.

Riorden, C. E., Mezritz, M., Slobetz, F., and Kleber, H. D. (1976). Successful detoxification from methadone maintenance: Follow-up study of 38 patients. *Journal of the American Medical Association, 235(24)*, 2604–2607.

Robins, L. N. (1978). Sturdy childhood predictors of adult antisocial behaviour: Replications from longitudinal studies. *Psychological Medicine, 8(4)*, 611–622.

Robins, L. N., Helzer, J. E., Hesselbrock, M., and Wish, E. (1980). Vietnam veterans three years after Vietnam. In L. Brill and C. Winick (Eds.). *The yearbook of substance use and abuse*. New York: Human Sciences Press.

Rohsenow, D. J., Niaura, R. S., Childress, A. R., Abrams, D. B., and Monti, P. M. (1990–91). Cue reactivity in addictive behaviors: Theoretical and treatment implications. *International Journal of the Addictions, 25* (7A and 8A), 957–993.

Rosenbaum, M. (1982). Getting on methadone: The experience of the woman addict. *Contemporary Drug Problems, 11*, 113–143.

Ross, H. E., Glaser, F. B., and Germanson, T. (1988). The prevalence of psychiatric disorders in patients with alcohol and other drug problems. *Archives of General Psychiatry, 45*, 1023–1031.

Ross, R. R., and Fabiano, E. A. (1985). *Time to think: A cognitive model of delinquency prevention and offender rehabilitation*. Johnson City, TN: Institute of Social Sciences and Arts, Inc..

Ross, R. R., and Gendreau, P. (Eds.). (1980). *Effective correctional treatment*. Toronto: Butterworths.

Rotgers, F. (1992). Coercion in addictions treatment. In J. W. Langebucher, B. S. McCrady, W. Frankenstein, and P. E. Nathan (Eds.). *Annual Review of Addiction Research and Treatment, 2*, 403–416.

Rounsaville, B. J. (1986). Clinical implications of relapse research. In F. M. Tims and C. G. Leukefeld (Eds.). *Relapse and recovery in drug abuse* (NIDA Research Monograph No. 72). Washington, DC: NIDA, pp. 172–184.

Rounsaville, B. J., Bryant, K., Babor, T., Kranzler, H., and Kadden, R. (1993). Cross system agreement for substance use disorders: DSM-III-R, DSM-IV and ICD-10. *Addiction, 88*, 337–348.

Rounsaville, B. J., Kosten, T. R., Weissman, M. M., and Kleber, H. D. (1985). *Evaluating and treating depressive disorders in opiate addicts* (NIDA Treatment Research Monograph). Rockville, MD: NIDA.

Rounsaville, B. J., Kosten, T. R., Weissman, M. M., Prusoff, B., Pauls, D., Anton, S. F., and Merikangas, K. (1991). Psychiatric disorders in relatives of probands with opiate addiction. *Archives of General Psychiatry, 48*, 33–42.

Rounsaville, B. J., Wiessman, M. M., Crits-Christoph, K., Wilber, C., and Kleber, H. (1982). Diagnosis and symptoms of depression in opiate addicts: Course and relationship to treatment outcome. *Archives of General Psychiatry, 39*, 151–156.

Rounsaville, B. J., Weissman, M. M., and Kleber, H. D. (1982). The significance of alcoholism in treated opiate addicts. *Journal of Nervous and Mental Disease, 170*(8), 479–488.

Rounsaville, B. J., Weissman, M. M., Kleber, H., and Wilber, C. (1982). Heterogeneity of psychiatric diagnosis in treated opiate addicts. *Archives of General Psychiatry, 39*, 161–166.

Rouse, J. J., and Johnson, B. D. (1991). Hidden paradigms of morality in debates about drugs: Historical and policy shifts in British and American drug policies. In J. A. Inciardi (Ed.). *The drug legalization debate.* Newbury Park, CA: Sage Publications pp. 183–214.

Saunders, B., Wilkinson, C., and Allsop, S. (1991). Motivational intervention with heroin users attending a methadone clinic. In W. R. Miller and S. Rollnick (Eds.). *Motivational interviewing: Preparing people to change addictive behavior.* New York: Guilford Press, pp. 279–292.

Savage, L. J., and Simpson, D. D. (1980). Posttreatment outcomes of sex and ethnic groups treated in methadone maintenance during 1969–1972. *Journal of Psychedelic Drugs, 12*(1), 55–64.

Schilling, R., Schinke, S., and Weatherly, R. (1988). Service trends in a conservative era: Social workers rediscover the past. *Social Work, 43(1)*, 5–9.

Schippers, G. M., Romijn, C., and Hermans-van Wordragen, R. (1990). Engaging adolescent drug abusers and their families into treatment: Dutch versus American results. In J. J. Platt, C. D. Kaplan, and P. J. McKim (Eds.). *The effectiveness of drug abuse treatment: Dutch and American perspectives.* Malabar, FL: Krieger pp. 209–217.

Schreiber, M. (1992). The drug problem in the Federal Republic of Germany: Measures taken by the German government, with special emphasis on pilot projects and the AIDS problem. In G. Bühringer and J. J. Platt (Eds.). *Drug addiction treatment research: German and American perspectives.* Malabar, FL: Krieger, pp. 59–66.

Schuckit, M. A. (1985). Genetics and the risk for alcoholism. *Journal of the American Medical Association, 254*(18), 2614–2617.

Schuckit, M. A. (1992). Advances in understanding the vulnerability to alcoholism. In: O'Brien, C. P. and Jaffe, J. H. (Eds.). *Advances in understanding vulnerability to alcoholism.* New York: Raven Press, Ltd, pp. 93–108.

Secretary, Department of Health and Human Services (1991). Drug abuse and drug abuse research. *Third triennial report to Congress.* Rockville, MD: NIDA.

Sellers, E. M., Naranjo, C. A., Kadlec, K. E., and Woodley-Remus, D. V. (1988). Weight loss induced by serotonin uptake inhibitors (SUI) in male heavy drinkers. *Psychophar-macology, 96(suppl)*, 311 (abstract).

Sells, S. B. (1979). Treatment effectiveness. In R. L. DuPont, A. Goldstein, and J. O'Donnell (Eds.). *Handbook on drug abuse.* Rockville, MD: National Institute on Drug Abuse, pp. 105-117.

Sells, S. B., Demaree, R. G., Simpson, D. D., Joe, G. W., and Gorsuch, R. L. (1977). Issues in the evaluation of drug abuse treatment. *Professional Psychology, 8*, 609-640.

Shaffer, J. W., Kinlock, T. W., and Nurco, D. N. (1982). Factor structure of the MMPI-168 in male narcotic addicts. *Journal of Clinical Psychology, 38*(3), 656-661.

Shaffer, J. W., Nurco, D. N., and Kinlock, T. W. (1984). A new classification of narcotic addicts based on type and extent of criminal activity. *Comprehensive Psychiatry, 25*, 315-328.

Shaffer, J. W., Nurco, D. N., Hanlon, T. E., Kinlock, T. W., Duszynski, K. R., and Stephenson, P. (1988). MMPI-168 profiles of male narcotic addicts by ethnic group and city. *Journal of Clinical Psychology, 44(2)*, 292-298.

Shaffer, J. W., Wegner, N., Kinlock, T. W., and Nurco, D. N. (1983). An empirical typology of narcotic addicts. *International Journal of the Addictions, 18*(2), 183-194.

Sharpe, L. G. and Jaffe, J. H. (1990). Ibogaine fails to reduce naloxone-precipitated with-drawal in the morphine-dependent rat. *Neuroreport, 1(1)*, 17-19.

Sheehan, M., Oppenheimer, E., and Taylor, C. (1986). Why drug users sought help from one London drug clinic. *British Journal of Addiction, 81*, 765-775.

Sheehan, M., Oppenheimer, E., and Taylor, C. (1988). Who comes for treatment: Drug misusers at three London agencies. *British Journal of Addiction, 83*, 311-320.

Sherman, J. E., Zinser, M. C., Sideroff, S. I., and Baker, T. B. (1989). Subjective dimensions of heroin urges: Influence of heroin-related and affectively negative stimuli. *Addictive Behaviors, 14*, 611-623.

Shikles, J. L. (1989). *Preliminary findings: A survey of methadone maintenance programs.* Statement of the United States General Accounting Office before the House Select Committee on Narcotics Abuse and Control. Washington, DC: House of Representatives.

Shinn, M., and Weitzman, B.C. (1990) (Eds.). Urban homelessness [Special issue]. *Journal of Social Issues, 46(4)*.

Siegel, S. (1983). Classical conditioning, drug tolerance, and drug dependence. In Y. Israel, F. B. Glaser, H. Kalant, R. E. Popham, W. Schmidt, and R. G. Smart (Eds.). *Research advances in alcohol and drug problems, Vol. 7.* New York: Plenum, pp. 207-246.

Simon, R., Bühringer, G., and Strobl, M. (1992). Trend anaylsis of treatment service data from the EBIS information system. In G. Bühringer and J. J. Platt (Eds.). *Drug addiction treatment research: German and American perspectives.* Malabar, FL: Krieger, pp. 127-138.

Simpson, D. D. (1981). Treatment for drug abuse: Follow-up outcomes and length of time spent. *Archives of General Psychiatry, 38*, 875–880.

Simpson, D. D. (1990). Treatment evaluation research using a national data base. In J. J. Platt, C. D. Kaplan, and P. J. McKim (Eds.). *The Effectiveness of Drug Abuse Treatment: Dutch and American Perspectives*. Malabar, FL: Krieger, pp. 221–230.

Simpson, D. D., and Joe, G. W. (in press). Motivation as a predictor of early dropout from drug abuse treatment. *Psychotherapy*.

Simpson, D. D., and Marsh, K. L. (1986). Relapse and recovery among opioid addicts 12 years after treatment. In F. M. Tims and C. G. Leukefeld (Eds.). *Relapse and recovery in drug abuse*. (Research Monograph No. 72). Washington, DC: NIDA, pp. 86–103.

Simpson, D. D., and Sells, S. B. (1982a). Effectiveness of treatment for drug abuse: An overview of the DARP research progream. *Advances in Alcohol and Substance Abuse, 2(1)*, 7–29.

Simpson, D. D., and Sells, S. B. (1982b). *Evaluation of drug treatment effectiveness: Summary of the DARP follow-up research* (NIDA Treatment Research Monograph). Washington, DC: U.S. Government Printing Office.

Simpson, D. D., and Sells, S. B. (Eds.) (1990). *Opioid addiction and treatment: a 12-year follow-up*. Malabar, FL: Krieger.

Simpson, D. D., Joe, G. W., and Lehman, W. E. (1986a). *Addiction careers: Summary of studies based on the DARP 12-year follow-up* (NIDA Treatment Research Monograph). Washington, DC: NIDA.

Simpson, D. D., Joe, G. W., Lehman, W. E. K., and Sells, S. B. (1986b). Addiction careers: Etiology treatment, and 12-year follow-up outcomes. *The Journal of Drug Issues, 16(1)*, 107–121.

Singh, B. K., Joe, G. W., Lehman, W., Garland, J., and Sells, S. B. (1982). A descriptive overview of treatment modalities in federally funded drug abuse treatment programs. *International Journal of the Addictions, 17*(6), 977–1000.

Sisk, J. E., Hatziandreau, E. J., and Hughes, R. (1990). The effectiveness of drug abuse treatment: Implications for controlling AIDS/HIV infection. Washington, DC: Office of Technology Assessment.

Skinner, H. A. (1982). The Drug Abuse Screening Test. *Addictive Behaviors, 7*(4), 363–371.

Skinner, H. A., and Goldberg, A. E. (1986). Evidence for a drug dependence syndrome among narcotic users. *British Journal of Addiction, 81*, 479–483.

Sorensen, J. L. (1990). How can opiate addicts taper from methadone maintenance? In J. J. Platt, C. D. Kaplan and P. J. McKim (Eds.). *The effectiveness of drug abuse treatment: Dutch and American perspectives*. Malabar, FL: Krieger, pp. 85–92.

Sorensen, J. L., Constantini, M. F., Wall, T. L., and Gibson, D. R. (1993). Coupons attract high-risk untreated heroin users into detoxification. *Drug and Alcohol Dependence, 31(3)*, 247–252.

Sorensen, J. L., Gibson, D., Bernal, G., and Deitch, D. (1985). Methadone applicant dropouts: Impact of requiring involvement of friends or family in treatment. *International Journal of the Addictions, 20*(8), 1273–1280.

Sorensen, J. L., Hall, S. M., Loeb, P., Allen, T., Glaser, E. M., and Greenberg, P. D. (1988). Dissemination of a job seekers' workshop to drug treatment programs. *Behavior Therapy, 19*, 143–155.

Stanton, M. D. (1980). A family theory of drug abuse. In D. J. Lettieri, M. Sayers and H. W. Pearson (Eds.). *Theories on drug abuse: Selected contemporary perspectives* (NIDA Research Monograph No. 30). Washington, DC: NIDA, pp. 147–156.

Stanton, M. D., Todd, T. C., and Associates (1982). *The family therapy of drug abuse and addiction*. New York: Guilford.

Steer, R. A. (1982). Symptoms discriminating between heroin addicts seeking ambulatory detoxification or methadone maintenance. *Drug and Alcohol Dependence, 9*(4), 335–338.

Steer, R. A. (1990). Psychopathology and depression in heroin addicts. In J. J. Platt, C. D. Kaplan, and P. J. McKim (Eds.). *The effectiveness of drug abuse treatment: Dutch and American perspectives*. Malabar, FL: Krieger, pp. 161–167.

Steer, R. A., Iguchi, M. Y., and Platt, J. J. (1992). Use of Revised Beck Depression Inventory with intravenous drug users not in treatment. *Psychology of Addictive Behaviors, 6(4)*, 225–232.

Steer, R. A., Platt, J. J., Hendricks, V. M., and Metzger, D. S. (1989). Types of self-reported psychopathology in Dutch and American heroin addicts. *Drug and Alcohol Dependence, 24*, 175–181.

Steer, R. A., Platt, J. J., Ranieri, W. F., and Metzger, D. S. (1989). Relationships of SCL-90 profiles to methadone patients' psychosocial characteristics and treatment response. *Multivariate Experimental Clinical Research, 9(2)*, 45–54.

Stephens, R. C., and Cottrell, E. (1972). A follow-up study of 200 narcotic addicts committed for treatment under the Narcotic Addict Rehabilitation Act (NARA). *British Journal of Addiction, 67*(1), 45–53.

Stewart, J., DeWit, H., and Eikelboom, R. (1984). Role of unconditioned and conditioned drug effects in the self-administration of opiates and stimulants. *Psychological Review, 91*(2), 251–268.

Stimson, G. V., and Oppenheimer, E. (1982). *Heroin addiction: Treatment and control in Britain*, London: Tavistock.

Stitzer, M. L., and McCaul, M. E. (1987). Criminal justice interventions with drug and alcohol abusers: The role of compulsory treatment. In E. K. Morris, and C. J. Braukmann (Eds.). *Behavioral approaches to crime and delinquency: A handbook of application, research, and concepts*. New York: Plenum, pp. 331–361.

Stitzer, M. L., Griffiths, R. R., McLellan, A. T., Grabowski, J., and Hawthorne, J. W. (1981). Diazepam use among methadone maintenance patients: Patterns and dosages. *Drug and Alcohol Dependence, 8*(3), 189–199.

Stockwell, T. (1988). Can severely dependent drinkers learn controlled drinking? Summing up the debate. *British Journal of Addiction, 83*(2), 149–152.

Strang, J., Griffiths, P., Powis, B., and Gossop, M. (1992). First use of heroin: Changes in route of administration over time. *British Medical Journal, 304*, 1222–1223.

Substance Abuse and Mental Health Services Administration (SAMHSA; June, 1993).

Preliminary estimates from the 1992 National Household Survey on Drug Abuse, Advance Report Number 3. Rockville, MD: U.S. Dept. of Health and Human Services.

Sutker, P. B., and Allain, A. N. (1988). Issues in personality conceptualizations of addictive behaviors. *Journal of Consulting and Clinical Psychology, 56*(2), 172–182.

Swan, N. Two NIDA-tested heroin treatment medications move toward FDA approval. *NIDA Notes, 8(1)*, 4–5.

Swift, W., Williams, G., Neill, O., and Grenyer, B. (1990). The prevalance of minor psychopathology in opioid users seeking treatment. *British Journal of Addiction, 85(5)*, 629–634.

Szapocznik, J., Kurtines, W. M., Foote, F., Perez-Vidal, A., and Hervis, O. (1986). Conjoint versus one-person family therapy: Further evidence for the effectiveness of conducting family therapy through one person with drug-abusing adolescents. *Journal of Consulting and Clinical Psychology, 54*(3), 395–397.

TenHouten, W., Stern, J., and TenHouten, D. (1971). Political leadership in poor communities: Applications of two sampling methodologies. *Urban Affairs Annual Review, 5,* 215–254.

Terry, C. E., and Pellens, M., (1970). *The opium problem.* Montclair, NJ: Patterson, Smith.

Tims, F. M. (1982). *Assessing treatment: The conduct of evaluation in drug abuse treatment programs.* (NIDA Treatment Research Report). Rockville, MD: NIDA.

Tims, F. M., and Leukefeld, C. G. (1986). *Relapse and recovery in drug abuse* (NIDA Research Monograph No. 72). Washington, DC: NIDA.

Tobeña, A., Fernández-Teruel, A., Excorihuela, R. M., Nuñez, J. F., Zapata, A., Ferré, P., and Sánchez, R. (1993). Limits of habituation and extinction: Implications for relapse prevention programs in addictions. *Drug and Alcohol Dependence, 32,* 209–217.

Torborg, M., Bellassai, J. P., and Yezer, A. M. J. (1986). *The Washington DC urine testing program for arrestees and defendants awaiting trial: A summary of interim findings.* Presented at the National Institute of Justice sponsored conference, Drugs and Crime: Detecting Use and Reducing Risk, Washington, DC.

Toro, P. A., and Wall, D. D. (1989). *Assessing the impact of sampling and measurement methods in research on the homeless.* Unpublished manuscript (cited in Fischer and Breakley [1991]).

Treaster, J. B. (April 17, 1993). Two judges decline drug cases, protesting sentencing rules. *New York Times,* p. A1.

Treaster, J. B. (August 1, 1993). With supply and purity up, heroin use expands. *New York Times,* pp. A1, A41.

Treaster, J. B. (October 5, 1993). U.S. reports sharp increase in drug-caused emergencies. *New York Times,* p. B11.

Turner, C. F., Miller, H. G., and Moses, L. E. (Eds.) (1989). *AIDS sexual behavior and intravenous drug use.* National Academy Press, Washington, DC.

Turner, J. A., and Romano, J. M. (1984). Evaluating psychologic interventions for chronic pain: Issues and recent developments. In C. Benedett (Ed.). *Advances in Pain Research and Therapy.* New York, Raven.

U.S. Congress, Office of Technology Assessment. (September, 1990). Effectiveness of drug abuse treatment: Implications for controlling AIDS/HIV infection. (Pub. No. OYA-BP-H-73). Washington, DC: United States Government Printing Office.

Vaillant, G. E. (1966a). A 12 year follow-up of New York narcotic addicts: I. The relation of treatment to outcome. *American Journal of Psychiatry, 122*, 727–737.

Vaillant, G. E. (1966b). Twelve-year follow-up of New York narcotic addicts: II. The natural history of a chronic disease. *New England Journal of Medicine, 275*(23), 1282–1288.

Vaillant, G. E. (1966c). 12-year follow-up of New York narcotic addicts: III. Some social and psychiatric characteristics. *Archives of General Psychiatry, 15*, 599–609.

Vaillant, G. E. (1966d). A twelve-year follow-up of New York narcotic addicts: IV. Some characteristics and determinants of abstinence. *American Journal of Psychiatry, 123*(5), 573–584.

Vaillant, G. E. (1973). A 20-year follow-up of New York narcotic addicts. *Archives of General Psychiatry, 29*(2), 237–241.

Vaillant, G. E. (1983). *Natural history of alcoholism: Causes, patterns and paths to recovery.* Cambridge, MA: Harvard University Press.

Vaillant, G. E. (1988). What can long-term follow-up teach us about relapse and prevention of relapse in addiction? *British Journal of Addiction, 83*, 1147–1157.

Van Bilsen, H. P. J. G. (1991). Motivational interviewing: Perspectives from The Netherlands, with particular emphasis on heroin-dependent clients. In W. R. Miller and S. Rollnick (Eds.). *Motivational Interviewing: Preparing people to change addictive behavior.* New York: Guilford Press, pp. 214–224.

Van Bilsen, H. P. J. G., and van Emst, A. J. (1986). Heroin addiction and motivational milieu therapy. *International Journal of the Addictions, 21*(6), 707–714.

Van Bilsen, H. P. J. G., and van Emst, A. J. (1989). Motivating drug users. In G. Bennet (Ed.). *Treating drug abuse.* London: Routledge & Kegan Paul.

Van Dyke, C., Stesin, A., Jones, R., Chuntharapai, A., and Seaman, W. (1986). Cocaine increases natural killer cell activity. *Journal of Clinical Investigation, 77*(4), 1387–1390.

van de Wijngaart, G. F. (1991). *Competing perspectives on drug use: The Dutch experience.* Amsterdam: Swets and Zeitlinger.

van Limbeek, J., Geerlings, P. J., Wouters, L., Beelen, W., de Leeuw, M., Heinemeyer, M., Edelbroek, W., van Rooyen, R., and Goris, A. (1990). The prevalence of psychopathology among drug addicts in an outpatient methadone maintenance and detoxification clinic in the Hague. In J. J. Platt, C. D. Kaplan, and P. J. McKim (Eds.). *The effectiveness of drug abuse treatment: Dutch and American perspectives.* Malabar, FL: Krieger, pp. 169–175.

van Limbeek, J., Wouters, L., Kaplan, C. D., Geerlings, P. J., and von Alem, V. (1992). Prevalence of psychopathology in drug-addicted Dutch. *Journal of Substance Abuse Treatment, 9*, 43–52.

van Vliet, H. J. (1990). Separation of drug markets and the normalization of drug problems in the Netherlands: An example for other nations? *The Journal of Drug Issues, 20(3)*, 463–471.

Vollmer, H. C., Ellgring, H., and Ferstl, R. (1992a). Prediction of premature termination of therapy in the treatment of drug addicts. In G. Bühringer and J. J. Platt (Eds.). *Drug addiction treatment research: German and American perspectives.* Malabar, FL: Krieger, pp. 253–269.

Vollmer, H. C., Ferstl, R., and Ellgring, H. (1992b). Individualized behavior therapy for drug addicts. In G. Bühringer and J. J. Platt (Eds.). *Drug addiction treatment research: German and American perspectives.* Malabar, FL: Krieger, pp. 333–352.

Waldorf, D. (1973). *Careers in dope.* Englewood Cliffs, NJ: Prentice-Hall.

Waldorf, D. (1983). Natural recovery from opiate addiction: Some social-psychological processes of untreated recovery. *Journal of Drug Issues, 13(2),* 237–280.

Waldorf, D., and Biernacki, P. (1981). The natural recovery from opiate addiction: Some preliminary findings. *Journal of Drug Issues, 11,* 61–73.

Walsh, D. C., Hingson, R. W., Merrigan, D. M., Levenson, S. M., Cupples, L. A., Heeren, T., Coffman, G. A., Becker, C. A., Barker, T. A., Hamilton, S. K., McGuire, T. G., and Kelly, C. A. (1991). A randomized trial of treatment options for alcohol-abusing workers. *New England Journal of Medicine, 325*(11), 775–782.

Ward, D. A. (1979). The use of legal coercion in the treatment of alcoholism: A methodological review. *Journal of Drug Issues, 9,* 387–393.

Warren, R., and McLellan, R. W. (1982). Systematic desensitization as a treatment for maladaptive anger and aggression: A review. *Psychological Reports, 50*(3, pt 2), 1095–1102.

Watters, J. K. (1988). A street-based outreach model of AIDS prevention for intravenous drug users: Preliminary evaluation. *Contemporary Drug Problems, 14,* 411–423.

Webster, C. D. (1986). Compulsory treatment of narcotic addiction. *International Journal of Law and Psychiatry, 8,* 133–159.

Weddington, W. W., and Carney, A. C. (1987). Alprazolam abuse during methadone maintenance therapy (letter). *Journal of the American Medical Association, 257*(24), 3363.

Weissner, C. M. (1990). Coercion in alcohol treatment. In Institute of Medicine. *Broadening the base of alcoholism treatment.* Washington, DC: National Academy Press, pp. 579–609.

Wells, E. A., Hawkins, J. D., and Catalano, R. F. (1988a). Choosing drug use measures for treatment outcome studies. I. The influence of measurement approach on treatment results. *International Journal of the Addictions, 23*(8), 851–873.

Wells, E. A., Hawkins, J. D., and Catalano, R. F. (1988b). Choosing drug use measures for treatment outcome studies. II. Timing baseline and follow-up measurement. *International Journal of the Addictions, 23*(8), 875–885.

Wesson, D. R., Havassy, B. E., and Smith, D. E. (1986). Theories of relapse and recovery and their implications for drug abuse treatment. In F. M. Tims and C. G. Leukefeld (Eds.). *Relapse and recovery in drug abuse* (NIDA Research Monograph No. 72). Rockville, MD: NIDA, pp. 5–19.

Westermeyer, J. (1989). Nontreatment factors affecting treatment outcome in substance abuse. *American Journal of Drug and Alcohol Abuse, 15(1),* 13–29.

Wexler, H. K., Blackmore, J., and Lipton, D. S. (1991). Project Reform: Developing a drug abuse treatment strategy for corrections. *Journal of Drug Issues, 21(2)*, 469–490.

Wexler, H. K., Falkin, G. P., and Lipton, D. S. (1990). Outcome evaluation of a prison therapeutic community for substance abuse treatment. *Criminal Justice and Behavior, 17(1)*, pp. 71–92.

Wexler, H. K., Falkin, G. P., Lipton, D. S., and Rosenblum, A. B. (1992). Outcome evaluation of a prison therapeutic community for substance abuse treatment. In C. G. Leukefeld and F. M. Tims (Eds.). *Drug abuse treatment in prisons and jails* (NIDA Research Monograph No. 118), Rockville, MD: NIDA, pp. 156–175.

Wexler, H. K., Lipton, D. S., and Johnson, B. D. (1988). *A criminal justice system strategy for treating cocaine-heroin abusing offenders in custody.* Washington, DC: U.S. Dept. of Justice.

Wikler, A. (1948). Recent progress in research on the neurophysiological basis of morphine addiction. *American Journal of Psychiatry, 105*, pp. 328–338.

Wikler, A. (1965). Conditioning factors in opiate addiction and relapse. In D. M. Wilner and G. G. Kasselbaum (Eds.). *Narcotics.* New York: McGraw-Hill, pp. 85–100.

Wikler, A. (1973). Dynamics of drug dependence: Implications of a conditioning theory for research and treatment. *Archives of General Psychiatry, 28*, 611–616.

Wikler, A. (1980). A theory of opioid dependence. In D. J. Lettieri, M. Sayers, and H. W. Pearson (Eds.). *Theories on drug abuse: Selected contemporary perspectives* (NIDA Research Monograph No. 30). Washington, DC: NIDA, pp. 174–178.

Wikler, A., and Pescor, F. T. (1967). Classical conditioning of a morphine abstinence phenomenon, reinforcement of opioid-drinking behavior, and "relapse" in morphine-addicted rats. *Psychopharmacologia, 10*(3), 255–284.

Wille, R. (1983). Processes of recovery from heroin dependence: Relationship to treatment, social changes and drug use. *Journal of Drug Issues, 13*, 333–342.

Willenbring, M. L. (1992). Integrating qualitative and quantitative components in evaluation of case management. In R. S. Ashery (Ed.). *Progress and issues in case management* (NIDA Research Monograph No. 127). Rockville, MD: NIDA, pp. 223–250.

Willenbring, M. L., Whelan, J. A., Dahlquist, J. S., and O'Neal, M. E. (1990). Community treatment of the chronic public inebriate: I. Implementation. In: M. Argeriou and D. McCarty (Eds.). *Treating alcoholism and drug abuse among the homeless: Nine community demonstration grants.* Binghamton, NY: Haworth Press, 79–98.

Wilson, G. S. (1989). Clinical studies of infants and children exposed prenatally to heroin. In D. E. Hutchings (Ed.). *Prenatal abuse of licit and illicit drugs: Annals of the New York Academy of Sciences, 562*, 183–194.

Winick, C. (1962). Maturing out of narcotic addiction. *Bulletin on Narcotics, 14*, 1–7.

Winick, C. (1965). Epidemiology of narcotics use. In D. M. Wilner and G. G. Kasselbaum (Eds.). *Narcotics.* New York: McGraw-Hill, pp. 3–18.

Winick, C. (1980). A theory of drug dependence based on role, access to, and attitudes toward drugs. In D. J. Lettieri, M. Sayers, and H. W. Pearson (Eds.). *Theories on drug abuse: Selected contemporary perspectives* (NIDA Research Monograph No. 30). Washington, DC: NIDA, pp. 225–235.

Winick, C. (1988). Some policy implications of the New York State Civil Commitment Program. *Journal of Drug Issues, 18*, 561–574.

Wise, R. A. (1988). The neurobiology of craving: Implications for the understanding and treatment of addiction. *Journal of Abnormal Psychology, 97*(2), 118–132.

Wish, E. D. (1988). Identifying drug-abusing criminals. In C. G. Leukefeld and F. M. Tims (Eds.). *Compulsory treatment of drug abuse: Research and clinical practice* (NIDA Research Monograph No. 86). Rockville, MD: NIDA, pp. 139–159.

Wish, E. D., and Johnson, B. D. (1986). The impact of substance abuse on criminal careers. In A. Blumstein, J. Cohen, J. A. Roth, and C. A. Visher (Eds.). *Criminal careers and career criminals*. Washington, DC: National Academy Press, pp. 52–88.

Wish, E. D., and O'Neil, J. (1991). Cocaine use in arrestees: Refining measures of national trends by sampling the criminal population. In S. Schober and C. Schade (Eds.). *The epidemiology of cocaine use and abuse* (NIDA Research Monograph No. 110). Rockville, MD: NIDA, pp. 57–70.

Wish, E. D., Chedekel, M., Brady, E., and Cuadrado, M. (1986). *Alcohol use and crime in Manhattan*. Presented at the American Academy of Forensic Sciences Annual Meeting, New Orleans, LA.

Wisotsky, S. (1991). Beyond the war on drugs. In J. A. Inciardi (Ed.). *The drug legalization debate*. Sage Publications, pp. 103–129.

Woodward, A., (1992). Managed care and case management of substance abuse treatment. In R. S. Ashery (Ed.). *Progress and issues in case management* (NIDA Research Monograph No. 127). Rockville, MD: NIDA, pp. 34–53.

Woody, G. E., McLellan, A. T., Luborsky, L., and O'Brien, C. P. (1985). Sociopathy and psychotherapy outcome. *Archives of General Psychiatry, 42*, 1081–1086.

Woody, G. E., McLellan, A. T., Luborsky, L., and O'Brien, C. P. (1987). Twelve-month follow-up of psychotherapy for opiate dependence. *American Journal of Psychiatry, 144*(5), 590–596.

Woody, G. E., McLellan, A. T., Luborsky, L., O'Brien, C. P., Blaine, J., Fox, S., Herman, I., and Beck, A. T. (1984). Severity of psychiatric symptoms as a predictor of benefits from psychotherapy: The Veterans Administration-Penn Study. *American Journal of Psychiatry, 141*(10), 1172–1177.

Woody, G. E., O'Brien, C. P., and Greenstein, R. (1975). Misuse and abuse of diazepam: An increasingly common medical problem. *International Journal of the Addictions, 10*(5), 843–848.

Woody, G. E., O'Brien, C. P., McLellan, A. T., and Luborsky, L. (1986). Psychotherapy as an adjunct to methadone treatment. In R. E. Meyer (Ed.). *Psychopathology and addictive disorders*. New York: Guilford, pp. 169–195.

Wouters, L., and van Limbeek, J. (1990). Analyzing symptom patterns: Preliminary results with two computer programs. In J. J. Platt, C. D. Kaplan, and P. J. McKim (Eds.). *The effectiveness of drug abuse treatment: Dutch and American perspectives*. Malabar, FL: Krieger, pp. 231–242.

Wright, J. D., and Knight, J. W. (1987). *Alcohol abuse in the National Health Care for the*

Homeless client population. Amherst: University of Massachusetts, Social and Demographic Research Institute.

Ziegler, H. (1992). Treatment facilities in Germany: Number and type of services, organization, and funding. In G. Bühringer and J. J. Platt (Eds.). *Drug addiction treatment research: German and American perspectives.* Malabar, FL: Krieger, pp. 115–125.

CUMULATIVE AUTHOR INDEX
FOR VOLUMES 1 AND 2

CUMULATIVE SUBJECT INDEX FOR VOLUMES 1 AND 2